SACRED EYES

L. ROBERT KECK

Resources for Creative Personal and Social Change

Knowledge Systems, Inc.

ACKNOWLEDGEMENTS

A very special "thank you" to Tom Williams, M.D., whose vision and generosity made an important difference at an early and crucial stage in this project.

Others who have my gratitude for reading portions of the manuscript at various stages of its development and offering helpful suggestions are: Rita Arditti, Ph.D., Nancy Brown, Marjorie Chambers, Ph.D., Lou DeWine, Ph.D., Ester Ekus, Ph.D., The Reverend James Keck, Krista Keck, Sidna Leavenworth, Gail Lyons, Marilee Pallant, Jeff Sherrill, Ph.D., Nicholas Tormey, Ph.D., Bishop James S. Thomas, and David Tressemer, Ph.D.

The poem at the beginning of the Epoch II Introduction (pg. 38) is reprinted from *The New Eden* by Dr. Michael W. Fox published by Lotus Press, Sante Fe, NM. © 1989 by Michael W. Fox.

The two quotes by R.M. Filke (pp. 184-185) come from "Letter to a Young Poet" by Ranier Maria Rilke, translated by Stephen Mitchell. ©1984 by Stephen Mitchell. Reprinted by permission of Random House, Inc.

The quote on pages 232-233 is reprinted from *Black Elk Speaks*, by John G. Neihardt, by permission of the University of Nebraska Press. Copyright 1932, 1959, 1972 by John G. Neihardt; ©1961 by the John G. Neihardt Trust.

Published by Knowledge Systems, Inc.

For a free catalog or ordering information
call (317) 244-8806, fax (317) 248-1503
or write Knowledge Systems,
7777 West Morris Street
Indianapolis, IN 46231 USA

First Edition
Second printing, April 1994

Library of Congress Cataloging-in-Publication Data

Keck, L. Robert, 1935-
    Sacred eyes / L. Robert Keck.
       p.   cm.
    Includes bibliographical references and index.
    ISBN 0-941705-23-4 (cloth) : $18.95
    ISBN 0-941705-26-9 (pbk) : $12.95
    1. Religion and science. 2. Evolution--Religious aspects.
3. Emotional maturity--Religious aspects.   I. Title
BL240.2K45   1992
218--dc20   92-34187
                                                              CIP

THIS BOOK IS DEDICATED TO

DIANA. . .

> . . . wife, lover, companion, and soul-mate. She personifies
> the archetypal unity of feminine-nature, and
> is a skilled artisan in the high calling
> of compassionate service to others.
> It is an incredible pleasure to live and love with her,
> and to learn from her.

AND TO "SPIRIT OF THE DAWN". . .

> . . . our Wheaten Terrier, who sat by my side,
> literally, for almost all the hours that went into the writing of
> *Sacred Eyes*. He would tolerate only so much work and
> head-tripping before he would demand play and heart-
> tripping—a therapeutic balancing.

TABLE OF CONTENTS

AN INVITATION TO VIEW THE ENTIRE HUMAN JOURNEY, AND YOUR OWN LIFE, WITH SACRED EYES

Nothing here below is profane for those who know how to see. On the contrary, everything is sacred.

—TEILHARD DE CHARDIN

WE ARE LIVING IN AN EXTRAORDINARY TIME, a crucial juncture in history. It is an incredibly exciting, dangerous, and opportune time, the magnitude of which is unparalleled in the long human journey. The impending end of a century, and of a millennium, give symbolic emphasis to something we all sense—this is a major turning point for humanity.

To be able to see what is important in a time like this, to be able to perceive the difference between the superficial and the substantive, and to be able to envision what is being born and what is dying in the womb/tomb of transformation, we must be able to look deeply into soul-level territory.

If we look deeply into humanity's soul we can see a new hope emerging, in spite of all the despair that so characterizes the surface. If we look deeply into our soul we can see an emerging spiritual meaning and purpose, in spite of what dominates mass culture—institutions and dogma that are all but bankrupt for the faithful, and a spiritual malaise permeating the lives of those who have left organized religion. If we look deeply into the soul of our times we

1

can see an epoch-sized transformation of the human psyche—a growth spurt in spiritual maturity—in spite of the chaos of clashing revolutions and counter-revolutions filling the daily newspapers. It is through the cultivation of sacred eyes that we can accomplish this depth of vision.

Everything starts with how we view the world. With cynical eyes we see the evidence, and there is plenty of evidence, of how far we fall short of perfection. Cynical vision, however, is a cop-out. After all, in the chaos that inevitably accompanies a transformational time we can pick out ample illustrations to justify cynicism. But cynical eyes just don't see the larger picture—they provide a truncated vision, bereft of hope.

In like manner pessimistic eyes see the evidence to support despair about the future. Indeed, the larger picture includes negative evidence, but it also includes much more. Pessimistic vision sees only a partial picture and offers an unrealistic and distorted view of the future.

It is with sacred eyes that we can see the larger, more realistic, picture. Sacred eyes can penetrate down through the opaqueness of the materialism and the reductionism that has so characterized our recent look at scientific evidence and the historical record to perceive human evolution's meaning and purpose. Sacred eyes can penetrate the chaos of our current time in history to see the "pattern that connects" all the seemingly disparate revolutions. Sacred eyes can penetrate the superficiality of our day-to-day activities, and gain insight into our personal integrity with the soul of humanity and the time of our lives. And sacred eyes can envision the emerging values of the 21st century, already developing in the cauldron of humanity's soul, but just now bubbling to the visible surface.

As Teilhard de Chardin reminds us in the opening quote, everything is sacred if we but look into its soul—the entire universal context, the long evolutionary journey of humanity, these incredible times at the end of the 20th century, and our own personal stories. With sacred eyes we can see the beauty, the divinity, and the meaning and purpose in this collective journey, as well as our own reason for being. With sacred eyes we can see the larger context without overlooking the details of the moment. With sacred eyes we can see the reasons for tough optimism and pragmatic hope within the chaos of our times.

Sacred eyes look to the big questions, and certainly our times call for living and loving the big questions. We simply can't afford anymore to have our vision constricted to the small questions—

questions limited to me or mine, this or that small group, narrow dogmas or doctrines of this or that religion, or even questions having to do only with the human element on this profoundly ecologically interrelated planet. It is a time wherein we have become aware of a world so comprehensive and so interrelated that the questions that concern us must be no less than global in scope and soul-level in depth and profundity—the really *big* questions.

The big questions that sacred eyes explore, having to do with the breadth and depth of life, are:

1. Is there meaning and purpose to the large and long journey of human evolution? Are we going somewhere, or are we just aimlessly wandering around throughout history? Has evolution been strictly by chance and a "survival of the fittest," or can we perceive a meaningful and purposeful progression?

2. Is there something special about this particular time in history—1960 to the turn of the millennium? Experts in virtually every field, along with historians and cultural analysts, are saying that there is. If so, what is it that makes this time in history so unique?

3. If this is such a transformational time in history what is it that is being transformed? What is it that is dying and what is it that is being born? How do we distinguish between that which is on the way out and that which is on the way in? What is transient and what is enduring?

4. How do we individually fit into this time in history? Are our personal stories on the same page as humanity's story?

This book has been in development for fourteen years, as I've tried to look deeply into those big questions and bring it all together into a grand synthesizing vision that would be easily readable and understandable. This book is not written for scholars or specialists per se, but rather for anyone who considers living this life to be a thoughtful and conscientious endeavor. This book is for those who have an intellectual hunger, a spiritual curiosity, and who want to live and love the big questions.

It has been an incredibly meaningful journey for me personally, as I have felt compelled to make sense of my life in the midst of the extraordinary history in which my life was taking place. In addition, it is my fervent hope that this book will also enrich the spiritual journey of you, the reader.

It has been fourteen years of research into what might be called "Deep Value Trend Analysis." I became fascinated with the fact that virtually every science, every field of endeavor, every public institution, and every historian and cultural analyst was saying that the latter part of the twentieth century was a transformational time. Was there, I wondered, a "pattern that connects" all the seemingly disparate revolutions? If we looked deeply enough, could we find a common force that is fueling all the various revolutions, and informing all the various perceptions of transformation?

Many futurists analyze the content of newspapers and the activity on the culture's surface in order to ascertain the trends of today, and then extrapolate them into the future as a means of predicting our tomorrows. My hunch is that with such a process we can confuse trends with temporary fads, aberrations, and backlash. The waters on the surface may swirl a great deal, and a superficial picture may confuse us as to the real direction of the river. A larger and deeper picture can give us a more accurate analysis.

For instance, social movements inevitably swirl to and fro on the surface. There is often a dramatic beginning to a social movement, then a period of backlash when the movement appears to have waned, if not reversed. Looking only at the surface we may be fooled into thinking, when viewing a temporary backlash, that the movement is over. Only by looking deeply, throughout a broad sweep of culture, can we distinguish between the temporary whimsies and the long-term major changes taking place. Only with Deep Value Trend Analysis can we know the values that will endure into the twenty-first century so as to really shape our future.

The feminist and environmental movements are cases in point. Both had dramatic eruptions onto the surface of our culture in the 1970s. Both movements have gone through ebbs and flows, both have experienced superficial support and then neglect, and both are currently experiencing backlash. But make no mistake about it— and I hope this book will make clear the reasons why—they are both deep substantive movements, representing fundamental changes in values within the deep psyche of humanity, and they *will* play major roles in defining our future.

Without accurate Deep Value Trend Analysis, businesses will miss the mark in their long-range planning, politicians will engage in counter-productive and ill-advised social legislation, institutions will, at best, spin their wheels rather than facilitating future growth and development, and religions will be nothing more than museums celebrating the past.

Without this kind of depth analysis, politicians and business leaders were surprised by the eruptions, and the strength of feelings, associated with the Clarence Thomas-Anita Hill hearings, or the level of interest in sexual harassment. Without this kind of depth understanding, people and nations were surprised by the fall of the Berlin Wall, or the dissolution of the Soviet Union. Without the depth vision of sacred eyes, life appears to be nothing but a series of surprises, seemingly attacking us "out of the blue" and without meaning or purpose.

In my research into Deep Value Trend Analysis, I looked thoroughly into many different fields, listened carefully to their experts, read voluminously throughout their literature, and tried to break through the inevitably parochial jargon to discern what are the deep value changes being represented in their respective revolutions. Eventually, the deep "pattern that connects," the soul-level transformation of values that is the emergent Epoch III, began to appear.

When it became evident that humanity was going through an epoch-sized value transformation I was driven to try to understand what values are fading and what values are coming into prominence. That eventually led to a long and deep examination of history to see *when* we adopted the values that are now on their way out, and what values preceded *that* ancient turning point.

What became clear is that humanity has been on an evolutionary journey of maturation similar to that of the individual. Collectively, as we do individually, we grew up through a childhood—what I am referring to as Epoch I—in which our purpose was to develop physically. We had a particular value system attendant to that childhood, a value system which was basically feminine. Consequently, when we arrived at the point in our childhood development—somewhere between 100,000 and 50,000 years ago—when we realized we were part of a larger world and subject to forces beyond ourselves we started expressing our appreciation for the life giving and life sustaining powers of the feminine. The focus of our worship, therefore, was the Mother Earth Goddess.

Starting about 10,000 years ago we began the first epoch-sized transformation of the human psyche as we matured into our collective adolescence—Epoch II. The purpose of our adolescence was ego and mental development, the value system was essentially masculine, and we switched our worship from the Mother Goddess to a Father God.

The end of the twentieth century represents only the second epoch-sized transformation of the human psyche as the organic maturational energies deep within our soul call us to move out of adolescence and into adulthood—Epoch III—for the purpose of spiritual maturation. Human life has a built-in propensity for growing toward health and wholeness in body, mind, and spirit.

We are now at the crucial juncture of adding spiritual maturity to the remarkable evolutionary journey that has brought us to our current stage of physical and mental development.

Our mental development, particularly over the past three hundred years, has been considerable. The knowledge we have gained about the universe, and ourselves, is quite remarkable and the technology we have developed is awesome. Nevertheless, there is now increasing evidence that our adolescent value system has run its course. It is now counter-productive and increasingly dangerous.

If we don't grow up—soon—we may abort the human evolutionary journey. Our adolescent immaturity, with physical and mental development out of balance with spiritual development, has us on the brink of a "teenage suicide." The short view, and the self-centered view, of adolescent vision has brought us dangerously close to killing ourselves—either suddenly in a nuclear holocaust, or slowly by maiming our life-support system. For human evolution to continue into health and wholeness, physical and mental development must now be matched with spiritual maturity.

The process for such growth and maturation is organic. It is not that we have to create that process with our minds and through strength of will make ourselves evolve. Evolution—or, in this particular metaphor, maturation—is emerging naturally from the soul of humanity. We only have to welcome that energy, cooperate with it, and do what comes naturally—grow up.

The 1960s was the decade when the energy of necessary maturation burst forth from the collective soul. We had repressed the move into adult maturity long enough. What seemed like total chaos at the time was a bursting forth of life's innate drive toward health and wholeness. The last refuge of our adolescence was blown away, and what was "blowing in the wind" was the drive toward a higher order, the maturation of human life, the next evolutionary step toward getting our act together in body, mind, and spirit.

This transitional time is our collective "dark night of the soul." It is a *dark* night because what we have known is dying. The former day is no longer. Light has ceased to shine on, and enlightenment has ceased to emit from, the value system of our adolescence. Consequently, we experience a lot of darkness and death.

It is a dark night of the *soul* precisely because this is soul-level stuff we're dealing with—deep values—and only the second large shift of deep values in all of human history. And it is of the soul because this maturation has to do with spiritual development.

The Greek word for "soul" is the same word as for "butterfly." In Chapter Six, where we will explore more fully this "dark night of the soul," we will explore the metaphor of the caterpillar becoming the butterfly. For many of us in this chrysalis time, those of us who primarily feel our former identity, it feels like a time of death and destruction, a time of disintegration. But if we can respond to the butterfly energy that is also within the chrysalis, we can begin to welcome our new identity.

There is no guarantee that we will make it out of the chrysalis alive. As already indicated, we have the capacity to commit suicide before we attain adult maturity. We have that freedom, and certainly there is plenty of evidence to indicate that our adolescent values include a propensity for self-destruction. The innumerable crises that characterize our daily lives and threaten virtually every traditional public institution are evidence of the danger. But a crisis of transformation has opportunities as well as dangers.

Yes, we have the capacity to self-destruct, to be driven by the smallest and most immature part of ourselves. But we also have the capacity to welcome the evolutionary energy emerging from our soul, to respond to the highest and best in us, and to co-create the new "possible human," as Jean Houston put it. We can choose one hell of an exit, or we can choose one heaven of an ascent. The faith inherent in this book is that Spirit is offering the latter, and we have the extraordinary privilege to be living at a time in which we can participate in such an epoch-sized transformation.

Since the only other transformation of deep values took place thousands of years ago, we don't exactly have people living who can tell us how it was to live through such a change, or people to provide experienced leadership for the transmigration. We are in uncharted waters, trying to negotiate the considerable distance from the humanity we have known to an entirely new form of humanity, a challenge of gargantuan proportions.

This book is my attempt to provide something of a map for that journey, and hope and faith for that challenge. For if we can accurately perceive the values that will be the heart and soul of the new Epoch III human, we can see more clearly where we are going. Our passage will go more smoothly if we can identify the values we are leaving behind, understand the inevitable resistance of those with vested interests in the status quo, as well as discern the values that are drawing us into our future.

There are five major values emerging from humanity's soul which will define our spiritual maturity in Epoch III and which will shape the content of our lives as we move toward, into, and beyond the 21st century:

1. HOLISM AND SYNERGY

The Epoch II patriarchy, with its developmental agenda of ego and mental maturation, has valued analysis, separation, categorization, compartmentalization, and specialization. Once we separated the world into parts, we arranged them in hierarchical order—our part having power over, and being better than, their part.

Epoch III will see a fundamental change as we mature beyond the need for such patriarchal and hierarchical proclivities. In Chapter Eight we will examine how thorough-going the changes will be as we discover holism and synergy. We will experience miraculous breakthroughs never before imagined as we explore wholeness, balance, ecological interrelatedness, and the synergy of wholes being more than the sum of the parts. A new human being emerges as we get our act together in body, mind, and spirit.

2. EMPOWERMENT

The Epoch II value system fundamentally and extensively disempowered people. We mistakenly thought power had to do with having power over other people, or we projected power out onto externals—God, Christ, money, medicine, or machines. The individual was viewed as sinful, depraved, helpless, and powerless.

In Chapter Nine we will explore the Epoch III notion of power—a divinely ordained inner resource, a tap-root to the very core essence of the universe. What has been true for only a few extraordinary people in the past will become available for anyone in a new era of spiritual democracy—discovery of the power within oneself and within relationships that will transform life as we know it.

3. CHANGE

Change is certain and is happening to us at an escalating rate. Epoch II was unfamiliar with change, threatened by it, and resisted it at every turn. Those of us who grew up within Epoch II were raised in the illusion that life could basically stand still—the world for which we were being educated would be there when we arrived, we could start in one profession and stay there, etc.

Change, in Epoch III, will be a thoroughly permeating condition of life, and the ability to view change as "user friendly" will be one of the most important life-enhancing skills of Epoch III. We will discover how change—as a deep value emerging from our soul at this time in history—is precisely the process of growth, maturation, and transformation. That is the subject of Chapter Ten.

4. Re-Membering Human-Nature

Our childhood was one of being born from the womb of Mother Earth and we grew up in at-one-ment with nature. The animals were our brothers and sisters. We began the ego development of our adolescence, however, by separating ourselves from the rest of nature. We divided the previous wholeness and integrity and distinguished ourselves from others in what was a necessary state in the growth and development of human self-identity.

Now, however, having developed the adolescent ego we move on to the maturity of ego transcendence. In re-membering that which was dis-membered we will discover a marvelous new synergy between humanity and nature and, in the process, discover a new self-image regarding the nature of humanity. In Chapter Eleven we look beyond the "what to do" aspects of ecological and environmental responsibility, to "how to think" about the human-nature relationship.

5. Historical Integrity

Our adolescent propensity for separation and division created a general lack of integration. In dividing humanity from nature we lost our integrity with our innate feminine power. In dividing body from mind and spirit, we lost additional integrity. And with our discomfort with the flow of time, we lost integrity with the time of our lives.

A natural result of the other four emergent values in Epoch III will be the recovery of what I am calling historical integrity. We will discover anew how our body, mind, and spirit form a unity in this time, this place, this planet, and this person—a pregnant whole for the purpose of birthing spiritual growth and development.

It is of substantial spiritual consequence how you and I integrate with the unique challenges of this transformational time. In Chapter Seven following our discussion of the fading Epoch II, and again in Chapter Twelve following our exploration of Epoch III, we will shift from humanity's Biography to autobiography, from the large story to our individual stories. Why are you, with your particular body, mind, and spirit, with your unique cluster of gifts, living at this particular time, in this particular place?

I would offer one caution before we start this survey of evolutionary history and the emerging spiritual maturity—do not underestimate the nature or extent of these emergent Epoch III values, nor the degree to which they will transform our lives, our institutions, and our culture.

The five values which will dominate Epoch III, as identified above, are all much more than they may seem. It is tempting, at first blush, to think they are ridiculously simple and self-evident. It is tempting to think that we already have seen them and know them. Don't be fooled by that initial and superficial response.

Because we have seen the first "ripples" of the Epoch III "wave of the future," we may be tempted to think:

"Holism? Oh, I know all about holism. I participated in the holistic health movement."

"Empowerment? I know all about that. I've been working on my twelve-step recovery process for several years now."

Etc., etc., etc.

Our experience over the past three decades notwithstanding, we have not as yet even begun to imagine the full strength of this deep value transformation. To use a different metaphor, what we have seen to date is only the first glimmers of a light that would blind us if we were blasted with its full power. Our Epoch II minds could not handle the full Epoch III enlightenment. Like a cosmic rheostat we are getting the light in gradual degrees. We cannot conceive of what these five values will fully, and finally, look like. We only have a hint at this point in time. But if we attempt to absorb the glimmer now available, perhaps we will become more and more able to see the full enlightenment of Epoch III when it does appear in all its glory.

I certainly make no claim to understand these emergent values in their full or final form. My attempt in this book is just a timid beginning, but our challenge is to at least begin.

One of our toughest challenges in this extraordinary transitional time is to not think too small. It is time to unshackle our minds and our imaginations and to let our spirits fly into the rarefied atmosphere of the emerging Epoch III. It is time to enlarge our vision with sacred eyes so as to see the possible health, wholeness, and holiness awaiting us. The morning fog accompanies the dawn of this new day, but as the sun gets higher in the sky it will burn off the fog and we will begin to see more clearly.

As I was writing the paragraph above I found myself humming Cris Williamson's current version of an old hymn—words that will, therefore, provide our invocation for the journey which follows:

> Open mine eyes that I may see,
> Glimpses of truth thou hast for me.
> Open mine eyes, illumine me,
> Spirit Divine.

EPOCH I

THE BIRTH
AND CHILDHOOD
OF HUMANITY

Physical Development

CHAPTER 1

AN EXPECTANT UNIVERSE:
Father Sky

Strange developments are going on in astronomy. They are fascinating partly because of their theological implications, and partly because of the peculiar reactions of scientists. . . For the scientist who has lived by his faith in the power of reason, the story ends like a bad dream. He has scaled the mountains of ignorance; he is about to conquer the highest peak; as he pulls himself over the final rock, he is greeted by a band of theologians who have been sitting there for centuries.

—ASTRONOMER ROBERT JASTROW

I LIKE THE IMAGE JASTROW SUGGESTS. Not that we should go back to a pre-scientific way of viewing the world—we should not and we will not. We are not going back, either religiously or scientifically. I like the image because it suggests a summit meeting between scientists and theologians in our attempt to understand the universe.

Another scientist of substantial note, Albert Einstein, also recognized the need for such a summit meeting. "Religion without science is blind," he said, and "Science without religion is lame."

Religion has contributed much of value to the growth and development of humanity. At the same time, religion has often based its security on holding tightly to past dogma, refusing to look at new information provided by science. That kind of religion is, indeed, blind.

Similarly, although there was great historical value in science's rejection of religious dogma as a barrier to learning new things about the universe, it, too, was inadequate on its own to bring us the full and complete life of meaning and purpose. In fact, it was precisely at the point of meaning and purpose that science has been "lame." Many scientists have considered any talk of meaning and purpose, in our exploration of the universe, as totally inappropriate. Teleology is the word for considering design or purpose in the universe, and for many scientists that is a four-letter word, in effect if not in actual letter count. They have considered meaning and purpose to be something left over from our religious and immature past, not something for the rational and intellectual modern scientist.

Epoch II science was a necessary and valuable antithesis to the thesis of Epoch II religion. Now, however, is the time for synthesis, the time to mature into Epoch III, as both science and religion reach new heights in a synergy at the summit. At the summit no dogma will be imposed to stifle the grand and free search for more knowledge about the universe and humanity's place in it. At the summit there will be no dehumanizing sterility that fears talk of meaning and purpose. For the grand evolutionary achievement of the human mind and spirit strives to ask not only the "what's" and "how's" of the world, but also the "why's" and "wherefore's."

Epoch III is for soul-level stuff. And as we grow into adult maturity we will be more appreciative of balance, more tolerant of both/and solutions, and more aware of the value inherent in the esoteric as a balance to the exoteric, of the intuition as well as the intellect.

The synergy of science and spirituality will lift us to heights of human experience unimagined in Epoch II. We will be growing into an entirely new perspective of the cosmos, and a whole new self-image for humanity. We will begin to see a universe which has been expecting us, indeed, a universe which prepared for us. Dr. Paul Davies, a professor of theoretical physics, suggests that recent discoveries about the universe offer "powerful evidence that there is 'something going on' behind it all. The impression of design is overwhelming. Science may explain all the processes whereby the universe evolves its own destiny, but that still leaves room for there to be a meaning behind existence."[1]

One has to have an enormous belief in "coincidences" not to see meaning and purpose within the recent scientific discoveries of the universe. Stephen Hawking, whom many consider to be the most brilliant theoretical physicist since Einstein, says that, "The odds against a universe like ours emerging out of something like the Big Bang are enormous.[2] . . . In fact, a universe like ours with galaxies and stars is actually quite unlikely. If one considers the possible constants and laws that could have emerged, the odds against a universe that has produced life like ours are immense.[3] I think there are clearly religious implications whenever you start to discuss the origins of the universe."[4]

Recent discoveries suggest that the primary forces in the universe are in the precise balance to enable life to evolve. Any slight variation and life would have been impossible. For instance, there are four major forces creating and sustaining the universe, forces referred to as the "fundamental constants:" gravity, the strong nuclear force, electromagnetism, and the weak nuclear force. If, as the universe was developing, gravity had been any stronger, our universe would have been smaller and everything would have happened more quickly. The average star, for instance, would have existed for only about one year, certainly not enough time for life to develop. If gravity had been any weaker, matter would not have congealed into stars and galaxies at all. In other words, if the strength of gravitation had varied by as little as one part in 10,000,000,000,000,000,000,000,000,000,000,000,000,000, we would not be here to reflect upon the universe.[5] Instead, gravity has had precisely the right strength—just right to allow this universe to develop, evolve, and to give birth to life.

Likewise, if the strong nuclear force which acts on the quarks, neutrons, and protons of the atomic nucleus were any stronger, hydrogen would not exist and we could not have life as we know it. If the strong force were any weaker no other elements besides hydrogen could exist, and again, life would not have developed.[6]

The earth and our entire solar system is made up of protons and neutrons, yet there are no antiprotons or antineutrons. "Indeed," says Hawking, "such an imbalance between particles and antiparticles is yet another a priori condition for our existence."[7]

Dr. Davies looked at these and other data of a fine-tuned universe and concluded: "It is hard to resist the impression that the present structure of the universe, apparently so sensitive to minor alterations in the numbers, has been rather carefully thought out. . . . The seemingly miraculous concurrence of numerical values that nature has assigned to her fundamental constants must remain the most compelling evidence for an element of cosmic design."[8]

Physicist Freeman Dyson, similarly, says that the scientific evidence argues purpose rather than coincidence: "The more I examine the universe and study the details of its architecture, the more evidence I find that the universe in some sense must have known we were coming."[9]

To assign all these "coincidences" to blind chance is no explanation at all and rather a cop-out. The one eye of science has seen, and will continue to see, new vistas in this incredible universe. Likewise, the one eye of spirituality sees dimensions to which science is blind. Monocular vision, with whichever eye, has limitations. It is binocular vision which gives the depth dimension—two eyes working synergistically so that we see that the whole is more than what either eye can see singularly. It is why the title of this book refers not to one, but to two sacred eyes, a binocular sacred vision of depth.

Ours is a time of synthesis, of synergy, and of sacred vision. It is a new vision of this awesome and incredible universe—a vision that sees a divine purpose, a vision that now speculates on evolving life as being the very reason for this entire magnificent journey. It is the vision that perceives the glint in Father Sky's eye as He impregnated Mother Earth. And it is the vision that sets the stage for us taking a new look at our home planet and our cosmic Mother, the Earth.

I lie in the stillness of the night atop Winged Spirit Mountain, a few miles west of Boulder, Colorado, with an unencumbered view of the deep, big, black sky, dotted with innumerable shimmering stars. The quietness, the stillness of the air, and my deep relaxation all contribute to a calm but profound appreciation of the enormity of the universe of which we are a part. My mind wanders over the vastness and tries to comprehend.

All of those stars are as bright as our sun—some many times brighter. Yet, instead of one, which is so bright that we cannot look directly into it without being injured, and which illuminates our days, there are too many to count. The night is so dark because they are so far away. So there is the matter of distance and brilliance—the brilliance of the one which is close, the dark beauty of the many that are far away.

I am also looking back in time as I gaze out into the night sky. The light entering my eyes right now from our nearest star, Alpha Centauri, left there some four and a half years ago. Consequently, I am looking at that star as it appeared back then—it may not even be there right now. With other stars I am looking back hundreds of years—others, thousands of years. And there are stars out there, beyond my unaided eyesight, that have been sending their light in our direction for billions of years. I am looking at Father Sky in what is, in fact, a memory of what He used to be—just as I remember my deceased human father as I knew him some seventeen years ago.

My mind turns to our participation in that vast universe. In a very real sense, I am not looking at foreign territory, but at a familiar home—if I can only tap into cellular memory. For we are all, literally, children of the stars.

We are star children in a physical sense because material in every atom of our body was created in the long distant past, throughout the birth, life, and death of stars long preceding the birth of our own solar system. We simply don't know how many billions of years the star-stuff of our bodies goes back in time. Consequently, in a very real sense our bodies are not twenty years old, or forty, or eighty— the stuff of our physical body is billions of years old. We have gone through innumerable "incarnations" in the material universe, eventually ending up as part of this particular planet, born this time around from the womb of Mother Earth. We are literally the product of a cosmic union—the seed of Father Sky implanted in Mother Earth, giving birth to humanity.

And we are star children in a spiritual sense, because we know that we have an innate participation with all that is, the entire universe, in spite of our periodic lapse of memory or, as Einstein put it, our "optical delusion of separateness." We are not isolated spiritually. We participate in the meaning and purpose of the universe. As the astronomer Harlow Shapley expressed it, "We are brothers of the boulders, cousins of the clouds." So, when I look into the night sky I know that I am looking at familiar, and familial, territory. My spirit has soared there before.

The problem is that we have been accustomed to worshiping science and looking at the world through materialistic eyes. Consequently, when science tells us something about the material in our bodies—that we are physically star children—we tend to believe it. However, when someone suggests that we are spiritually star children, we assume he must be having some "mystical" experience—and that just doesn't convince us. Unless, of course, we have learned to see with sacred eyes the genetic heritage—physical and spiritual—we have as a gift from Father Sky. Thanks, Dad.

CHAPTER 2

THE PREGNANT WOMB OF GAIA:
Mother Earth

This concept of an organic universe, of a cosmos that lives and breathes, is an important one. It carries the seeds of a new and more tuneful understanding.

—SCIENTIST LYALL WATSON

OUR MOTHER, THE EARTH, had one hell of a beginning.

If we ever needed a good example of the fact that beauty can arise out of ugliness, that heaven can arise out of hell, or that a bright new day can emerge out of the darkest night of suffering, our Mother Earth provides one. Born Herself about 4.6 billion years ago She was a long way from being a fit mother.

Her first billion years were so horrendous, in terms of inhospitable conditions, that earth scientists call it the Hadean Aeon, after Hades, the Greek word for hell. She was "a desert without seas or shores, without soil or green leaves - a shimmering orb of red-hot rock from horizon to horizon."[1] Bombardments of meteorites pummeled the earth's surface, having free access because of the lack of any atmosphere.

The moon was only 11,000 miles away, compared to today's 250,000 miles. It circled the earth in six hours rather than today's twenty-eight days. And it raised massive tides of molten rock here on earth. Earth was spinning much faster in those days with days and nights of six hours duration. There was no oxygen and no life on the early earth—a violent, hellish sphere.

Additional hundreds of millions of years passed. The bombardment from outer space diminished and the earth cooled allowing clouds of water vapor to accumulate. She moved from the Hadean Aeon into the Archean Aeon, from which identifiable rocks are

17

exposed currently throughout much of the world. It was the beginning of the historical record and the beginning of life. Earth scientists consider it astonishing that "some of the earliest rocks preserved on the planet contain cells entombed within them. . . . The conclusion seems inescapable: Life arose almost as soon as the planet ascended from hell."[2]

Exactly how Mother Earth came to life about 3.9 billion years ago, how life emerged out of non-life, is still a mystery to the scientists. Some speculate that lightening bolts striking the primal planetary material stimulated life. Others think that our Mother was impregnated by comets from outer space bringing life spores to Earth in violent collisions. Perhaps we have not as yet hit on what really happened. We know only that Mother Earth has been alive since very shortly after the material of Her body coalesced in space. Significantly, scientists say that it is "virtually impossible even for biologists to give a concise definition of the difference between living and nonliving substance. . . [or to say]. . . this is where life ends and this is where the inorganic realm of non-life begins."[3]

More to the point, life and non-life are continually in transformative processes, moving back and forth. We have created, in our minds, an artificial distinction by thinking the words life and non-life refer to totally separate and distinct aspects of reality. Or as astrophysicist George Seielstad put it, "the separation of matter into animate and inanimate components is temporary. Life and non-life interpenetrate. Life and the land, sea, and air in which it exists are inseparable."[4] Seielstad estimates, for instance, that an "oxygen molecule in the atmosphere is, on the average, part of a living system for about one day of every decade. A hydrogen atom in ocean water spends about one minute of every year in a living organism."[5]

There is a marriage between heaven and earth, where the two—Father Sky and Mother Earth—become one. They make love in the most holistic, interpenetrating way imaginable. We are the children of that union. The stuff of our bodies, and of our minds and spirits, is star stuff—spending some time in Father Sky and some time in Mother Earth, before and after it is in human form.

Our personal identities, our self-images, are incredibly false, tragically truncated, and sadly lacking, if we leave out this interconnectedness with all space and all time. When we overlook this marvel of our cosmic heritage, we lack the appropriate awe, respect, and gratitude which life deserves.

"There is nothing inorganic," wrote Henry David Thoreau. "The earth is not a mere fragment of dead history, stratum upon stratum, like the leaves of a book, to be studied by geologists. . . but living poetry like the leaves of a tree, which precede flowers and fruit; not a fossil earth but a living earth."[6] Thus, with scientist James Lovelock as the primary catalyst, many are now calling our living Mother Earth by the name of Gaia, the name the ancient Greeks gave to the Earth Goddess.

After emerging from hell, the survivor Gaia started on a long journey of nourishing life. But it was not, however, quite the rough, tough, combative process our Epoch II adolescent mind's have thought it to be. With a typically adolescent mentality we have liked to think of evolution as being an intensively competitive process of "survival of the fittest." Increasingly, scientists are realizing that Gaia enabled the evolution of life through "continual cooperation, strong interaction, and mutual dependence. . . Life did not take over the globe by combat," suggests Lynn Margulis and Dorion Sagan, "but by networking."[7] A very motherly thing to do, I might add.

It is important what metaphors we choose and on which we fashion our philosophy of life. In our Epoch II adolescence we looked back on Epoch I as a violent and competitive time. That was just the way nature was, we thought—a dog-eat-dog tough world. And in thinking such we justified all sorts of mayhem as "natural." As Epoch III begins to emerge in our minds, however, we are beginning to realize that the vicious canine consumption mentality was no more "real world" in early evolution than cooperation and synergy.

The matter of how we choose metaphors for understanding the world, and their attendant consequences, is a subject that could sidetrack us for some time. But for now, back to the story at hand— the evolution of Epoch I.

The evolution of life on/with Gaia is a long and fascinating process. By 2,500 million years ago bacteria had populated every part of Gaia. But in light of our recent thinking about germs and bacteria, the notion that all of life has had a long and symbiotic existence with bacteria may come as a bit of a surprise. Our Epoch II adolescent mind has had us thinking that we were totally separate and distinct from other life forms. We have viewed self as completely different from non-self, inside as different from outside, and we thought we should protect ourselves from "foreign" invasion of germs, viruses, and bacteria. Now, however, we are learning that in our early stages of life we grew up out of bacteria, and that bacteria continues to be an integral part of us today. Biologists are now saying that "health is not so much a matter of destroying microorganisms as it is of restoring appropriate microbial communities. . . [for they are] our ancestors, [and] planetary elders."[8]

The increasing complexity of life progressed fairly well from 3.9 billion years ago until about 2 billion years ago. Then it ran into a crisis of major proportions—a crisis that was to be the catalyst for a new stage of growth.

The crisis occurred when, in our very early stages of life, we developed an excess of garbage—toxic garbage. As living cells split a molecule of hydrogen dioxide (water), they kept the atoms of hydrogen and threw the atoms of oxygen back into the water. Oxygen was the left-over garbage, and it was a deadly poison—so deadly that if there had been a lot of that garbage around during the early years life would not have been able to survive. Oxygen is deadly because it burns organic material.

The poisonous garbage, oxygen, accumulated for 500 million years and threatened the very continuation of life in the seas. (There was no life on land as yet.) Then it accumulated in the atmosphere, growing from one part in a million to one part in five—from 0.0001 to 21%. We were in a severe crisis. We would either be killed off by the crisis, or we would have to innovate. We innovated.

In a very heroic and entrepreneurial fashion, we not only learned to tolerate the poison, we learned to use it to our advantage. We learned that we could get energy out of the toxic garbage by inventing a new trick called respiration. It was an inspired act. Literally. We developed the technique of respiration and succeeded in moving to a new level in the evolutionary journey.

There was excess oxygen left over after our respiration and Gaia made beneficial use of it. She used the excess oxygen to build up a protective envelope around her—ozone. The ozone shield reduced the amount of ultraviolet light reaching Gaia's surface and allowed life to move from the sea onto the land.

Gaia's atmosphere is very special, for it plays an important role in the development and protection of life in general, and in humanity's evolutionary journey in particular. Again, there is a hint of meaning and purpose. "There is something about the air itself that is full of surprises," writes Lyall Watson, with doctorates in anthropology and ethology, "suggesting that it could never have arisen by accident nor persisted by chance. . . . In the eyes of a chemist, air is a mixture of gases. But it is a mixture so curious and incompatible, so inherently unstable, that it begins to look unreasonable. Or, what is even more exciting, to look as though it had a reason for being."[9]

Similar to the recent discoveries about the universe at large, science is realizing that there were a large number of "coincidences" about the way our Mother Gaia developed. She managed Her evolutionary process in very precise ways so as to be a fit mother. With sacred eyes we can look at the scientific evidence and see an awe-inspiring meaning and purpose to it all.

Gaia's atmosphere is certainly one example of Her self-regulating capability. Not only did She turn the garbage into a valuable resource for life, but managed the amount at precisely the right percentage for Her children's benefit. She allowed the oxygen to accumulate up to 21 percent of the atmosphere, and then kept it right there. If it were much less life could not exist. If oxygen had continued to increase, to as much as 25 percent, everything would burst into flames.

Another example is the way Gaia has managed Her nitrogen. Nitrogen comprises 78 percent of our atmosphere. If it were to fall to just 75 percent, we would have a global and permanent ice age killing off all life as we know it.

Similarly, with carbon dioxide. Carbon dioxide comprises only .03 percent of the atmosphere. Yet, without carbon dioxide life could not exist. If Gaia's atmosphere had any greater percentage of carbon dioxide, She would again descend into hell. For instance, if Gaia were a dead planet, carbon dioxide would comprise about 99 percent of the atmosphere.

Gaia is a living organism and the womb from which human life emerged. There are many ways, we are just now discovering, that She has regulated the conditions of Her life so that she would be a fit mother. But like typical adolescents, we have been a bit slow in developing an appropriate appreciation for the many ways in which our Mother has loved us.

Our human capacity to maintain our internal temperature homeostatically, in spite of external changes, was learned from our Mother Gaia. Gaia's heat lamp, the sun, has gone through many changes during the life of Gaia. It now gives Gaia up to three times as much heat as it did when Gaia was an infant—yet Gaia is not three times as hot now as then. Throughout billions of years, in spite of the changes of the sun, Gaia has maintained Her surface temperature within the relatively narrow limits which permit and encourage life.

The miracle of Gaia's life, and Her mothering capacities, does not stop with the atmosphere and the sun's heat. The salt of the earth, for instance, has remained healthfully constant throughout the years in spite of many other changes. Gaia's oceans are about 3.4 percent salt and have remained so for most of Gaia's lifetime—again, just the right percentage for life. If the percentage were to ever have risen to about 6 percent the oceans would be dead.

The oceans, in fact, give additional evidence of the marvelously mysterious capacities of Gaia's living self-renewal. For some time we had been aware of the fact that water is cycled up from the oceans into the atmosphere, then down onto the land, and back to the oceans. Only recently did we discover that Gaia's circulatory system is more complex, and deeper, than that. There appears to be an eight-million-year cycle in which the entire ocean goes down into the inner Gaia and back up through vents discovered on the ocean's floor. This process appears to warm and chemically renew the oceans.

We have heard astronauts exclaim about how beautiful Gaia appears from outer space—a sight which has caused a dramatic transformation of consciousness for many. Now an "aquanaut" exploring the deepest ocean terrain has a similar perception. Robert Ballard, an oceanographer/geophysicist and a senior scientist with the Woods Hole Oceanographic Institution, was also the discoverer of the hydrothermal vents at the bottom of the Atlantic Ocean. "The earth," he writes, "is a living, breathing thing, a giant organism. We live on it in a potentially parasitic, terminal situation. We could kill the host, blow it up, pollute it. We almost did that. Thank God it's got resilience."[10]

Gaia has, indeed, been resilient. She has also been an incredible Mother, nurturing and nourishing us from our bacterial incarnation to the human beings we are today. She has been a complex and hearty survivor. She has been profoundly capable of maintaining and encouraging life, in spite of a multitude of stressors—and She does so, not by being a static rock of resistance, but by being a changing, dynamic, shifting and moving survivor. James Lovelock suggests that, "for this to have happened by chance is as unlikely as to survive unscathed a drive blindfolded through rush-hour traffic."[11]

I am literally writing these words on the day that we in this culture celebrate as Mother's Day. Again, atop Winged Spirit Mountain, I look to the west where I have a fantastically beautiful and panoramic view of the majestic Continental Divide and to the east to Gaia's placid plains. The view, and this particular day, create a meaningful convergence. The spirit within the breeze brings an inhalation of deep gratitude for both my human mother and for our Earth Mother—Frances and Gaia. I have received nourishing inspiration from both, and to both I am feeling a special gratitude. They have both, in their own ways, given me life and loved me through the valleys of tough lessons and onto the mountain-tops of glorious celebrations. And I have all too often taken their love for granted. Each has forgiven my immaturities and my short-comings, and each has affirmed me with a quiet and profound wisdom. Thanks, Frances. Thanks, Gaia. I love you both.

Regardless of what your experience may be with your human mother, the one thing we definitely share, reader and writer alike, is that we are all children of Gaia. We are just beginning to awaken to the great debt we owe Her. But, hopefully, as we do awaken to Her forgiving, and fore-given, love, our capacities to return that love, and to appreciate our rich heritage and precious gifts will increase. The increase of such capacities are key elements in having a healthy planetary family and a healthy future for us all.

CHAPTER 3

HUMANITY'S CHILDHOOD

Life is now taking matter into its own hands.
—SCIENCE WRITER BRIAN M. FAGAN

WE NOW TURN TO HUMANITY'S STORY, a long and labyrinthine tale, the large-scale Biography of our species. And what a story it is.

As with our Father Sky and our Mother Earth, all the children of that union have stories with plots—another way of putting it is that they all have lives with a purpose. Not that we know what every life form's purpose is—we clearly don't. But our ignorance, nor the current scientific abhorrence of discussing purpose, do not suffice in making life purposeless.

Any discussion of purpose is a tricky and slippery one—a topic which has traditionally sent scientists and scholars into fits of apoplexy. However, a book purportedly dealing with spiritual evolution certainly cannot avoid the subject.

In the use of terms such as plot and purpose I am not suggesting that life's evolutionary journey is pre-programed in all details. That would mean that all we are doing is living out a pre-set process totally devoid of creativity, novelty, and self determination. I simply don't believe that is the case. On the contrary, the plot to humanity's story is the evolutionary journey toward health and wholeness—or in the metaphor used in this book, maturation. Although we will get into the subject of love more in Chapter Eight, suffice it here to say that we were created out of a cosmic love—a built-in attraction toward wholeness. Creativity and free will are major ingredients in that kind of loving plot or purpose. So, as we near maturity we have the capacity to write a variety of chapters, or at least as far as our story, write a variety of endings. Humanity's story is being written as we live it.

Our purpose is to attain a healthy co-creator participant role, and to contribute to the continued evolution of health and wholeness. The end of the twentieth century is that critical turning point of humanity coming of age into that co-creator maturity. But that's getting ahead of our story. The first epoch in our story is our childhood, the purpose of which was physical evolution. So let's return to that period in our history.

Humanity is one of the offspring resulting from that marriage of heaven and earth. Humanity's story, like that of Father Sky's and Mother Earth's, is filled with "coincidences" and "miracles," enough to lead paleontologist Stephen Jay Gould to speak of "the awesome improbability of human evolution."[1] We will examine first the working out of that physiological purpose, and then consider the value system that emerged late in our childhood.

Our Childhood's Purpose: To Become Physiologically Human

At an individual level, one of our primary characteristics, compared to other animals, is our extended dependence upon our mother. This has been true for us collectively as well. Although this, as any metaphor, can be pushed too far—for we are still dependent upon the earth to a very significant extent—this overview suggests that our childhood dependency lasted for almost all of the entire four and half billion year lifespan of Mother Gaia. It is only in the very recent period of adolescent development that we have asserted our "independence"—leaving home as we blast off into outer space.

To see this in historical perspective we can borrow Dr. Carl Sagan's idea of a "cosmic year." In his concept of a "cosmic year" the entire history of the universe is compressed into the span of one year. Consequently, assuming a fifteen billion year old universe, one "second" of this "cosmic year" represents about 475 actual years, one "minute" equals just under 30,000 years, one "hour" just short of two million years, etc. This way we can get a perspective of human evolution—our long gestation, birth, and childhood—within a framework of time with which we can relate.[2]

RY 1ST—THE BEGINNING OF THE UNIVERSE

MAY 1ST—FORMATION OF OUR GALAXY, THE MILKY WAY

SEPTEMBER 9TH—FORMATION OF OUR SOLAR SYSTEM

SEPTEMBER 14TH—THE BIRTHDAY OF GAIA, MOTHER EARTH

SEPTEMBER 27TH—THE BEGINNING OF LIFE ON/WITH/OUT-OF GAIA

Just as soon as Gaia emerged from Hell, She began giving birth to, and nourishing, life. As mentioned in the last chapter, no one knows for sure exactly how life got its start here, but it is clear that life and Gaia, after She emerged from Her hellish beginning, are indistinguishable. Gaia created an environment by life, for life.

It is, indeed, accurate to say that life constantly emerges "out-of" Gaia, given the fact that ninety percent of the carbon in our bodies has passed through the ocean-floor vents, coming from deep within Gaia.[3]

As mentioned before, the stuff of our bodies has gone through innumerable life-cycles of stars, and just maybe our Biography is even more complex than that. If there is life elsewhere in the universe—which certainly is probable, given the vast numbers of stars and planetary systems in the universe—we no doubt have more "incarnations" than we can possibly count. Imagine what we would know if we could just tap into the memory of each atom of our bodies? Talk about multiple personalities!

NOVEMBER 1ST—THE INVENTION OF SEX BY MICRO-ORGANISMS

Now we know whom to thank.

After micro-organisms invented sex they multiplied so much that before "November" was over, they had populated every nook and cranny of Gaia—a skin for Gaia of living matter.

DECEMBER 1ST—DEVELOPMENT OF GAIA'S ATMOSPHERE

It was this late in our "cosmic year" that we faced the oxygen crisis, combined inspiration with respiration, and began to breath in what had previously been toxic garbage.

DECEMBER 10TH—LIFE GRADUATED TO THE MULTICELLULAR LEVEL

DECEMBER 15TH—LIFE DEVELOPED ITS FIRST BRAINS AND NERVOUS SYSTEMS

DECEMBER 20TH—PLANTS BEGAN TO POPULATE DRY LAND

DECEMBER 21ST—THE FIRST INSECTS AND ANIMALS BEGAN TO ENJOY DRY LAND

Although some of us have continued to live our lives on dry land, we have never, in a very real sense, left the ocean. The concentrations of salts in our bodies—sodium, potassium, and chloride—are essentially the same as in the oceans. We sweat, cry, and have coursing throughout our bloodstream that which is basically seawater.

DECEMBER 23RD—THE FIRST TREES

DECEMBER 24TH—THE FIRST DINOSAURS

DECEMBER 26TH—THE FIRST MAMMALS

DECEMBER 27TH—THE FIRST BIRDS

DECEMBER 28TH—THE FIRST FLOWERS, AND THE EXTINCTION OF THE DINOSAURS

DECEMBER 29TH—THE FIRST PRIMATES

DECEMBER 30TH—THE FIRST HOMINIDS

DECEMBER 31ST—(AND THEN, ONLY VERY LATE IN THE DAY)—THE FIRST HUMANS

One of the discoveries that excites scientists is that of our distant relative "Lucy," who was feeling the earth, smelling the flowers, experiencing the animals, and raising her young about three million years ago. She walked upright, was about three-and-a-half feet tall, had a brain about the size of a chimpanzee's brain, and lived in North Africa. "Lucy" was given her name by the archeologists who discovered her remains because the Beatles' song "Lucy in the Sky with Diamonds," was playing on the radio at the time of their discovery.[4]

By 11:00 p.m. we had begun to use stone tools, had discovered fire by 11:46 p.m., and were painting on cave walls by 11:59 p.m. Our handyman incarnation has been labeled "Homo habilis." It was "Homo erectus" our upright relative who discovered fire and "Homo sapiens" who was named as being wise.

Actually, there are two subspecies of Homo sapiens. Sometime about two hundred thousand years ago we had a big-brained cousin whom we have labeled "Homo sapiens neanderthalensis" living near modern-day Dusseldorf in Germany. Since the valley in which we found the remains of our cousin was named after a seventeenth-century composer named Joachim Neander, we have given our cousin the name of "Neanderthal." Although our cousin's lineage became extinct, we continue to use his name in vain every time we want to insult someone who is not up-to-date. Nevertheless, our Neanderthal cousin was an artist, a poet, and one who buried the dead. (By this time we had a very distinct value system, and we'll get into that a bit later in our discussion.) Our particular lineage comes from the other Homo sapiens, whom we have egotistically labeled as doubly wise—Homo sapiens sapiens.

As of this writing there is a great deal of controversy about some of the specific details between the paleoanthropologists on the one hand and the biologists on the other. The former look at bones for their information, the latter at genetic material. The controversy arose when some biologists, ignoring the bones and looking at laboratory genetic research, postulated that all we current humans are descendents of one particular woman in Africa about 146,000 years ago. She was quickly, and understandably, dubbed "Eve." The scientists who take bones as the source of data say that our particular lineage started much earlier.

For our purposes, all this is rather academic and essentially unimportant. We are looking at the larger overview and can leave the squabble over the exact timing to the experts. As I have maintained throughout, with the stuff of our bodies being star-stuff it is quite arbitrary to mark our "birth" at 146,000 years ago, or four million years ago, or several billion years ago.

Nevertheless, in our illustration of the entire evolution of life compressed within the "cosmic year," this so-called "Eve" of recent genetic research came on the scene at about 11:55 p.m. on December 31st.

More to the point, I am suggesting that the childhood of humanity—the entire process of becoming physically human—took up the entire "cosmic year" except for the last five minutes. Talk about an extended childhood.

Our adolescence, which we will get to in our discussion of Epoch II, has taken place in just the last ten seconds of the year. Buddha was born five seconds ago, and Christ four seconds ago, whereas modern science, the methods we use to understand the universe, has been around for only about the last second of our "cosmic year." This extended childhood, as I have indicated, was for the purpose of physical development, and there are three ways of looking at physical development. One is that which we have been exploring so far, namely how we anatomically became what we know today as human. That process was completed only about 150,000 years ago.

The second way of looking at our physical development has to do with our growth geographically—how humans physically spread out over the Gaian body. About 75,000 years ago, we started migrating out of Africa and began the long process of populating the planet with "humanity the doubly wise." It appears that we first spread out to Southern Europe and the warmer areas of Asia. By 50,000 years ago we had reached Australia and New Guinea. We reached Siberia about 20,000 years ago, and apparently crossed the Bering land bridge into North America about that time. It appears that we had reached all of South America by about 9000 B.C. It was only about 2000 B.C. that we finally reached the world's remote oceanic islands.[5]

The third way of considering humanity's physical development has to do with our growth quantitatively—becoming so numerically significant that we begin to play an important role in Gaia's future. 50,000 years ago we humans numbered perhaps a few million. 10,000 years ago there were about ten million of us. But about 4,000 years ago we started to multiply much more rapidly. By 2,000 years ago we had reached three hundred million in number. By the year 1600 a.d. we were five hundred million strong, and today we number more than five *thousand* million. It is estimated that by the turn of the century humanity will number over six thousand million.

How fascinating it would be to have a motion picture of our childhood—a visual overview of the entire process of physical evolution. We could follow the "travelogue" as we spread out first as bacteria, covering the entire body of Gaia. Then, the evolutionary spurt in Africa in which we became physiologically human beings. And we spread out again to re-populate the planet.

The movie would have all sorts of fascinating sounds, but would not become a "talkie" until we developed our first human/Gaia "mother tongue" somewhere between 50,000 and 100,000 years ago. We could follow the remarkable process of moving into different areas of the globe, taking on different superficial physical characteristics and developing our parochial languages.

Perhaps, if we were actually able to view such a movie of our evolution, we would be inclined to consider more carefully all our bigotry and prejudice based upon how people look. Perhaps it has all been a test for us to see how silly and sad our distinctions of "our group" from "their group," how tragic our identifications of "enemies," and how abominable our negative judgment of people who don't look just like us as non-human or sub-human.

It is important to be clear about how this overview of humanity's development linking us with the entire history of the universe is to make the point of participation and responsibility, not an egotistic claim of central or higher importance. To recognize that we have participated in the entire evolution of the universe is not the same as claiming that the only or central purpose of the universe was the emergence of humanity.

I think it was Stephen Crane who once wrote:

> A man said to the universe: "Sir, I exist."
> "However," replied the universe, "The fact has not created in me a sense of obligation."

The universe, and the wonder of life, is far too marvelous and complex for us to be so simple-minded as to think we could even comprehend its total or central purpose. What we can say for sure is that we have participated in the entire process and that if we are to make the most of our opportunity and responsibility we need to search for our own meaning and purpose. To take seriously our relationship with all life is not to claim universal centrality, nor of being the pinnacle of evolution.

It is important for us to find an appropriate and healthy self-image as we come of age into adult maturity. As we have already mentioned, and will explore more in depth within the next few chapters, we had a particular self-image within our childhood and a very different self-image throughout adolescence. They will both set the stage, I hope, for the more mature and meaningful self-image that we will explore in Chapter Eleven. But we are getting ahead of the story.

Humanity's childhood was a time of unity and at-one-ment with Gaia, our Mother Earth. Father Sky impregnated our Mother Gaia and She gave birth to life in general and then, very late in the process, to humanity in particular. There certainly is a lot we don't know about the role of Father Sky in our earlier "incarnations"—at least ten billion years of ignorance—but we do know a lot about the role of Mother Gaia. She has given us birth and nurtured us through a very long childhood.

Eventually, very late in our childhood, we matured to the point of developing a value system and in giving thanks to (worshipping) our Mother Gaia.

Our Childhood Value System
and Focus of Worship

Who or what we worship is a direct result of our value system. Out of a maturing soul comes the deep value system, and out of the value system comes the focus of external worship.

As far as we can tell it was well after becoming physiologically human that we started manifesting a deep value system. It was somewhere between 100,000 and 50,000 years ago that we started burying our dead, apparently contemplating life after death. It is the first indication that our collective soul had matured to the point of developing a deep value system.

Discerning what those values were is not an easy task, considering what we have found from that time period to "read" and the particularly tinted lens through which we have attempted to do the "reading."

Science writer James Schreeve suggests a different metaphor by which to consider our bias in interpretation. "Everybody knows fossils are fickle," Schreeve writes. "Bones will sing any song you want to hear."[6] Throughout the entire period of scientific inquiry into our childhood years of 100,000 years ago to 5,000 years ago we have been listening to "songs" heard through adolescent and masculine ears. So, until just recently, most of the "evidence" has fit into an adolescent and masculine interpretation.

Another difficulty is created by the fact that most of what we have from our childhood are "hard" facts. It is only the hard material—teeth, bones, stone tools, pottery—that have survived the millennia. What do we miss when we try to interpret millions of years of our childhood without knowing what our dreams, visions, and loves were? Isn't it possible that we would learn as much from discussions around the campfire as with the stone tools left over? As much from the feelings of the heart and the thoughts of the mind as from the outer protective shell of ribs and skull? But no tape recordings or written journals come down to us from those childhood years.

It seems rather symbolic that a masculine culture trying to remember its childhood is only left with the "hard" rather than the "soft" facts. And the difficulty is compounded by our current materialism—we tend to think that only the hard material evidence matters.

Fortunately, soft things are sometimes revealed in the hard evidence—paintings on cave walls, for instance, and the figurines we molded or carved. We have discovered cave-wall paintings which are dated as far back as 30,000 B.C., many of which present women and the woman's role in the community.

What for a long time had been interpreted, by male scholars naturally, as male eroticism is now being seen, by more enlightened male as well as female scholars, as indicating the central role of women during our childhood and the worship of the Goddess. And the paintings of animals, which previously had been interpreted only as objects of the hunt by primitive man, are now viewed as symbols of humanity's sense of unity with nature.

Archaeological evidence from 25,000 to 30,000 years ago indicates that in the later years of our childhood, when we began to develop socially, culturally, and spiritually, we focused our appreciation, our meaning and purpose, our worship, on the Earth Goddess.

Riane Eisler sums up a great deal of such evidence and suggests that:

> instead of being random and unconnected materials, the Paleolithic remains of female figurines, red ocher in burials, and vagina-shaped cowrie shells appear to be early manifestations of what was later to develop into a complex religion centering on the worship of a Mother Goddess as the source and regeneratrix of all forms of life.[7]

Additional evidence of the Neolithic worship of the Goddess is found from ten thousand years ago in the area of modern Israel, as far east as India, as far west as England, and as far South as the Mediterranean island of Malta. Archaeology professor Marija Gimbutas points out that the symbolism used in their objects of worship show that Paleolithic and Neolithic humanity focused upon a Goddess that was integral to life on earth and always in transformation. The Goddess was

> in constant and rhythmic change between creation and destruction, birth and death. The moon's three phases—new, waxing, and old—are repeated in trinities or triple-functional deities that recall these moon phases: maiden, nymph, and crone; life-giving, death-giving, and transformational; rising, dying, and self-renewing. . . . The concept of regeneration and renewal is perhaps the most outstanding and dramatic theme that we perceive in this symbolism.[8]

British archaeologist James Mellaart has documented "a stability and continuity of growth over many thousands of years for progressively more advanced Goddess-worshiping cultures."[9] Mellaart did extensive excavations in present day Turkey, what in the seventh millennium B.C. was the plains of Anatolia, and discovered that, in addition to worshipping the Goddess, humanity had a value system which was very definitely "feminine" in content. To put it in order, we worshipped the Goddess precisely because our deep value system was essentially feminine.

> There had been no wars for a thousand years. There was an ordered pattern of society. There were no human or animal sacrifices. Vegetarianism prevailed, for domestic animals were kept for milk and wool - not for meat. There is no evidence of violent deaths.[10]

Other scholars suggest that recent discoveries show that Anatolia was not a cultural aberration, but apparently the norm. There is now sufficient evidence from other archaeological digs to show that much of the Near and Middle East, as well as parts of Europe, Asia and America, once were dominated by feminine values and worship was of the Great Goddess.[11]

The period of the gestation, birth, and early nurturing of the human family evidently was characterized by cooperation rather than competition, an ecological relationship with nature rather than an exploitative one, and the unconscious as dominant rather than rational consciousness. There was equality between the sexes, and it was essentially a peaceful time. People chose living sites for beauty, accessibility of good water and soil, and availability of good animal pastures, not for their inaccessibility and fortress value. Gimbutas notes that there are numerous indicators that these were matrilinear societies with a person's history traced back through the mother.

Although our childhood societies were matrilinear and had a dominance of feminine values, there is no evidence that they were matriarchies. There apparently was a greater sense of equality and cooperation and not the dominator kind of model we have experienced during our patriarchal adolescence. Dr. Marilyn French makes the distinction between "matriarchy" and "matricentric." "Matricentric societies are spontaneous, organic; the mother cares for the baby until it is able to move about easily by itself, find food, and protect itself without her. The mother 'rules' by greater experience, knowledge, and ability, but the intention of her 'rule' is to free the child, to make it independent."[12]

The art that resulted from the childhood of the race has a notable absence of imagery idealizing war, violence, or "noble warriors."

Rather, what seems to have been our focus back then was the life-giving qualities of the feminine, nature, and the awe and wonder of all life. "What is conspicuous in neolithic diggings," writes cultural historian Lewis Mumford, "is. . . the complete absence of weapons, though tools and pots are not lacking."[13] Archaeologist W. J. Perry adds that:

> It is an error, as profound as it is universal, to think that men in the food-gathering stage were given to fighting. . . . All the available facts go to show that the food-gathering stage of history must have been one of perfect peace. The study of the artifacts of the Paleolithic age fails to reveal any definite signs of human warfare.[14]

Think about how often we rationalize various forms of violence, competition, and selfishness as being "just human nature," or how often we justify all sorts of mayhem as being "only human." From such a perspective of human nature, it is understandable that we have taken a cynical and pessimistic view of the future—to avoid war and/or selfish destruction of the environment, within that view, would take a fundamental overhaul of our very nature.

Recent biological and archaeological findings, however, have shown cooperation to be fundamental to the evolution of life, and in our childhood we were not characterized by our recent propensity for violence. To recognize these current violent behaviors, dominant throughout the past five to seven thousand years, as adolescent behaviors rather than unchangeable innate "human nature" throws a much different light on our view of future possibilities. For a while we saw only recorded history, only the period of our adolescence, and thought that was the whole extent of the human journey and a fundamental description of "human nature." We were wrong.

Throughout our childhood there was an interesting use of symbols representing transformation and regeneration, such as the serpent and the butterfly. The cross, seen as a symbol of life not of death, and symbols of resurrection were also prevalent as long as 8,000 years ago. Eisler writes that, "If the central religious image was a woman giving birth and not, as in our time, a man dying on a cross, it would not be unreasonable to infer that life and the love of life—rather than death and the fear of death—were dominant in society as well as art."[15]

The symbol of the bull also provides another interesting contrast between our childhood and the more recent period of our adolescence. In Neolithic times the bull was the symbol of the male qualities, which were clearly given, like everything else, by the Goddess. Consequently, there were paintings and figurines of the Goddess giving birth to a young bull. Later, during our adolescence, Christianity turned the horns of the bull into the symbol of Satan or evil.

In summary then, the purpose of our long collective childhood (Epoch I) was to develop physically into human beings. After we developed physically, but before we entered adolescence, our childhood's deep value system emerged from our soul. The primary characteristics of that deep value system were:

1. An at-one-ment with nature—ecological and changing.
2. An emphasis upon life-giving and nurturing.
3. Equality among the sexes.
4. Peaceful and cooperative.
5. Matricentric and matrilineal societies.
6. And since this value system was essentially feminine, we worshipped what seemed to us to be the feminine power behind everything—The Earth Goddess.

EPOCH II

THE ADOLESCENCE OF HUMANITY

Ego and Mental Development

EPOCH II INTRODUCTION

The first people were like the animals;
They knew no shame, guilt, guile,
For they were innocent.
They were innocent because they were whole.
Being whole they lived their own truth.
Being truthful they were fulfilled.
Being fulfilled they were made whole.
Being whole they were holy.

Being holy they were wise.
Being wise they lived in peace
With each other. . .

And they were well in body and soul,
Enjoying peace
Until the Fall
And their alienation from the animals
Who, ever since, have feared them.

—Dr. Michael W. Fox

Transitions of deep value systems incubate in the soul for some time before being manifested in the superficial culture and in our daily lives. We may never know when the actual inner alchemy of transforming soul begins—all we can know is when that transformation begins to bubble up into a level of awareness, or in actually changing the way we go about our lives.

In the case of our transformation from childhood into adolescence, from Epoch I into Epoch II, the evidence indicates that even the evidence coming to the surface took several thousand years. The Epoch II purpose and value system started becoming evident in human activity in about 8000 B.C., although the transition was not completed until about 1500 B.C. on the more isolated islands of the Agean and Mediterranean.

The evolutionary and maturational purpose of our adolescence was to be ego and mental development. Ego development, a sense of self as distinct from others, necessitates a certain kind of vision—seeing oneself as separate from the other. In Epoch I we were one with the animals, one with nature—in Epoch II we discovered and manifested our separation.

It started in about 8000 B.C. with the domestication of plants and animals. We changed what had been a cooperative at-one-ment with the rest of nature, to one of separation, control, and manipulation of nature for our own purposes. We gradually came to view ourselves as above nature and ordained by God to have dominion over nature.

That separation from nature some 10,000 years ago can hardly be overemphasized in terms of its impact. It had both positive as well as negative impact on the succeeding millennia of human development—all of which, I am suggesting, was necessary for our maturation.

First of all, the positive. It is not popular, during the latter part of the twentieth century, to suggest anything positive regarding our separation from nature, or even to speak favorably of the human ego. I would argue, however, that the ego development of adolescence, although not always pretty nor pleasant, is a necessary stage of self-identity before the more mature ego-transcendence can be experienced. We would not be ready for the spiritual maturation of Epoch III had we not gone through the adolescent ego development of Epoch II.

Nevertheless, recognizing the necessity of adolescence does not gloss over the problems associated with it. Only in being clear about the pitfalls of immaturity can we move on into a healthier and more wholesome maturity. And the pitfalls resulting from our separation from nature are many and quite substantial. In separating from nature we started a binge of separation, distinction, categorization, and compartmentalization—we lost our sense of connection, of wholeness. In separating from nature we lost touch with our innate inner power, and began projecting our sense of power out onto other things and other people—the trail has led through the projection of essential power up into heaven, out onto saviors and other heroes, and eventually out onto machines and advanced technology. And in losing our sense of inner power—separating from nature separated us from our essential feminine power—we tried to control nature and others with rigid belief systems and violence. (All of this will resurface time and time again as we progress through our examination of Epoch II.)

The purposes of Epoch II, our collective adolescent ego development, started with the separation from nature, in the domestication of plants and animals, but eventually manifested in the transformation of our deep value system. We replaced the essentially feminine values of our childhood with essentially masculine values. (It will be important throughout our discussion of Epoch II, and particularly as we look to a healthier Epoch III, to remember that these are adolescent and immature versions of the masculine. It may be the only masculine we have known, collectively, but it is not a mature version of the masculine.)

The values that came to dominate Epoch II were reductionism, patriarchy, hierarchy, control, and the fascination of external power and/or power over others. The logical transformation of worship, of course, was from the Mother Goddess to a Father God.

As mentioned before, the soul-level transformation of human life took many thousands of years to fully manifest. Although the important first step may have been the domestication of plants and animals in about 8000 B.C., it was about 4500 B.C. before the violent transition from a feminine and peaceful childhood into a masculine adolescence erupted onto the surface.

At about 4500 B.C. violent nomadic bands—the "street gangs" of prehistory?—grew in number and in ferocity. They began to overrun the more peaceful settlements. Archaeological digs into these times show massive destruction and dislocation. Scholar Marija Gimbutas suggests that the evidence points to three major migratory waves of violent incursions—the first from about 4300 to 4200 B.C., the second from about 3400 to 3200 B.C., and the third from about 3000 to 2800 B.C. Apparently the more isolated Agean and Mediterranean islands of Crete, Thera, and Malta were able to avoid the violent introduction of humanity's adolescence until around 1500 B.C.

The dominant characteristics of the invaders were that they were ruled by male priests and warriors, and that they worshiped a masculine God rather than a feminine Goddess. They also had a form of social organization which emphasized hierarchy, authority, male dominance, and violence. As researcher and author Riane Eisler put it, all the conquering nomads had a value system which placed a "higher value on the power that takes, rather than gives, life. This was the power symbolized by the 'masculine' Blade, which (the) invaders literally worshiped. For in their dominator society, ruled by gods—and men—of war, this was the supreme power."[1]

What happened at this time in the collective psyche of adolescent humanity was very interesting. Virtually every grouping of humanity constructed myths by which to make sense out of the loss of our childhood and the onset of adolescence. We call them creation myths, although they are, in fact, stories representing our memories of a paradisiacal childhood, and our "Fall" up into the struggle of adolescence.

The beginning of the book of Genesis in the Bible—the Garden of Eden—is the Judeo-Christian version of this transition. It purports, of course, to be a description of the very beginning of all creation, but that clearly is not the case. It, like the many other creation myths, represents the relatively new ego-consciousness of humanity emerging in our early adolescence, dim memories of our pleasant childhood, and the recognition that a dramatic, and not so comfortable, separation took place as we left our childhood.

Consider, for instance, the timing of when the Judeo-Christian creation myth was written down. The Garden of Eden myth is actually two stories pulled together as one. The first one in the Bible (Genesis 1:1 through 2:3) is the later of the two stories, written down in about 400 B.C. The earliest creation story, written down in about 1000 B.C., ends up in the Bible as the second version (Genesis 2:4 and following). Nevertheless, both stories, the two in one, came along a considerable period of time after our transition from childhood into adolescence—a transition starting about 8000 B.C. and being completed about 1500 B.C.

Also consider how the basic components of the myth are found throughout the diverse human religious and mythological literature. Creation myths from many cultures have the same two dominant themes—a Paradise and then a Fall. Richard Heinberg, who devoted a decade to studying Paradise myths from around the world, reports that they are found "in virtually any inhabited place, with any ethnic group."[2] Heinberg suggests that the Western world alone has a heritage of at least five such creation stories of a Paradise followed by a Fall: The Judeo-Christian Garden of Eden, the Sumerian Dilmun, the Iranian Garden of Yima, the Egyptian Tep Zepi, and the Greek Golden Age. They all represent essentially the same collective human memory, the memory of an idyllic childhood and the traumatic transition into adolescence. They are different verses of the same song, or perhaps more accurately, the same song in different languages.

It is interesting to note that all these so-called creation myths— actually stories about our childhood to adolescence transition— date the beginning of the world sometime during violent intrusion of God cultures into the previously peaceful Goddess cultures. The

Eastern Orthodox Church dates the beginning of the world at 5508 B.C., whereas the early Syrian Christians put it at 5490 B.C. The 17th century Bishop, James Ussher, determined that the Bible dated the creation of the world at 4004 B.C., whereas the Hebrew calendar puts the beginning at 3760 B.C.

Although not among the dominant cultures of the Western world, yet clearly geographically within it, are the Native American Indians. A Cheyenne creation myth, for instance, has us starting out in a paradise, naked and innocent within fields of plenty, but we soon fell from our idyllic beginnings because of becoming knowledgeable. This "cause" of the Fall, along with stories of a flood and famine, are also found in the Bible—for instance, eating of the forbidden fruit from the tree of knowledge.

All the creation myths have common themes. We started life naked and feeling no shame, speaking with the animals, and with a peaceful harmony and cooperation with all of nature. With the Fall came awareness of our nakedness, shame, knowledge of separation from animals and nature, and floods. The matter of floods, which are present in so many of the creation myths, as well as the sinking of lost continents, may very well be deep memories of the floods that surely would have followed the melting of the last Ice Age, somewhere between 15,000 and 10,000 years ago.

Obviously the Fall, in traditional religious interpretation, has not been considered a good or natural event. It has been viewed in negative terms, for it represented disobedience to God. It was proof of, or the cause for, the depravity of humanity.

In contrast, however, I am suggesting that it is all part of the natural process of maturation. It is organic to the process of becoming an adolescent, a process which naturally follows childhood. The drive for independence, for separation of the self from the parent, of "doing it my way," is natural to the growth process. Only an immature preoccupation with obedience would view it as a negative.

Paul Tillich, the late and great Christian theologian, spoke of sin as separation. In that sense the Fall was, indeed, the Original Sin. But to the mainstream of the public understanding of the phrase, and to the majority of the institutions and leaders of the Judeo-Christian tradition, Original Sin meant the innate depravity of human nature.

On our path toward adult maturity, we must go through the process of becoming a separate, distinct, unique self. To become an "I" we have to begin to understand our differences and our separateness from the "other," particularly the parent. The process of defining self, to a great extent, comes through the process of contrast and distinction.

We simply never grow to maturity if we don't eat the fruit of the tree of knowledge and become aware of our distinction from others. It is the adolescent separation from the peaceful and protected childhood which is the natural developmental step preceding adult maturation. Only after the development of a distinct and seemingly independent self are we ready for the process of adult re-union— the re-uniting of separate selves in which we can experience the grace of synergy—when re-uniting selves experience the glorious "more than the sum of the parts."

Before 8000 B.C. we lived in harmony as brothers and sisters with the animals. It is interesting to note that practically all the creation myths have humans and animals speaking the same language. Jewish legends report that, "the animal world had a different relation to Adam from their relation to his descendents. Not only did they know the language of man, but they respected the image of God. . . all of which changed into the opposite after the fall of man."[3]

Dr. Michael Fox concluded his poem, used in introducing this discussion of the transition, by saying that we "were well in body and soul, enjoying peace, until the Fall. . . ," and it was our alienation from the animals that created fear. "The Eden of the eternal present that the animal world had known for ages was shattered at last," wrote Loren Eisley. "Through the human mind, time and darkness, good and evil would enter and poison the world."[4]

This separation changed our relationship with the animals from the sacred to the profane. It changed the nature of killing from the sacred to the profane—a move which has subsequently taken on such a gap that today's humans, in late adolescence, can hardly relate to the reality which humans and animals shared in our childhood years. In our Paleolithic hunter-gatherer childhood, the hunt was experienced as a sacred act of communion with the animals. Life and death, ours and theirs, was seen as a matter of reciprocity. Animals sometimes killed humans and humans sometimes killed animals, but killing was always done for the necessity of life, and we killed only what was needed.

There was a reverence for life and a primal "you are what you eat" belief system. You took on, it was believed, the qualities of the animal you killed and ate. Killing an animal, in our primitive childhood, was done out of profound respect for its power, and in eating it you gratefully absorbed its power and its characteristics.

Such a relationship can be maintained, however, only when all are free—when we started to control and manipulate the situation, everything changed. When we started raising animals, controlling them, preparing them for slaughter, which led inevitably to the dispassionate purchase of meat "products" wrapped in cellophane at the supermarket—well, you get the picture.

Many scholars point to the domestication of animals as the key turning point. Others suggest that it was the invention of agriculture at about the same time, approximately 8000 B.C. The fact is, they all fit together—we moved from "primitive" hunter-gatherers to "civilization," from food gathering to food production, from the hunt to the domestication of animals. "The Neolithic revolution was an enormous break with the past," writes Morris Berman, "since it altered a way of life that had lasted for more than a million years."[5] In our adolescent ego development, we separated and made the distinction between the wild and the tame, the self and nature, heaven and earth, divine and human. "It is very likely that Paleolithic society did not know war," says Berman, and "that the concept of an enemy, an unfriendly Other, is a Neolithic invention."[6]

It was the rise of civilization, settling down to raise food through the domestication of plants and animals, that was the key which opened the door to a masculine adolescence for humanity. "Mesolithic society may have seen the domestication of animals," writes cultural historian William Irwin Thompson, "and Neolithic society may have seen the domestication of plants, but what the age after the Neolithic sees is the domestication of women by men."[7]

Our relationship with nature, in all its forms, is intricately tied in with our feminine nature. It is our feminine nature which keeps us in touch with our natural affinity for, our organic roots in, the animal kingdom. The transformation of our relationship with nature, from one of cooperative involvement to control and manipulation, made it inevitable that we would leave the Goddess worship, proceed to denigrate women, and move into an adolescence characterized primarily by an unbalanced sense of the masculine. For when the masculine or the feminine is separated from its complementary side, it becomes distorted and eventually pathological.

But separation is what adolescent ego development is all about—at least in its beginning. So we rejected our Mother and our essential feminine nature, separated ourselves from animals and nature, proclaimed male dominance over women, and proceeded to develop our masculine, adolescent ego. In the process, we gave up the playful and peaceful garden for the violent work of the battlefield. Historically, as we have seen, the thundering, violent, warrior-priest led bands of nomads over-ran the peaceful, Goddess-wor-shipping cultures, and we were on our way into adolescence.

"Man cut the umbilical cord to the Great Mother with a sword," observes Thompson, "and the sword has been hanging over his head ever since."[8]

After we separated ourselves from nature, animals, and our feminine power, the inevitable implications for our adolescent years were the creation of a patriarchy, ego distinctions and sepa-rations, projection of essential power, the need for control, and the use of violence. For the first several thousand years of our adoles-cence we viewed the world through religious eyes, and thus mani-fested the Epoch II purpose and value system in religious ways. It is that to which we now turn our attention.

CHAPTER 4

EARLY ADOLESCENCE:
Seeing Through Religious Eyes

Unlike many of his contemporaries among the deities of the ancient Near East, the God of Israel shares his power with no female divinity, nor is he the divine Husband or Lover of any. He scarcely can be characterized in any but masculine epithets: King, Lord, Master, Judge, and Father. Indeed, the absence of feminine symbolism of God marks Judaism, Christianity, and Islam in striking contrast to the world's other religious traditions, whether in Egypt, Babylonia, Greece, and Rome or Africa, Polynesia, India, and North America. . . the actual language they use (Judaism and Christianity) daily in worship and prayer conveys. . . the distinct impression that God is thought of in exclusively masculine *terms.*

—RELIGIOUS SCHOLAR ELAINE PAGELS

RELIGIOUS EYES AND SACRED EYES are not necessarily the same. Sometimes they may facilitate seeing the same things, but all too often they are as different as night and day.

Religious eyes see well in the daylight, focus best on that which is overt, clear, and brilliant. Religious eyes see what shines in the light of the current paradigm. Religious eyes see the externals of theological concepts, traditional dogma, ritual, professional leadership, and the buildings to which one goes to worship.

Sacred eyes, in contrast, see the sometimes dimly lit meaning and purpose, the subtle nuances, and focus on the symbols, myths, and legends that reveal the unconscious. If religious eyes see the shell, sacred eyes see the essence. If religious eyes see the body, sacred eyes see the soul. If religious eyes see current orthodoxy, sacred eyes see the larger, and longer, spiritual meaning and purpose.

During our early adolescence we were definitely seeing reality through religious eyes, whereas during our later adolescence we

viewed the world through scientific eyes, and often thought anything spiritual was passe. It is with sacred eyes that we view the
meaning and purpose, the spiritual essence, within both. It is with
sacred eyes that we see the soul of our times. In our evolutionary
developmental stage of adolescence, we definitely saw the world
primarily through religious eyes.

Consistent with our adolescent ego need for creating divisions,
over the years we created many in-groups and out-groups, and
over the centuries we became more and more diversified religiously. We could probably survey any of the various world religions to illustrate the nature of Epoch II—for all the current major
religions were created early in and have maintained dominance, at
least for the religious mainstream, throughout Epoch II. But we
can't follow the developing histories of all cultures and all religions.
Consequently, we will use the Christian tradition for illustrative
purposes. In doing this we are not suggesting any exclusivity or
superiority, but only recognizing that most of us in the Western
world have our roots in this particular tradition. It also happens to
be the tradition that I know best, and about which I can speak more
knowledgeably than any other.

Creation of a Patriarchy

When we shifted from the worship of the feminine Earthly
Goddess to the worship of the masculine Heavenly God, we created
a patriarchy with an elaborate rationale for the elevation of the
masculine over the feminine, of men over women. In the early years
of Christianity there was actually a diversity of values and theologies, including a lingering and more balanced relationship with the
feminine. But those most influential in the early church seemed
hell-bent on ushering in a patriarchy.

Irenaeus, bishop of Lyons in Gaul in the latter part of the second
century, was considered by some to be the most influential of all the
early Fathers, and Irenaeus did not believe that it was right for
women to act as priests. Tertullian, another major Father of the
church in the late second century and early third century, expressed
a similar dislike of women in official Church activities.

> These heretical women—how audacious they are. They
> have no modesty; they are bold enough to teach, to engage in
> argument, to enact exorcisms, to undertake cures, and, it may

> be, even to baptize. . . .It is not permitted for a woman to speak
> in the church, nor is it permitted for her to teach, nor to baptize,
> nor to offer (the Eucharist), nor to claim herself a share in any
> *masculine* function—not to mention any priestly office.[1]

By the third century, Christianity had effectively moved along strictly masculine lines, rejecting more androgynous gospels for inclusion into the official Bible. One needs only to examine how the church deals with women in the twentieth century, and how slow it has been to change, to see how powerful the patriarchy has been in maintaining itself. And although changes throughout our adolescence seem almost lightning fast in contrast to the pace of change in our childhood—a few millennia versus billions of years—they seem downright sluggardly in the context of our current volatility.

Ego Separations and Distinctions

As already mentioned, separation and drawing distinctions are a natural part of ego development, and one of the prime agenda items for our adolescence.

An interesting aside, related to humanity's development of ego consciousness, has to do with our first use of mirrors. The archaeological evidence regarding the introduction of mirrors appears to coincide with our transition from childhood into adolescence. And that seems to make sense. Seeing a reflection of oneself certainly helps in the process of recognizing the difference between self and other, while at the same time, egocentricity certainly likes a mirror around by which to fuel its vanity.

The earliest identifiable mirror dates from about 4500 B.C. with others dated throughout the succeeding millennia. "It is, however," writes historian of science Morris Berman, "from the sixth century B.C., when one sees the growing appearance of ego-consciousness in Greece, that Greek mirror production really took off."[2]

As already mentioned, the Garden of Eden story, and practically every other creation myth, links our Fall into adolescence to an act of disobedience. It is the natural way we begin to assert ourselves as independent from the parent. In a preponderance of creation myths, the act of disobedience is symbolized by the eating of the fruit from the tree of knowledge of Good and Evil. And such is the initiation rite—or in the traditional interpretation, the punishment—which thrusts us into adolescence.

We went on to divide reality up into many different pieces. And we did it in grand style, starting with the division of the world into sacred and profane, separating heaven from earth and human from the divine. We continued this process all the way up to the present with a binge of specialization, compartmentalization, and categorization.

Religiously, the adolescent rejection of the parent coupled with the shift from the feminine to the masculine resulted in replacing a very present and nurturing Mother with a transcendent and often vengeful Father. Our "cosmic egg" had a great Fall, broke into pieces, and all the King's men and all the King's horses can't put Humpty Dumpty back together again. At least not during our adolescence. And in one sense, it just goes with the adolescent territory.

In our childhood all of life was sacred. But after separating ourselves from nature we created a chasm between the sacred and the profane, heaven and earth, divine and human, spirit and matter, good and evil. In our childhood what distinctions we had were horizontal. We were different than the other animals, but we all participated in the same processes of birth, life, death, and rebirth. In our adolescence, however, we went vertical and, consequently, hierarchical. Good things were "up there," whereas bad things were "down here." Higher and lower had a value judgment. And men were to be "over" nature and women.

Projection of Essential Power

A natural consequence of all this separation, division, and hierarchical value judgment was that we projected our notion of power, and the essential power of the universe, externally. The essential power was thought to be "out there" in God, Divinity, Spirit, and a Savior. We humans, in contrast, were helpless and powerless.

It is ironic that with the advent of adolescence, when we tried to assert our independence and power, we would give away our power. But we gave it away in separating reality and projecting power externally, and then tried to reclaim control of the power through religious belief, ritual, the intercession of a Savior, and the exclusive conduit power of the priesthood and the church. When we separated heaven and earth, we created the need for intermediaries.

Most of Christianity responded, I believe, by misunderstanding the Christ revelation. Instead of being able to see Jesus as a revelation of what humanity essentially is and is capable of becoming, instead of seeing Jesus as an example of full humanity—one of us who was a role model precisely because he was fully human—many fell into an adolescent form of hero worship. By assuming we were separate from the Divine we needed a hero to bridge the gap between divine and human—a hero, in other words, to be our Savior across that gap. Instead of seeing Jesus as an example of what we are created to become, we projected divine power externally.

Such projection also paved the way for an institution to arise as the official conduit of this power gap. First, we created a power gap, then a hero to worship, and finally an imperialistic institutional parent to take care of us.

A careful study of the evidence regarding Jesus would seem to indicate that he was not anywhere near as patriarchal as our adolescent eyes viewed him to be. He had relationships with women, the implications of which the church quickly forgot. He was quite a critic of institutional tradition and ecclesiastical authority and arrogance which, understandably, the church ignored. He said that we would do greater things than he, which we don't hear much about, for it doesn't fit very well into hero worship. And the evidence seems to indicate that he never considered himself a Savior.

Most protestant and Roman Catholic scholars alike agree that Jesus did not see himself as divine in any special sense, but rather proclaimed that such divinity is inherent in all of us. Jesus, as scholar Thomas Sheehan points out, "did not assert any of the messianic claims that the New Testament attributes to him, and went to his death without intending to found a new religion called 'Christianity.'"[3]

The fact is that his followers, through the first couple of centuries after his death, gradually and progressively embellished the divine status of Jesus. The further we move from Jesus' actual lifetime the more his divinity is embellished and the earlier it is established. For instance:

- It was about 50 a.d., almost twenty years after Jesus death, when Paul becomes the first biblical writer to suggest that it was a miraculous *resurrection* which proved that Jesus was divine, different from other humans, and the expected Savior.
- Forty years after Jesus' death, in about 70 A.D., the Gospel of Mark was written and became the earliest Gospel we have in

the Bible. In Mark, Jesus gained his divine status at his baptism.
- Another fifteen years pass, to about 85 A.D., and the Gospels of Matthew and Luke were written. They place the evidence of Jesus' divinity at his birth, a virgin birth. In other words, a virgin birth for Jesus was first mentioned in the Christian scriptures some eighty-five or ninety years after Jesus' actual birth. If Jesus had actually had a literal and historical virgin birth one would think it would have been important enough for Paul or Mark to mention, both of whom were writing earlier than Matthew and Luke.
- In the Gospel of John, written about 110 A.D., Jesus is proclaimed to be divine because of being the *pre-existent* Son of God.

So, the farther we move away from Jesus' actual life, the earlier his followers place his acquisition of special status. It is also interesting to note that the Gospel of John jumps from the pre-existent divinity of Jesus to his baptism, with no mention of a special birth, even though it was written some 25 years after Matthew and Luke.

Jesus, I believe, was a powerful revelation of the unity of heaven and earth, of spirit and matter, and of the integrity of divine and human. He was the incarnation of an important message of integrity and love. Adolescent humanity, however, got some of the message but unfortunately missed a lot because of immaturity.

The church as institutional parent and self-proclaimed official conduit for salvation also participated in, contributed to, and indeed was dependent upon the separation of heaven and earth, divine and human, Christ and the average person. It was from such separation, and the assumption that all divine power was unavailable to the individual except through special intercession, that it derived its authority and maintained its power. If anyone thought or said, "I can do it myself," it was heresy. The church's position was, only through an external God and Christ can we be "saved," and the church is the only conduit through which we can gain access to that external and saving power.

The church also separated inner personal experience from outer religious and institutional authority. It was not interested in the individual's inner experience of dreams or other mystical reality. It was not interested if the person had "searched their soul" on any given matter of religious importance. It was interested only in belief, in conformity to the doctrine and dogmas of the Church, and in maintaining subservience to the Church's authority.

The Attempt to Control
through Belief Systems and Violence

A strong case could be made for the notion that separation from nature and an unbalanced masculinity leads inevitably to the need to control. My purpose is not to take a lot of time here to lay out such an argument, but simply to focus on the evidence that, for whatever reason, Christianity exerted a great need for control, through rigid belief systems and the use of violence.

An emphasis upon belief, rather than faith, represents a need for control. Faith is an open-ended willingness and courage to go with the flow, knowing that whoever or whatever is in charge is a friendly sort of Soul. A need to have a neat and seldom, if ever, changing belief system is a need to have it all figured out. Reliance on a set belief system is the security blanket of insecure people. Adolescent insecurity also tries to make the symbolic literal, the mythic historical, and the psychological and spiritual reduced to matter.

An insistence on *conformity* of belief is another sign of our insecurity—wanting to make sure that we are not alone, that we have the support of companions in our beliefs. It is also the way institutions try to create and maintain their power. You are "in" or "saved" if you agree with the party line—you are out and lost if you are a maverick. If you are a maverick, you are dubbed a heretic. The root meaning of heresy and of heretics is "to choose." And making choices about what one believes presents a threat to the institution.

Christianity, in its early years before the institutional church got its foothold, was not monolithic in regards to belief systems. For the first three centuries Christianity actually had a great deal of diversity.

The Gnostic Gospels, for instance, contain many sayings by Jesus and his disciples which criticize as naive misunderstandings any belief in a literal Virgin Birth and a literal bodily resurrection. Gnosticism, of course, was rejected as heresy, and none of the gospels made the official Bible.

The Gnostic Gospels purported a holistic belief that the kingdom of God was within—that to know oneself at the deepest level was simultaneously to know God. They presented Jesus as a spiritual guide, one who spoke of illusion and enlightenment, whereas the literature that became orthodoxy speaks of sin and repentance. The Gnostic Gospels also included an androgynous God and a very different perspective of women than what became Christian orthodoxy.

And like an immature adolescent male, the Church justified all sorts of violence by which to enforce its authority and the party line. An objective look at Christian history reveals what evil can be perpetrated on others when a significant part of the self is disowned and repressed, when "our way is the right way" is coupled with the arrogance of thinking that God is on our side. The adolescent propensity for an unbalanced masculinity, violence, simplistic belief systems, and immaturity reached pathological proportions and gruesome manifestations in the Middle Ages.

So crucial was right belief that the Church decreed, in 1215, that heretics should not only be excommunicated but also should be put to death. This notion that people should be put to death for what they believed, or failed to believe, and the theological concept of dominion over women and nature—which inevitably translates into a *fear* of women and sexuality—laid the theological foundations for one of the sickest, most hideous, and tragic periods in Church history, the witch-craze.

The Church and State, in the 14th through the 17th centuries, conspired to systematically exterminate those who were believed to be witches, the majority of whom were women. The estimates range from half a million to nine million women who were burned, hanged, drowned, or otherwise tortured to death.

The rationale, as Erica Jong explains, was that these so-called witches "flew through the air to Sabbats where they met the Devil, had intercourse with him, and swore their undying allegiance to him."[4] They were assumed, therefore, to be directly responsible for all the difficulties that society was experiencing: plagues, blighted crops, and dying babies.

> During the three centuries of the witch-craze the tortures used to extract "confessions" from supposed witches were so hideous that one hesitates even to recount them. It is safe to say that once the accusation of 'witch' was made, the poor accused had no escape. It was only a question of how long the torture would go on, how many others would be implicated, and whether or not the so-called witch would receive the mercy of strangulation before being burned. . . .[5]
>
> What could a witch expect once the accusation was made? At the very least, tests like "swimming". . . or else weighing and pricking; at worst, ordeals like *strappado*, thumbscrews, the boot, the Black Virgin. Swimming meant that the accused was bound crosswise hand to foot and cast into a body of water. If she sank, she was said to be innocent; if she floated, she was the devil's own child (that is: God's water had rejected her).

Weighing meant that the witch was weighed against a Bible or certain other weights—and whether she was found to be heavier or lighter, she was presumed guilty. (If heavier, she was possessed by an earth spirit; if lighter, by a spirit of fire.) Pricking was an ordeal in which witch-hunters sought those places on the witch's body that were "the Devil's marks," thus insensitive to pain. In their hunger for victims, some Inquisitors even used retractable witch-prickers. The blade slid into the handle under pressure and the witch's ouchlessness was "proof" of her guilt.

Strappado consisted of tying the victim's arms behind her back, hanging weights to her feet, and violently hoisting her up in the air several times until she confessed or died. (Arms came out of sockets and trysts with the Devil came out of the unlikeliest mouths.) The boot was a vicious leg-breaker; the thumb-screws are self-explanatory; and the Black Virgin. . . was a hinged life-size iron form with spikes inside to pierce—but not kill—the victim when it closed around her. Little wonder that so many "confessed."

During the witch-craze, these tortures were perpetrated by those who considered themselves the only true representatives of God on earth. The Devil would have far to go to equal their ferocity.[6]

And there was more. Our adolescent violence was not limited to the witch-craze. Along with women in general, and "witches" in particular, a group known as the Cathars was also the focus of torture and death, as an out-of-control patriarchy tried desperately to gain and maintain control. Cathars were capable of bodily ecstasy, visions, and trance; "and that provided a focus of attack for what the crusaders feared and hated most: their bodies, the natural world, the wild and the primitive, the interior Other who now threatened them at every turn."[7]

Matters such as these are always complex, and this is not to suggest that the causes are singular or simple. There are usually political, economic, and territorial issues as well as the psychological and spiritual reasons to justify such violence. Nevertheless, what we are looking at in this book is the big, soul-level, picture of humanity's evolutionary journey. In that light, all the above are understandable in an adolescent and immature, distorted and patriarchal Epoch II.

Entire towns that were suspected to be Cathar strongholds were put to the sword. It is hard to imagine the self-righteousness, and the combination of rage and fear, that gave the crusaders their degree of violence—it is reported that some butchered babies with glee so as to protect the world from them growing up to be Cathars.

When the Bishop of Citeaux was asked by the pope's crusaders what they should do with the citizens of a given town, about whom they were unsure regarding their heresy, the Bishop said: "Kill them all, God will recognize his own." Twenty thousand people were put to death—the entire town.[8] So zealous were these Christian protectors of right belief that some people were actually tried and convicted for heresy after their death, and then the body was exhumed and burnt.

Berman points out that "at the very same time that the machinery for persecuting witches began to fall into place, the literate classes of western Europe became obsessed with werewolves."[9] There was a great fear of slipping back into an animal state. It is probably all related to the irrational fears resulting from our separation from nature and the feminine. For anything, or anyone, who could be defined as "animal" was justifiably given special inhumane treatment. Think about how we always defined "primitive" peoples, or any enemy, as animals—check out our cartoon descriptions of the Japanese during World War II.[10] After defining them as such, any act of extermination was justifiable.

I am not suggesting a total rejection or denigration of our adolescence, any more than I would suggest that the process for any one of us moving into an adult maturity has to be based upon a total rejection of our adolescence. There were many good things that were part of our adolescent development collectively, just as there is for us individually. The point, however, is that if we are to mature we must identify our immaturities, if we are going to experience a transformational new birth into greater health and wholeness, we must know what must be left behind.

There have been many books written exclusively extolling the virtues and benefits that our society has derived from the five thousand years of the Judeo-Christian tradition. That is simply not the purpose of this book. In this analysis we are looking at the large sweep of the Big Story, with an emphasis upon the major transformational times in the development of humanity, the natural and necessary crises that set the stage for transformation, what the essential elements were, and what we need to give up if we are to move on. Many of the best elements of the Judeo-Christian tradition will be identified, and built-upon, as we move into Epoch III. They were, however, all too subtle and secondary in Epoch II.

We don't want to overly romanticize our childhood, nor overly condemn our adolescence. It is difficult in this kind of overview, and summarizing of vast amounts of material, not to oversimplify. The point is to identify the essential elements that need maturation, so as to set the stage for our discussion of the enormous changes taking place at the end of the twentieth century—the transformation from adolescence into adulthood, from Epoch II into Epoch III.

The Judeo-Christian history to date, with its adolescent and masculine value system, laid a substantial foundation of unbalanced masculinity, dominion over nature and women, separation of reality into separate unrelated pieces, fascination with external power, the over-emphasis upon left-brained belief systems, and a horrendous amount of violence with which to enforce it all.

Although the value system may be essentially the same for the Judeo-Christian mainstream, because of sheer numbers, it was the Christians more than the Jews who had the power with which to impose their values on the culture at large. The year 1348 seems to be when Jews were singled out for their first persecution, and they joined, simply because they were Jews, witches and heretics in the list of scapegoats for the fears of those in power. The rationale for the torture and murder of Jews, however, was not because of heresy, per se, but because they were accused of causing the Black Plague of the 14th century.

As we shall see later on, a "dark night of the soul," or some other manner of crisis, usually acts as a catalyst for a time of transition, a transformation. The 14th through the 17th centuries represent the transition, spiritually, from seeing the world through religious eyes to seeing the world through scientific eyes. And there were substantial crises in our collective psyche which gave us the impetus for change—excesses in the dominant value system, a major reformational shock in the life of the Church, and a major shock to our need to our perception of control, namely, the Black Plague.

The Black Plague gave Europe a major case of helplessness. We had the compulsive need to be in control, were trying desperately to gain control through rigid belief systems and violent enforcement, when we found ourselves totally helpless in the face of a killing disease. Even those of us who had the "right" belief system were dying.

We tried to gain control of it, and here is where we first persecuted the Jews. We singled out a minority as the cause of our troubles. The Black Plague, which was killing vast numbers of us, must have been caused by the water we were drinking, we thought. In September of 1348 a group of Jews at Chillon on Lake Geneva, in the South of France, were accused of poisoning the wells. They denied it until we tortured them long enough, and then they confessed. Their confessions were sent to neighboring towns and the torturing and the killing spread.

"In Basel," science writer ...Charles L. Mee, Jr. reports, "all the Jews were locked inside wooden buildings and burned alive. In November, Jews were burned in Solothurn, Zofingen and Stuttgart. Through the winter and into early spring they were burned in Landsberg, Burren, Memmingen, Lindau, Frieburg, Ulm, Speyer, Gotha, Eisenach, Dresden, Worms, Baden and Erfurt. Sixteen thousand were murdered in Strasbourg. In other cities Jews were walled up inside their houses to starve to death. That the Jews were also dying of the plague was not taken as proof that they were not causing it."[11]

In spite of all the scapegoating, the torture, the killing, we couldn't get control of the plague. Throughout the 14th century we kept dying, and felt increasingly helpless. In all, about forty-four million people died of the Black Plague, wiping out about one-third of Europe.

The excessive violence of the crusades, the excessive role claimed by the Church in parenting our spiritual lives, and the excessive sense of helplessness we felt in the face of the Black Plague all contributed to this being a major transformational time. The Protestant Reformation was a reaction against the institutional abuses of the Church—the insistence that the Church and the clergy were the exclusive bridge for the gap between heaven and earth. Instead of reforming a unified church, we increased our adolescent propensity for separation. The Protestant Reformation resulted in one catholic church becoming split into so many sects and denominations that it is hard to keep track of any precise number.

The point is that coming out of this time in the middle ages in Europe we shifted from our early adolescence into our late adolescence—from finding our primary meaning and purpose viewed through religious eyes to viewing life primarily through the lens of scientific inquiry. The orgy of violence and rigid belief systems in the Church, and the extreme helplessness felt in the face of the Black Plague, gave our collective psyche the sense that we could not gain control of our lives through religion. But, we thought, perhaps through science we could. Now that we had separated heaven and earth, and finding that loyalty to heaven did not result in control of our lives, we started looking to science to figure it all out and enable us to gain control.

> As the Black Death waned in Europe, the power of religion
> waned with it, leaving behind a population that was gradually
> but certainly turning its attention to the physical realm in
> which it lived, to materialism and worldliness, to the terrible
> power of the world itself, and to the wonder of how it works.[12]

We turned, therefore, from being saved by a Messiah, the Church, and the spiritual realm, to being saved by science, the mind, and knowledge about the material realm. But even though we changed the lens through which we looked at life we continued with essentially the same adolescent value system. From the magic of a Savior who could heal and take us to heaven, to the "magic bullet" of medical science, we continued to look externally for the power that saves, the power that gives meaning and purpose to our lives, the power that makes sense out of our existence. We continued in an unbalanced masculinity, feeling out of control and searching desperately for ways to gain control. We continued to believe that right belief was the way to gain control—only now it was scientific right belief. And we simply developed greater tools—you know how adolescent males love to play with machines—to violate nature, animals, and women.

I hope that I'm not misunderstood, in this chapter and the next, as bashing Christianity, masculinity, or science, per se. My intent is not to reject any of those three—after all, I'm not a masochist. However, in order to make a transition into a healthier and more mature future, we need to understand the immaturities of our past. Just because Christianity and science have been adolescent to date, does not mean we should totally reject them. We just need the organic and natural maturation of them into adulthood. And just because masculinity has been unbalanced and immature doesn't mean half of the human family need to feel ashamed of their sex. We men just need to grow up—indeed, the entire society needs a more mature notion of the masculine.

The Epoch III synthesis of a mature science and a mature spirituality will be discussed throughout Chapters Eight, Nine, Ten, and Eleven. For now, however, in our overview of history we need to cover the seventeenth through the twentieth centuries, the latter stages of our adolescence in which we switched our worship to science.

CHAPTER 5

LATE ADOLESCENCE:
Seeing Through Scientific Eyes

A whole series of disciplines has grown and flourished over the last four hundred years. Alchemy gave way to chemistry, astrology to astronomy, mythology to psychoanalysis, and . . . storytelling to professional academic history. . . The essential feature of this mode of understanding is that of psychic distance, the existence of a rigid barrier between observer and observed. If you get emotional about a subject you are analyzing, if you do experience identification or resonance, you disqualify yourself as a professional observer or analyst.

—HISTORIAN OF SCIENCE, MORRIS BERMAN

IN THE SEVENTEENTH CENTURY WE SWITCHED THE LENS through which we viewed the world, from religious to scientific. We continued, however, the same adolescent, and unbalanced masculine, value system. Although, on the surface, science would seem to have given us a very different view of reality—and in some important respects it did—nevertheless, we remained in our adolescence masculine values. We simply switched our worship from God and the Church to the scientific capacity to make sense of the world. We turned our loyalty from the Church's priesthood, to the "priesthood" and "saints" of modern science.

Still operating out of the psychic poverty which resulted from our separation from nature, we continued our attempt to control everything in and about us. Paradoxically, as part of our adolescent ego development, we had the need to exert our own independence, while at the same time we continued our projection of essential power externally. We simply switched from projecting power onto an other-worldly Father in heaven, and heaven's earthly conduits of saviors and the Church, to projecting power onto this-worldly scientific knowledge, materialism, and rationalism.

Although scientific knowledge was this-worldly, it was the province of a privileged "priesthood." The scientific "priests" had the knowledge, and generally used a specialized jargon to keep the knowledge within the club. It takes only a cursory look at the history of medical science to see how this was played out. Until the recent erosion, the arrogance of the medical "priesthood," the specialized knowledge protected by a specialized jargon, understood only by the insiders, kept the populace ignorant, powerless, and dependent.

In the last chapter we focused primarily on one religious tradition to illustrate our early adolescence. Similarly, medical science can be used as an illustration of how the masculine adolescent value system has been lived out in the scientific era.

Christianity had its "Church Fathers" who contributed to the essential direction that institution took, and so did science. The most influential of all the "Scientific Fathers" were Francis Bacon (1561-1626), René Descartes (1596-1650), and Isaac Newton (1642-1727). We will touch on their influences, very briefly, as we examine the roots of the value system of medical science.

As mentioned earlier, the major agenda for our adolescence was that of ego and mental development. We developed physically in our childhood and mentally in our adolescence. Consequently, although the 17th through the 20th centuries are still identified as in our adolescence, and although we kept essentially the same value system, we did make some changes in our way of thinking as we grew up.

The left-brained preoccupation of Christianity in rigid belief systems, as of against a dynamic faith, became in science a left-brained preoccupation with rationalism and empiricism. Thus reason alone as the source for knowledge, and the testing of that reason in the world of experience, became the dogma. As cultural historian William Irwin Thompson put it, "it was no longer a question of believing, but knowing, and . . . scientists in their new ways of knowing the world succeed(ed) in taking charisma away from (the) Church."[1]

But, as we shall see, although science was in many ways a maturation in our adolescent mentality, it was still a dogmatic loyalty to a particular way of thinking. It saw mystical knowledge as a mistake, emotional knowledge as unreliable, "soft" data as less valid than "hard," dreams as an unimportant garbage dump, and intuition—well, intuition was never used alone, it was always referred to as "woman's intuition" which, for science, made it less than important. And as Morris Berman has pointed out, science's ego never preceded the word "objective" with the word "mere" as it did with "subjectivity." The immature masculinity of our adolescence, as it was played out in science, had us removed and separate from nature, the observer separated from the observed, and we were to be unemotionally objective. We were to be "real men," and that included you women as well, if you were to be legit in the "real world"—read, in the materialistic, rationalistic, and scientific world.

Although the early Church was not short of the "how" of salvation, namely, through Christ and the Church, the primary focus in our early adolescence was upon the religious "whys" of life. Science, however, shifted the focus totally away from the "whys" and onto the "what's" and "how's." "Why," in our adolescence, was considered an other-worldly question, whereas "how" and "what" were this-worldly. And if the scientific lens did anything to us it was to look here, and not there. We focused our gaze on matter rather than spirit, on earth rather than heaven, on physics rather than metaphysics.

In so doing, we rejected religion. Obviously, we kept doing the religious thing, we had the Protestant Reformation, and we have had the past four hundred years of various, smaller ebbs and flows in the life of the Church. There were many fine things accomplished by the institutional Church, and many loving lives devoted to religious work. In the largest sweep of history, however, and for the mainstream of human development, we turned our loyalty from religion to science. Science replaced religion as the primary authority about life. Most of us became more interested in materialism than in spirituality, more interested in the "whats" and "hows," than in the "whys." Although many of us kept going to religious institutions and paid homage to the holy writ, we didn't really believe its cosmology in place of the one science gave us, and I think if we are honest we would admit that our "theology" was more scientific than early adolescent religious.

Science made sense of the world with a "3-M theology"— masculinity, machines, and materialism—developed by its three patron "saints," Francis Bacon, René Descartes, and Isaac Newton. Medical science, in particular, worshiped at this theological altar.

Science, in relationship to nature, continued what Christianity had started. Early Christianity gave divine sanction to humanity for having dominion over nature. Our scientific "saints" took it a step further—they told us to force nature to reveal Her secrets. Notice how we always knew that nature represented our feminine side?

Bacon used the imagery of a torture chamber, suggesting that like a prisoner, we would only get all the answers we wanted when nature was "straitened and held fast, so nature exhibits herself more clearly under the trials and vexations of (mechanical devices) than when left to herself."[2]

Bacon saw nature as a rebellious female, and understood the task of men "to bind her to your service and make her your slave."[3] He referred to nature as a "common harlot," and believed that, left to her own devices, she would go back to the wild—something that modern science was to prevent. Nature must, therefore, be "re-strained and kept in order"—by men, of course. For, "matter is not devoid of an appetite and inclination to dissolve the world and fall back into the old Chaos." In Bacon's perspective, "nature takes orders from man and works under his authority," and therefore she can be "forced out of her natural state and squeezed and molded."[4]

Historian of science, Carolyn Merchant, in her important book *The Death of Nature*, does a masterful job of summarizing Bacon's influence in the early days of the scientific revolution. She per-ceives, rightly I think, how Bacon's influence was essentially sexist regarding the scientific relationship with nature. He continually used bold sexual imagery in describing man's purposes with na-ture, and had great influence on:

> the modern experimental method—constraint of nature in the laboratory, dissection by hand and mind, and the penetra-tion of hidden secrets—language still used today in praising a scientist's "hard facts," "penetrating mind," or the "thrust of his argument." (Bacon's influence) legitimates the exploitation and "rape" of nature for human good.[5]

Morris Berman, with whose quote we started this chapter, agrees with Merchant regarding Bacon's influence.

> The overall framework of scientific experimentation, the technological notion of the questioning of nature under duress, is the major Baconian legacy.[6]

The second of the three major scientific "saints," René Descartes, gave us the most influential metaphor for our adolescent explora-tion of nature—the machine. Although Bacon's ideas of forcing nature, as female, to reveal her secrets has had an important influence down to the present, changing nature from organic to inorganic made the process of manipulating nature even easier.

Whereas Bacon looked at nature as female, and suggested the "torture" and "vexing" of her in order to secure her secrets, Descartes and Newton turned nature into a machine. And then there was nothing that one could feel guilty about—no longer violating the feminine, we were only tinkering with a machine. And you know how adolescent males love to play with machines.

The machine metaphor became the dominant way of thinking about nature, and it set the stage for the major sub-themes of science—nature as separate from us and to be studied with distant objectivity; nature as devoid of spirit; the search for absolute certainty; analysis and reductionism; and the notion that everything is running down, as does a machine. Merchant writes,

> The removal of animistic, organic assumptions about the cosmos constituted the death of nature, the most far-reaching effect of the Scientific Revolution," writes Merchant. "Because nature was now viewed as a system of dead, inert particles moved by external, rather than inherent forces, the mechanical framework itself could legitimate the manipulation of nature.[7]

Descartes and Newton were the primary influences in this regard. "I consider the human body as a machine," wrote Descartes. "My thought . . . compares a sick man and an ill-made clock with my idea of a healthy man and a well-made clock."[8]

The machine metaphor also made inevitable the splitting of mind and body, matter and spirit. "There is nothing included in the concept of the body that belongs to the mind; and nothing in that of mind that belongs to the body," asserted Descartes.[9]

And such separations continued the adolescent patriarchy. "If the original need of patriarchy had been to split the human from nature. . . ," observes Marilyn French, "Cartesian splitting of the mind from the body refined and reinforced the original division. For men were mind, women body. Man was now a mind disconnected from his body, abstracted and presumably without desire or will. He was an impartial, objective observer of the rest of creation, notably matter. . . . Man could observe matter, tinker with it, mutilate it, experiment with it, and himself remain untouched and untouchable. Inert matter could not reciprocate or revenge man's depredations."[10] Our increasing ecological awareness, toward the end of the twentieth century, is beginning to call that into question.

Descartes essentially divided up the human being and doled out the parts to different disciplines. So the results of "Cartesian reductionism" were that the soul or spirit was given to the Church, the body to medical science, and a dis-spirited mind to the eventual medical branch of psychiatry. This led, in medical science, to a binge of specialization, categorization, and compartmentalization. The human being was not only split up in the large categories of body, mind, and spirit, but the body was then divided up into the plethora of specialities we have today—experts knowing more and more about less and less.

I won't dwell on it here, but you can see how such a process leads inevitably to external expertise and disempowering the individual. In such an adolescent separation there is this expert who has authority over this piece of your body and that expert who has authority over that part. We have arrived at the point of having, for every part of the machine, a "medical mechanic" whose use of specialized knowledge and jargon makes you feel rather dumb about your own body. Talk about the old cliche of "divide and conquer." What was lost in this process was you—you in the role of integrator. We'll return to this, and deal with it more extensively, in Chapters Eight and Nine.

One more good news/bad news consequence of Cartesian reductionism, as it was lived out in medical science, was the belief in the "single cause" theory of disease. The good news is that Pasteur demonstrated the connection between some germs and some diseases, which led eventually to dramatic breakthroughs in some infectious diseases. The bad news is that this led us to at least two undesirable consequences.

One is that we came to fear bacteria as our enemy. Remember when the first astronauts came back from the moon and we put them into isolation? We feared they might bring back germs which we were unprepared to fight. That is a symbol for how paranoid we have often been about germs—spraying disinfectant into every nook and cranny of our lives. We now know that we constantly live in harmony with legions of bacteria, and that bacteria actually make up ten percent of our dry body weight. The important matter is balance and harmony, not extermination.

The medical community, however, has largely been preoccupied with identifying the precise germ that caused a disease, and then in developing the "magic bullet" to kill the invader. Sometimes it worked. Certainly with some infectious diseases it worked miracles. But perhaps it has also led us astray when it comes to diseases that include psychosocial factors as well.

The difficulty is that of applying one theory, one way of seeing reality, to everything. We were convinced germs caused illness, we developed an elaborate medical system of research which looked at germs for the explanation of almost everything, and were not about to consider alternative ideas. As Abraham Maslow once put it, "If the only tool you have is a hammer, you tend to treat everything as if it were a nail."

The other consequence to "Pasteur's germ theory of illness" is that we thought that was the whole story. We forgot about how spiritual, emotional, and other metaphysical matters might play a role in getting sick or in restoring health and well-being.

A machine universe did not need God. It is a bit ironic, since the scientific fathers were actually very religious men, but they started what amounted to the desacralization of the world. A machine is spirit-less. God was seen as a distant watch-maker who set everything in motion, but was not needed for the day-to-day operation. God created such a good machine, this thinking went, that He was not necessary as an ever-present maintenance mechanic. The notion of an active and involved God was a notion from an earlier, more immature, animistic time, whereas the world machine runs very well by itself, thank you.

"The universe of perfect law and sublime order was self-running and self-lubricating," as one professor of physics and astronomy put it. "From the self-running mechanistic universe, God withdrew into a vague background of abstract being and remained there as the indispensable architect of it all."[11] "God created the universe in the beginning," our scientific adolescent mind reasoned, "and thereafter time had ticked away as in a well-oiled clock. The Apocalypse, the Coming, and the End were out of sight, for the celestial machinery could never wear out."[12]

Scientific materialism is so much the orthodox religion of our time that most of us hardly think to question it—indeed, to question it is tantamount to heresy. Of course matter is where the action is. Of course there is no spiritual essence in matter. Of course spirituality and religion are for the psychologically immature. Of course we don't consider spiritual matters in the causation or treatment of disease—to do so would be to go back to the Middle Ages. Of course it is the scientist to whom we turn for the really important answers of life. As someone once put it, "What matters is matter—as for mind, never mind."

In the nineteenth century process, movement, change, and transformation were introduced into the scientific world-view. A machine universe, however, could only change in one direction, in the direction of deterioration. Therefore, although one might think it would be natural for medical science to take its clues from evolving life, it didn't. Medical science took its basic sense of life from the machine metaphor and focused on deterioration and pathology.

Even a biologist, Joseph Needham, wrote, "In science, man is a machine; or if he is not, then he is nothing at all."[13]

Many in the medical establishment have scoffed at the "holistic health" and "wellness" movements. And it is no surprise that they would. Both hit at two of the greatest deficiencies of medicine—the separation of the body from mind and spirit, and the almost exclusive focus on illness.

Modern medicine has accomplished a great deal, and individual medical practitioners are often quite loving and compassionate people who entered the profession to help people. Nevertheless, the institution of medicine is a natural extension of the value system set in place by the scientific fathers of three to four hundred years ago.

Medical science is unquestionably patriarchal. It has a great need to control both disease and the people being treated. It is mechanistic, materialistic, and reductionistic in its approach to disease and healing. It has had, until recently, an unquestioned authority, an insistence upon itself as the only official conduit for the "salvation" of health and well-being—demonstrated by the way the American Medical Association influences laws that deal with so-called "alternative healers." And it has a left-brained, subtle but rigid dogma with an all too frequently arrogant "priesthood."

Doesn't it follow that physicians who learn their trade primarily by studying laboratory animals and cadavers, and who spend most of their time with sick people, would know more about the functioning of a dis-spirited body than of a live, healthy, optimally functioning person with an active synergy of their body, mind, and spirit? Isn't it strange that we call them *health* professionals?

Don't get me wrong. We definitely need professionals who are knowledgeable about and skilled in the diagnosis and treatment of disease. Some well-selected physicians are certainly part of my own valued consultants. But there are some major changes needed if the medical profession and the institution of medicine are to move from adolescence into mature adulthood, from a partial and patriarchal past into a healthy, whole, and balanced future.

That medical science is built on the Cartesian separation of mind and body is almost so obvious that it doesn't make much sense in taking time and space here to document the case. Practically all the research done in the name of medicine is on the matter of the body, and not on mental, emotional, or spiritual factors that may contribute to the onset and/or the treatment of disease. And even when the "mind" is considered, it is usually the brain that is being talked about—the physiology or biochemistry of the brain, rather than anything so esoteric as the role of love in healing. (Despite the fact that there is considerable evidence to the contrary.)

Sigmund Freud, the father of psychoanalysis and the one most influential in our medical schools regarding the role of the mind said that, in order to be scientific, psychoanalysts have to be "incorrigible mechanists and materialists."[14] The only thing that counts is the physical brain's biochemistry. It should be no surprise to us, therefore, that Freud thought the religious impulse of humankind "must be classed among the mass delusions" of human existence.

The unbalanced masculine aggressiveness which characterizes medical science gets its start in medical school. "Medical schools, especially in the United States," writes Fritjof Capra, "are by far the most competitive of all professional schools. . . . They present high competitiveness as a virtue and emphasize an 'aggressive approach' to patient care. In fact, the aggressive stance of medical care is often so extreme that the metaphors used to describe illness and therapy are taken from the language of warfare. For example, a malignant tumor is said to 'invade' the body, radiation therapy 'bombards' the tissues to 'kill' the cancer cells, and chemotherapy is often likened to chemical warfare."[15]

The dean's office at the University of California/San Francisco School of Medicine conducted a survey on how medical school changed the student's self-concept. The majority of the students said that before entering medical school they were intellectually honest, competent, organized, calm, enthusiastic and happy most of the time. After two years of medical school almost half perceived themselves as less competent, more demoralized, more angry, more confused, more anxious, more depressed, and more ambivalent than before.[16]

One medical student was profoundly candid in his graduation speech:

> Medical school felt like a family where the mother was gone and only the hard father remained at home. The medical school culture values competition, aggression, logic, striving, objectifying, intellect, and power—while, at the same time, devalues relatedness, receptivity, creativity, sensitivity, subjectivity, feeling, and nurturance. The mechanical is emphasized over the humanistic, objective over subjective, thinking over feeling, efficiency over creativity.
>
> If we become inefficient and slightly fuzzy-headed after thirty straight hours of work, we feel we have failed to measure

up to the standards of medicine. If on the other hand, we succeed in driving ourselves, keeping our performance up to snuff, then we begin to see ourselves as a separate breed, superior to the rest of humankind. This display of superhuman endurance. . . ultimately manifests as contempt for those patients who complain about their life and troubles on a cushy eight hours of sleep. In some of us it leads to arrogance.[17]

A practicing physician, Dr. Thomas Preston, adds his experienced perspective regarding that arrogance in the medical profession:

> Since the first physicians were in effect priests, their cultural descendants have inherited the priestly vestments of aloofness, special powers, and access to the supernatural.[18]
>
> There is nothing worse in the practice of medicine, or anything more destructive and degrading to both patient and physician, than the control the physician exercises over the patient under an unequal contract. The physician demands that the patient give up two fundamental rights, the right to know and the right to decide.
>
> This practice is shamelessly, if unconsciously, accepted by physicians and taught as a matter of course to medical students. It is a direct outgrowth of not viewing problems from the patient's perspective and is rationalized as "knowing what is best and using every means to attain it."[19]

Dr. Preston also suggests that medical training prepares a physician not only to be uncomfortable with uncertainty but to consider it unprofessional. This belief in certitude, and the elimination of self-doubt, trains the physician-to-be in delusions of being omniscient and omnipotent.

A physician-sociologist team at Detroit's Wayne State University School of Medicine has studied the doctor-patient relationship—recording and analyzing the interactions during office visits by patients. They found a consistent pattern in which the doctor focused upon the physical signs of disease and overlooked the psychosocial factors. As a result, they concluded, physicians missed an estimated 30 to 70 percent of the symptoms.[20]

The Wayne State researchers found a second problematic pattern in the videotaped interviews between physician and patient to be the matter of doctor arrogance. Doctors interrupted the patients an average time of 18 seconds after they had started to describe their problems—half of the patients being interrupted immediately after mentioning the first symptom.[21]

This physician arrogance is manifested in an impatience with people who want to talk about their problems, or who ask too many questions. Medical textbooks have even indicated that patients who come to their doctor with a written list of symptoms demonstrate "almost a sure sign of psychoneurosis," and have identified it as a syndrome, giving it a French term which means "the illness of the little paper."

In vivid contrast to this desire by physicians that patients submissively worship at the altar of medical knowledge, increasing research indicates that it is the assertive person who has better results in dealing with disease. In a study of women with metastatic breast cancer, for instance, the longest survivors had poor relationships with their physicians—as judged by the physicians.[22]

This adolescent version of power infects doctor and patient alike. On the one hand is the arrogance of the medical establishment, but just as important is the subservience and complicity of the patient population. The combination is deadly, sometimes literally so.

One excess resulting from this combination is financial. Since the subject of the financial crisis in health care is a multilayered one, and one which has been dealt with by many authors, I won't take our time to deal with it in any detail here. Needless to say, typical market restraints simply don't work with the medical profession. In this case, the "supplier" creates the "demand," to a great extent, by determining medical tests, prescribing surgery or drugs, and suggesting office visits—"I would like to see you again next month." The average patient has not been assertive enough to question any aspect of this process—after all, they are the experts, and "Big Daddy" (read, the company or Medicare, etc.) is paying for it.

The use of surgery and drugs are other excesses that the physician controls and most patients go along with. Physicians write an average of ten drug prescriptions for every man, woman, and child in the U.S. every year.[23] "It's one thing," says Dr. Sidney Wolfe of the Health Research Group, "to involve the risks of taking drugs that are effective in treating a symptom or curing a disease. . . but quite another thing to take drugs that are ineffective. Our research indicates that one out of every eight prescriptions is for a drug not considered effective by the government's own standards."[24]

In a culture which is giving so much attention to the "wild" drugs, those that are illegal, such as crack cocaine and other street drugs, it is ironic that the "tame" drugs, those prescribed by our medical priesthood, do so much harm. Americans spend almost $2 billion on prescription drugs each year, and 10 percent to 20 percent of those cause adverse side effects. Those so-called side effects put an estimated 1.6 million people in the hospital and kill about 160,000 Americans each and every year.[25]

No drug is safe, even though it is prescribed by an accepted expert. Some drugs even cause other diseases. A rheumatologist, Dr. Scott Kale, for instance, writes that as many as 10 percent of lupus cases are caused by drugs prescribed for other problems.[26]

The Health Research Group also estimates that there are a minimum of 3.2 million unnecessary operations each year, with an unnecessary loss of 16,000 lives.[27] There is an obvious economic incentive when an operation like coronary bypass surgery is performed on fee-for-service patients three times more frequently than on patients who are on prepaid plans.[28] In the ten years from 1975 to 1985 bypass surgery, at $25,000 to $50,000 per operation, became a favorite revenue producer for hospitals and surgeons—the number of operations per year soaring from 57,000 to more than 200,000.[29] In the 1980s, for instance, an average of 230,000 bypass operations were performed annually, yet the National Heart, Lung and Blood Institute judged that at least 25 percent of them were unjustified.[30] Research has also verified that the five year survival rate of those heart disease patients who had bypass surgery was no better than those who did not.[31]

The National Institutes of Health reports that of the 750,000 hysterectomies performed annually, "22 percent are unjustified and, moreover, only 10 percent of all the hysterectomy operations were uncontestably warranted."[32] And there are many other such operations which, the medical profession's own research shows, are performed excessively. Dr. Schneider, reflecting on the unnecessary operations being performed, and the resulting deaths, suggests that "a cool, analytical look at the situation as it is today dictates considerable caution on the part of the wise consumer. Unskeptical faith can be fatal."[33]

Unquestionably, medical science has provided us many benefits. It has provided some marvelous advances in our understanding of disease and our skill of diagnosing and treating illness. There certainly has been remarkable progress in treating serious trauma. But all this notwithstanding, if we are mature enough we have to recognize the short-comings so that we can make improvement. Although it has been characteristic of our adolescence, we can no longer afford the immature defensiveness of the total acceptance or total rejection, "love it or leave it" mentality. In spite of its successes, medical science has been the manifestation of an adolescent value system which must be transcended if we are to experience the health and wholeness possible in Epoch III.

A clear-eyed look at medical science reveals that it has been most successful for white males, the group most favored by the dominant adolescent paradigm. That's the way a paradigm works. It favors those in power, and those in power tend to keep it that way. Medical science has been less favorable for women, minorities, and those less educated. As Dr. Robert Schneider put it, "The uneducated, the poor, the ethnic groups with language barriers have more surgical scars."[34]

Women come out second best, not only in positions of power and authority in the medical establishment, but in the research methodologies. An inordinate amount of research is focused on men. "Remember the cholesterol study?" asks columnist Ellen Goodman. "Its 4,000 subjects were men. Remember the smoking study? The 15,000 subjects were men. How about the aspirin study? Its 22,000 doctors were all male."[35] The fact is that women are treated on the basis of this and other similar research, without really knowing if the sex difference should make a difference in medication, dose, etc. The National Institutes of Health reportedly spends less than 14 percent of its budget on women's health issues, even though women make up more than half of the population.[36]

A paradigm also tends to blind us regarding effective cost analysis. Because we believe medical science to be *the* way to fight disease, we rarely stop to ask if it is cost-effective. It seems that only the defense department and the medical establishment can get away with such excess—which should not surprise us in an unbalanced masculine adolescence.

As I write these words there are new efforts emerging to attempt correction in some of these areas. Increasingly, we see the evidence of our gradual recognition regarding humanity's collective adolescent immaturities. Increasingly, we can see a recognition of, and a reaching out for, the collective growth spurt emerging in our time. We still, however, have a long way to grow.

In 1970 President Nixon declared war on cancer—there's that military terminology again. With almost no emphasis upon prevention—that's not what the medical establishment is best at—the cancer-research lobby convinced the U.S. Congress that, with plenty of money, it would eliminate the disease of cancer by 1976, "as an appropriate commemoration of the 200th anniversary of the independence of our country."[37]

Isn't it convenient how we have forgotten that promise? 330,000 Americans died of cancer in 1976. By 1986, after throwing many billions of dollars into the medical research establishment, 462,000 Americans were dying every year from the disease. "Survival rates for the most common types of cancers—those which make up 90 percent of the cases—have remained virtually unchanged over the last twenty-five years."[38]

There was a major study published in *The New England Journal of Medicine* which concluded that the odds of dying of cancer have actually increased over the past three decades, and that our emphasis on improving treatment "must be judged a qualified failure." "We're not saying treatment is no good," said Dr. John C. Bailar III, the director of the study. "What we're saying is that cancer treatment is not getting a whole lot better." The report recommends an increased emphasis on prevention.[39]

A 1990 study of cancer death rates, and the success of cancer treatment, found that death rates for almost all forms of cancer are on the rise. And, importantly, the researchers emphasized that *the increase is not because people are living longer or have better cancer detection.* Dr. Devra Davis of the Mount Sinai Medical Center in New York, who led the study, admitted: "The sad truth is we don't really know what's causing a lot of these changes."[40]

Questioning the cost-effectiveness of our investment in the medical approach to cancer would seem to be logical. We might also question the paradigm which assumes that cancer has only a physical causation and treatment. Perhaps, just perhaps, we have been looking where the paradigmatic light is, and not where the answer is. Stay tuned—more on this in the discussion of Epoch III.

Another sign of the innate pathology of the so-called health establishment is how unhealthy its prime professionals are. Tragically, every year in these United States of America we lose the equivalent of seven entire medical school classes to physician suicides, drug addiction and alcoholism.[41] Of all the drug addicts in treatment 15 percent are physicians, more than three times the rate for the general public. Suicide accounts for more than forty percent of all premature deaths among physicians, with male doctors between the ages of 25 and 40 being three times as likely to kill themselves as men in other professions. And it is very revealing, regarding the patriarchy as well as the pathology of the profession, that women doctors of the same age group are four times as likely to kill themselves.[42]

One major study which penetrated the professional and institutional facade of physicians described the doctors as victims. It found that physicians carry a tremendous feeling of being alone, walled in by the culture they have helped to create. One researcher, anthropologist John-Henry Pfifferling, reflected on the study:

> Nearly every doctor I got to know was troubled to some extent, some very seriously so. I discovered that doctors feel they have no one to talk to, nowhere to turn for help or support. *They're* supposed to be the helpers; *they're* supposed to provide support. But most of them had never been able to share their loneliness with anyone, particularly within the medical system.[43]

All the physicians studied had feelings of being alone and distant from others, with one-third having serious emotional problems. The study concluded that very few physicians are what could be called healthy, and most were barely surviving.

Physicians are killing themselves, and the medical establishment has more and more people mad as hell at it for its excesses and greed. In a healthy society this would be one of the most vital and beloved institutions. It would have a professional leadership who walked their talk as personal examples of health and wholeness. But we are not there yet.

As stated earlier, medical science is but one example of our late adolescent "3-M theology"—masculinity, machines, and materialism. Almost every aspect of life in Epoch II has worshiped this theology. All around us, however, are signs of a dying Epoch II and of the birth of Epoch III—the putrid smell of a rotting value system as a new and more healthy value system emerges to take its place.

The process of death and new birth, when it involves humanity and when it is soul-level stuff, comes in the form of a "dark night of the soul." It is the inevitable precursor to our transformation of adolescence into adulthood, the transition from Epoch II into Epoch III. It is the time in which we are now living. It is the condition which gives us our current challenges. And it is the subject to which we now turn.

CHAPTER 6

INTO THE DARK NIGHT OF THE SOUL

All the tumult and seeming chaos, when viewed in the light of historical perspective, can be seen to represent not only the death agonies of an old order but also the birth pangs of a new epoch—a new golden age which assuredly will outshine those of the past.
—HISTORIAN L. S. STAVRIANOS

THE DECADE OF THE 1950S WAS THE TWILIGHT of a very calm and serene day. It was a day of innocence, of conformity, of niceness. Everybody liked Ike and the churches were full every Sunday morning. We were unaware that tomorrow would be significantly different. We thought simply that a day was ending like any other day, a decade ending like any other decade. We marveled at the beautiful sunset, oblivious to the fact that it was impurity in the air which created the lovely color, and which foretold the horrors of the impending storm in our dark night of the soul.

We who were growing up in the majority culture during the 1950s were not, by and large, bad people. We were just naive and oh so innocent. "But the innocence of that period," wrote George Leonard, one of the most perceptive journalists of that time, "was the innocence of unawareness, of injustice unredressed, of inequities barely imagined."[1]

In the 1950s we gave little thought to the fact that a quarter of the people in our nation lived under an American apartheid—separate eating, separate drinking fountains, separate restrooms, and separate swimming pools. A black man could be lynched if he was not appropriately humble, if he did not shuffle in a certain way, or if he dared to look a white man, let alone a white woman, in the eyes.

74

We gave little thought to the environment, to animal rights, or to the second-class status of women. There were no such things as rape crises centers, no attention to battered wives, no affirmative action, no equal opportunity employment, and the terms "date rape" or "spousal rape" were not in our vocabulary and likely would have been considered contradictions in terms. In 1957 a national survey found that 80 percent of us—and that number included women as well as men—believed that women who chose to remain unmarried were "sick," "neurotic," or "immoral."[2]

But in the 1960s repressed pathologies erupted from our collective unconscious and we entered our dark night of the soul. Our innocence was shattered and our naivete smashed by the lightning bolts of racial violence, the thunder of a war we couldn't win, and the stormy confrontations of the civil rights movement, the women's movement, the peace movement, and the ecology movement.

There is a built-in bias in nature for maintaining life in the short-term by protecting the status quo—homeostasis. And seemingly paradoxical is the fact that there is also a built-in bias in nature for transformation—order, a higher order, emerging out of chaos.

What at times seemed like total chaos in the 1960s was a bursting forth of the inevitable drive for a higher order. The capstone of our immature adolescence was blown away, and what was "blowing in the wind" was the spirit of balance, the spirit of maturation, and the spirit of health and wholeness.

The decade of the '60s represents the beginning of our dark night of the soul, the catalyst for our collective maturation from adolescence into adulthood, from Epoch II into Epoch III, and from a primary agenda of ego and mental development to one of spiritual development. Those institutions and individuals who resist the winds of change, who try to defend, preserve, and protect an unbalanced, partial, and patriarchal past, will find themselves facing the fierce winds of a hurricane—nature's way of blowing out the stale air and blowing in the new. Those who inhale this spirit of wholeness will find it to be a breath of fresh air, the inspiration of their lives, the inspiration of this transitional time, and the inspiration for a new maturity.

The purpose and function of a dark night of the soul is to make us face the pathologies which had previously been hidden far down in our unconscious, and to reveal hints of the emerging trends. Over the past three decades we have become aware of what darkness we have had to face and what sickness we have had to heal if we are to see the light of a new, healthier, and more mature day. So we find ourselves experiencing a variety of illnesses as our soul tries to purge immature pathologies from the body politic.

Sick in the Night

We are sick in the night with paranoia, scapegoating, and projection of our fears out onto anyone who is of a different nationality, race, religion, or sexual orientation. We are neurotic with a compulsion to pour vast amounts of money into weapons and other defense mechanisms. We are obscene in our spending of 1.8 million dollars *per minute* on weapons, while fifteen million children under age five die each year because they don't have enough food or medicine. We are immature adolescent parents who choose to invest in weapons rather than in our children—in America alone, one hundred infants die every day.

Concern about children, according to this adolescent patriarchal mentality, is women's work, while protecting our ownership of guns is man's work. The National Rifle Association (NRA) suggests that "the crusade against semiautomatic rifles reflects a deep split in values between those who honor the traditional warrior virtues and skills as vital necessities for a nation's survival and those who deplore them as proof of a willing reversion to the bestial. . . . Our female-dominated, spastic society has been working overtime for a generation to discredit manhood."[3]

The first question such a statement raises is—If we *were* a female-dominated society with any semblance of a maternal instinct, would we be spending so much money on weapons while our children die? The second question is—Is the NRA's notion of "manhood" one that mature males want as a guiding principle? Needless to say, my answer to both questions is an obvious and resounding, "No!"

We are sick in the night with an adolescent self-centeredness that has outlived its usefulness and its healthiness. Like a vast teenage society, advertisers convince us that we have material needs to be "in," and we respond with compulsive consuming. We act like pathological binge consumers, thinking that the world is one huge, well-stocked refrigerator, the contents of which we devour while numbing ourselves before late-night television—which is why the naturalist Loren Eisely called us "the world eaters."

We "eat," in a very short time, what it took Mother Gaia millions of years to produce. Prior to the early 1800s, for instance, our consumption of copper and iron was directly proportional to the increase of population—as the population doubled, our use of those metals doubled. But from the early 1800s to the early 1900s our numbers increased threefold whereas "the consumption of copper increased 80 times and iron 100 times."[4] Our consumption of oil, as another example, caused resources expert M. King Hubbert to observe, "It is hard to know which is more remarkable, that it took 600 million years for the Earth to make its oil, or that it took 300 years to use it up."[5]

It is interesting to note that what we consider to be the driving forces of a healthy economy are synonymous with the Middle Age's "seven deadly sins"—greed, avarice, envy, gluttony, luxury, lust, and pride. If enough people are, therefore, "sinful" enough and addicted to the produce, consume, and dispose cycle, we call it a healthy economy. Yet, any rational critique of this would have to label it an adolescent propensity for immediate gratification with no thought for tomorrow. The U.S., for instance, has about six percent of the world's population, yet consumes about thirty percent of the world's production of energy and raw materials. If this is so healthy, why is it the world would be in real trouble if every other nation followed our example?

We are cutting down forests without regard to the ecological consequences, eliminating animals' natural habitats without thought, exterminating species without conscience, and massivly killing and experimenting with animals without compassion.

The Worldwatch Institute and the Windstar Foundation are two organizations dedicated to the development of what they call a "sustainable society;" in other words, a society mature enough to live with our children and our children's children in mind. Isn't that simply a definition of mature adults and sensitive parents?

> A sustainable society is one that satisfies its needs without jeopardizing the prospects of future generations. Inherent in this definition is the responsibility of each generation to ensure that the next one inherits an undiminished natural and economic endowment. This concept of intergenerational equity, profoundly moral in character, is violated in numerous ways by our current society.[6]

Matthew Fox reminds us that for Native peoples the criteria for morality in one's choices is the impact that it will have on those living seven generations from now. With that criteria, how moral are our current choices?

We are sick in the night with an unbalanced and adolescent masculinity which knows only violence as a way of expressing frustration. We not only express pathological proportions of violence in our relationship with nature and animals, but we beat a woman every 18 seconds, rape a woman every six minutes, with domestic violence against women occurring more often than rapes, muggings, and automobile accidents combined.

We are, indeed, sick in so many other ways that it would make this book too long, and certainly too negative, if I tried to enumerate them all or even elaborated upon those I mentioned. My point is not to make a thorough survey of our troubles, but to point out what is perhaps all too obvious—we have so many self-destructive tendencies that many people are getting depressed, unsure that we will even see the light of a new dawn. Our dark night of the soul is very, very dark, and we may commit suicide before morning. With our propensity for violence and the availability of nuclear weapons we could commit a massive and sudden suicide. Or, with our adolescent self-centeredness and short-range vision, we could commit a slow suicide by killing off our ecological life-support.

If things are so bad, one might ask, why even write a book with an essentially hopeful message? Cynicism, despair, and depression are all too frequent companions these days within the human family. Are we even willing to consider hope? If the ship is going down anyway, does all this simply represent a philosophical discussion on the deck of the Titanic? What's the use, anyway?

As serious as the questions of survival are, disaster is not automatic. Trends are not destiny, no matter how powerful they may seem at the time. Things can change. *We* can change. We *do* change. Change is what living things do—naturally. What we invest our time and energies in can create a self-fulfilling prophecy. And I certainly do not intend to contribute to the most negative and cynical thinking and help us move toward a disaster.

Besides, I think there is ample reason for tenacious hope and tough-minded optimism. A basic theme of this book is that there is a natural process to life—maturation—and life has a built-in bias for moving us toward health and wholeness. Make no mistake about it, we have the power to ruin things if we are hell-bent on destruction. But that is not the only power we have. We also have the power to be heaven-bent on growth, development, and maturation, for the purpose of health and wholeness. We can be attracted to the highest and best in us, just as we can sink to the lowest and worst.

Important in this discussion about sickness in our dark night of the soul is a discernment between causes and symptoms. We will not emerge from this transitional night and see the dawn of a new day unless we identify and deal with the root causes of our sickness. In fact, it may very well be that this lack of discernment is precisely why we are still sick in the night, still in an immature adolescence, even after three decades.

In our adolescence those in power have been so prone to projection and scapegoating that problems and solutions have been defined at the symptom level. It has been identified, over and over again, how *those other people* are the problem. In the '60s we had a "Negro problem" and a "Vietnam problem," in the '70s we had the problems of having to put up with those "radical feminists" and "radical environmentalists," and in the '80s we became aware of the "drug problem" and the "gay and lesbian problem." Consequently, we launched ambitious efforts at treating the symptoms and declared war on our "enemies."

We lynched the black man, kept the woman "in her place," and excluded the Jews and gays from our clubs. Nixon declared war on cancer in the 1970s, and Reagan declared war on drugs in the 1980s. But we conducted our war against drugs by targeting the drugs "they" export, while continuing, indeed expanding, the export of "our" drugs.

Consider tobacco, for instance. It is one of our country's favorite and most protected drugs, and the entire scene is dripping with hypocrisy and inconsistency. We target massive dollars for our war against the import, sale, and use of cocaine and heroin, while we subsidize the growth, export, and sale of tobacco. Yet, "the U.S. surgeon general has determined that nicotine—the drug in to-bacco—is as addictive as cocaine or heroin."[7]

If tobacco is as addictive as cocaine or heroin, then we must justify the unevenness of our concern over the fact that the latter must kill more people. Right? Wrong! The National Center for Disease Control report that there were 434,175 smoking related deaths in 1988. In contrast, the National Institute on Drug Abuse in 1988 listed the figures for the annual deaths attributable to heroin/morphine as 4,000, cocaine killed 2,000, and marijuana 75.[8] In other words, one of our most favorite and protected drugs kills seventy-one times the number of people killed by the drugs on which we have declared war.

Tobacco takes more American lives *every year* than we lost in World War II. We were patriotic about "saving the world for democracy" yet allow officially sanctioned killing to continue here at home. Tobacco products, for instance, are excluded from our government's regulatory agencies. "By law, the Consumer Product Safety Commission can't touch tobacco even though, by the agency's own assessment, 'Cigarettes are responsible for more deaths than the combination of all of the other products that have come under the commission's purview.'"[9] Tobacco is excluded from the Toxic Substances Act, the Fair Labeling and Packaging Act, the Federal Hazardous Substances Act, and the Controlled Substances Act.

In spite of the hypocrisy involved in our determination of what is legal and what is illegal, American adults are increasingly turning their backs on cigarette smoking. Per capita smoking for adults steadily decreased throughout the eighties. Consequently, the tobacco companies target two other markets—youth and foreign exports.

It is generally accepted that about 90 percent of smokers are addicted before the age of twenty. Therefore, the subsequent and inevitable deaths of our children and youth are assured when they become addicted to tobacco. Where is the outrage? Where is the recognition of our hypocrisy? We vent enormous amounts of anger and pour large sums of money into the detection and prosecution of illegal drug "pushers," while executives of tobacco companies are revered community leaders. Yet the latter are unquestionably "pushers" making huge profits off addicting our children to a killing drug. We let them addict, and then kill, hundreds of thousands of our children every year in America. Where is the outrage?

And speaking of hypocrisy—consider our exportation of tobacco. Flagging sales at home have the tobacco companies looking to foreign markets, particularly Asia. It is understandable, given that now only 27 percent of American men smoke, whereas the rate in Japan is 63 percent, and in China it is 70 percent. But, again, what about our lack of national integrity? We condemn other countries who allow the export of their drugs into this country while we encourage, indeed support, the export of our drugs to kill people in other countries.

Tobacco claims an estimated 2.5 million lives a year worldwide, and the U.S. government—not just the tobacco companies, but our government—aids in the expansion of our export. "With overseas smoking rates rising precipitously, the World Health Organization (WHO) predicts that developing nations will face a 'cancer epidemic' by the turn of the century."[10] Yet, while the Reagan administration was carrying out a campaign to "Just say 'No' to drugs," it intervened in 1985 on behalf of U.S. tobacco companies to force

Far Eastern countries to allow the increase of our export of tobacco into their countries.[11]

My point is that the focus on symptoms rather than causes and the scapegoating and projection of our own repressed pathologies, along with the resulting hypocrisy, will not solve our problems. We will think we are gaining on this one, and then another one erupts from our unconscious depths—and we will project the problem out onto another scapegoat, and declare a war on "them" or "it." We can lance a boil but if we don't get at the poison in the system another boil will simply erupt at another point on the body politic.

This is not an argument against ever treating symptoms. Without going into every circumstance, of course it is appropriate to deal with the symptom. It is to say, however, that if that is *all* we do, we should not be surprised if we never make a substantive gain on health and wholeness, if we never cure our pathologies. I think it was Dr. David Bressler, when he was directing the UCLA pain clinic, who said that taking drugs for pain, simply treating the symptom, is akin to driving your car down the highway and, when the red oil warning light comes on, grabbing a hammer and smashing the warning light, thinking, "Now *that* problem is taken care of."

I suspect that being out of balance is a cause of more problems—political, economic, religious, personal health, etc.—than we are usually willing to recognize. And my point here is that our adolescence has now come to the point of being so out of balance that we are thrust into a dark night of the soul. We developed physically, then mentally, but we need a spiritual maturation if we are to be in balance.

Spiritual Tossing and Turning

Because our current experience of darkness is, precisely, a dark night of the *soul*, it is fundamentally a spiritual crisis. It is a time when spiritual maturation is needed for a whole and balanced life. Our current spiritual immaturity oozes out of a variety of boils all over the body politic. The boils may appear to be different "problems," but the poison in the system is our spiritual immaturity.

Such an observation, in the American culture of the late twentieth century, may fall on deaf ears. That we are least aware of this as a sickness in our culture is, however, evidence for, not against, it being the deep fundamental cause of our current pathologies.

Let's consider, briefly, what has been happening spiritually in our dark night of the soul. We know, intuitively, that both the cause of our problems and the major agenda emerging for a healthier future is spiritual. Consequently, we have been tossing and turning in our night sickness trying to find the spiritual health that will make us whole. Understandably, however, the initial tossings and turnings have not shown us the way out of this dark night of the soul. So far, they have been adolescent responses to an uncomfortable sickness in the night; they are not the mature solutions, but by looking at them with sacred eyes we can begin to see our way into the dawn.

1. TOSSING AND TURNING EAST:
In the 1960s we started, first of all, tossing and turning to the East. As so often happens, our youth live out that which is repressed in our unconscious; and in the 1960s our youth started turning to Eastern religions in large numbers, living out what was still unconscious for most of us—the bankruptcy of our adolescent Christianity.

To simply switch religions is not, however, the way to cure our spiritual sickness, nor a way to find the dawning light of spiritual maturity. In stark contrast to Freud's distrust of religion, Carl Jung had some profoundly helpful insights regarding the unconscious and our spiritual lives. Jung expressed grave concern over Westerners trying to find spiritual health by simply adopting Eastern religions. He felt, for instance, that genuine yoga cannot be practiced in the Christian world. And even though a Westerner claims not to be a Christian, it is something else again to be free of the deep psychic impact of the Christian influence in the West. Jung wrote:

> The trouble is that Western man cannot get rid of his history as easily as his short-legged memory can. History. . . is written in the blood. I would not advise anyone to touch yoga without a careful analysis of his unconscious reactions. What is the use of imitating yoga if your dark side remains as good a medieval Christian as ever? If you can afford to seat yourself on a gazelle skin under a Bo-tree or in the cell of a gompa for the rest of your life without being troubled by politics or the collapse of your securities, I will look favorably upon your case. But yoga in Mayfair or Fifth Avenue, or in any other place which is on the telephone, is a spiritual fake."[12]

Jungian author, Lucindi Frances Mooney, speaks to the same point when she writes: "To reject one's own culture is tantamount to rejecting one's own inner, hidden nature. In effect, we try to storm

Eastern temples, instead of seeing the value of rebuilding our own."[13]

2. TOSSING AND TURNING TO THE RIGHT:

As we continue to toss and turn with spiritual sickness in the night, some of us turn to the Right, to fundamentalism. Fearing the change that our unconscious knows is coming, those of us who turn to the Right think that the problem is change itself. We think that the way out of the dark night of the soul is through the rear-view mirror, a retreat into yesterday. The problem, we think, is that we left the good old values—the answer, therefore, is to go back and do them better and harder. Consequently, in times of change, we are drawn to the "back to the basics" movements—religiously, politically, educationally, etc.

If we can just go back to the good old days, this thinking goes, we will escape the anxieties of change. But turning to the Right is a turn toward rigidity, not flexibility, a turn back into the petrifaction of death, not the evolution of life. Fearing change, we look for the security blanket of stasis, of rigid doctrine, of literal biblicism, of a past that was known, rather than a future which is unknown. Belief translates into security and is preferred over the insecurity of faith in an emerging future.

The rise of fundamentalism in the waning decades of the twentieth century is not a trend nor a wave of the future, it is a reaction. It is a perceptive reaction, in one sense, for more than some others who are asleep in our dark night of the soul, fundamentalists recognize that things are changing, and they don't like it. Change is perceived as a threat.

Historically, fundamentalism is a predictable reaction. Every time we have gone through a transitional juncture in history there have always been those who feared change and turned to the Right. Historian William Irwin Thompson writes that:

> We know from studies of cultural history that when a way of life is vanishing, people hold on to it and try to give it a more intense expression. When knighthood is about to disappear from the waning Middle Ages, armor becomes extremely elaborate; the celebration of the armored knight mounted on his horse becomes an unconscious farewell. Whether it is the Ghost Dance of the American Indians or the return to nature in the romanticism of industrial Europe, the "Silver Swan" madrigal of Morley or the *Art of the Fugue* of Bach, it is the supernova of a star in its death.[14]

The expansion of fundamentalism in our time, and its energized abhorrence of anything that smacks of "New Age," is powerful, albeit unconscious, evidence that a new day is indeed on its way. Fundamentalism's expansion, like a supernova, is evidence of its impending death. And its preference for literalism is its attempt to control the shifting turf under its feet. We are experiencing an earthquake in our paradigm, and fundamentalism thinks that if we hold on firmly enough to the old structures everything will not crumble. Turning to the Right may feel for a while like security, but it is doomed to failure. Down deep we know it, but we try to shore up the falling structure and our growing anxieties and doubts by seeking enough converts. In numbers, we think, there will be security. In that, the Right is wrong.

The perceptive social critic, Michael Harrington, suggests that:

> God, one of the most important political figures in Western history, is dying. . . . With a few lapses into liberalism, or even radicalism, God has been a leading conservative in Judeo-Christian society. His death not only means empty churches and bereft individuals but also marks the rending of the social fabric. This insight is corroborated, not contradicted, by the recent revival of fundamentalism whose desperate orthodoxy tries to will the departing deity back into existence.[15]

3. TOSSING AND TURNING TO THE LEFT:

The rest of us continue to toss and turn in our dark night of the soul. Turning East or Right doesn't appeal to all of us, so some of us turn to the Left—in this case, to the left-brain. Many of us who turn to worshiping science and rationalism think that turning to the left-brain is *the* answer to the chaos of our time and the sickness in our depths. Whereas the fundamentalists think that our problem is change, those of us who turn to the left-brain think that the problem is our past loyalty to religion and other such childish, superstitious, and fuzzy-headed thinking. If we are just logical and rational enough, this thinking goes, we can get out of our current difficulties.

Nevertheless, a half-brained approach is just not sufficient for an experience of wholeness. The left-brainers rightly perceive that adolescent religion was just that, adolescent, but mistakenly think that mature adult life can be experienced without spirituality. The left-brainers mistake various notions *about* God as accurate descriptions *of* God and existing organized religion as the only possible expression or facilitation of spirituality. The left-brainers assume that to reject *those* notions and structures means to reject *all* spiritual questing. Tossing and turning to the Left, however, is a truncated, reactionary, and inadequate response to our dark night of the soul.

Take, for instance, the rich world of mythology and the role myth plays in a fully actualized and healthy individual or culture. The lack of depth in a left-brained approach to life is revealed in the way the dominant culture deals with the word "myth." What the left-brainers and much of our culture, including the popular press, call a mistake or a falsehood—as in "we need to separate out the truth from the myth in this story"—is the very life-blood of the spiritually mature.

The left-brainers—and also, interestingly enough, those who turned Right—like to deal with literal, historical, fact—not with symbolic truth. So when the Ogalala Sioux medicine man, Black Elk, tells a mythological story the left-brainers want to know if it really happened. Black Elk, in contrast, after he told the story of the White Buffalo Woman, said: "This they tell, and whether it happened so or not I do not know; but if you think about it, you can see that it is true."[16] It takes sacred eyes to see that kind of truth, and left-brainers don't look at the world through sacred eyes.

Our myths tell us about the big questions in life—how the world came into being, what we are here for, and how we move from one stage of life to another. Bill Thompson calls myth the "history of the soul," and David Feinstein and Stanley Krippner say that myths provide "meaning for the past, purpose in the present, and direction for the future." Joseph Campbell made an important and powerful contribution to our movement out of adolescence and into a more mature adulthood by his scholarship in the world's mythologies. And the incredible popularity of his work in the 1980s was one of the clear signals that we are getting ready for the dawn of a new day.

Myths are true, often profoundly so. When we learn to listen to their inner meanings, when we can see the spiritual and psychological symbolism in them, myths can be the vehicles which carry us into a meaningful and purposeful tomorrow. When we incarnate the spirit of myth into our lives, then myths can become literally and historically true as well.

Unfortunately, we have a ways to go before we greet the dawn. This morning's newspaper used the word "myth" four times, in four different stories, and in every case it was used to mean "false." The left-brainers create a culture living in a symbolic and mythic wasteland, and it is a poverty which threatens the health of our soul.

Jungian author Helen Luke suggests that:

> The sickness of our society is not due to the threat of the bomb, to the ineptitude or corruption of the Establishment, to wars, or to the machinations of Communists or Capitalists. These evils are effects, not causes; they have always existed and are no worse because of the enormous scale on which they now operate. Our sickness is fundamentally due to the breakdown of the symbolic life which all the great religions have existed to maintain, so that we are left with eyes that see not and ears that hear not beyond the literal facts and voices of our environment. We hear only the dark news of the broadcaster, and our inner ear is deaf to the song of angels.[17]

4. TOSSING AND TURNING DOWN UNDER:

If the dominant culture is tossing and turning to the Left during our dark night of the soul, the counter-culture is tossing and turning Down Under—specifically, to the underground depths that have been so devalued and ignored by the dominant culture. The very inadequacy of a left-brained culture to provide meaning and purpose is testified to by the increase, in the latter part of the twentieth century, of people turning Down Under.

Anyone observing our culture in this dark night of the soul is struck by how many people have been drawn to the esoteric traditions—the underground currents of mainstream religions. The increased interest in Gnosticism, the early Christian mystical group; in Sufism, the Moslem mystical tradition; in the Cabala, Jewish mysticism; in the Hermetic traditions such as alchemy, astrology, and the Tarot; in the Egyptian Mystery Schools; and in Goddess worship, the underground in a patriarchal culture.

The same point is made with the explosion of interest in Native American spirituality and shamanism. The earth-centered spirituality of the Native Americans, and the "journeying" to the lower world of the shaman, are in direct contrast to the patriarchal, dominator-of-nature, left-brained bias of the dominant culture.

It follows that the mainstream has to use labels to reject, devalue, and make the undercurrents off limits. Consequently, Gnosticism is considered a Christian heresy, esoterica is considered fuzzy-headed, and our mainstream psychoanalytic professionals consider shamanic experiences as pathological. The left-brainers dismiss anything out-of-hand that they label "occult"—which interestingly means "hidden." Likewise, myth is falsehood, metaphysical is unintellectual, mystical is anti-scientific, and dreams are the garbage-heap of the mind. Left-brainers just don't understand, nor appreciate, the depths, the heights, that which is "hidden" from the dominant paradigm, and that which can only be seen in the darkness.

The point here, of course, is that there is an inadequacy to any of these partial tossings and turnings in our dark night of the soul. None is comprehensive enough to provide our path toward wholeness. All are partial reactions to our adolescent immaturities. One can find the simplistic and fundamentalistic mindset in those turning Down Under, just as in those turning to the Right. And Jung's comment about Westerners turning to yoga is applicable to those dilettantes of esoterica. In similar fashion, Dr. Roger Walsh, a professor of psychiatry and philosophy at the University of California at Irvine, and one of the most knowledgeable and friendly students of shamanism, reminds us that it is questionable if a Westerner can usefully be called a shaman, unless he or she can be fully embedded into the social, cultural, and mythological setting from which shamanism emanates.

5. TOSSING AND TURNING OFF:

As many as are tossing and turning East, Right, Left, or Down Under, there are even greater numbers who have simply turned Off. Spiritual malaise—literally, mal-ease—may be the most prevalent of our choices during our dark night of the soul.

What may be the true silent majority is not so much *for* or *against* any of the other groups, as simply Turned Off with the whole affair. Those Turned Off are not interested in either joining nor condemning Eastern religions, are not prone to get too excited about the Right's fears, are not much interested in the arrogant mind-games of the left-brainers, nor are they true-believers in the esoteric traditions. Although surveys show that a great many of us believe in astrology, Tarot, various forms of esoterica, mysticism, and the paranormal, those of us who are Turned Off are not very energized about anything. We're not activists for any particular category listed above, we're just Turned Off.

A lot of us who are Turned Off, in fact, go to church. But we do it for the social benefits, the business contacts, or for the kids. We certainly don't want a serious theological discussion, or to be pressed about the ethics of our decisions throughout the week. We may be religiously involved, but we are Biblically illiterate, theologically naive, and spiritually adolescent. We certainly don't believe in the three-story universe of the Bible, and if we worship anything it is contemporary scientific knowledge about the universe, but we don't want to discuss the conflicts between the Bible and modern science. We don't believe in most of what we "confess" or sing about in church, but we don't want to talk about it. Don't bother us with those things. We're Turned Off.

The word enthusiasm literally means to be possessed by God. Where is the enthusiasm for anything spiritual among those of us who are Turned Off? Zilch. Enthusiasm for anything spiritual is not in favor these days. As Harrington observed:

> Serious atheists and serious believers have more in common with one another than with mindless, *de facto* atheists. . . and routine churchgoers. Both have looked into the same void at the center of this incredible age. . . . The committed believers and unbelievers now have the same enemy: the humdrum nihilism of everyday life in much of Western society. . . . The God of the Judeo-Christian West is in his death agony and that is one of the most significant political events of this incredible age.[18]

The death of God has been proclaimed before. It never affected those turning East, for they were busy trying to find God inside. It sent those who turned Right into an existential fever, for from their literal perspective their security blanket was being taken away. Since those of us who turn Right tend to think in literal terms, we are constitutionally unable to consider the death of God in symbolic terms.

Those of us who turn to the left-brain have no interest at all in any discussion of the death of God, for religion is only for the psychologically immature in any case. For those of us who turn Down Under, the mainstream God is, for all practical purposes, dead anyway. And for those of us who Turn Off—well, we're just not interested.

But as we will look at more in detail later, a night ends and a new day begins only if we are willing to let go of the darkness. Death precedes new life. Normal and healthy life moves on, but we will never move on into adult spiritual maturity unless we are willing to give up childish and adolescent notions of God—in other words, to let those notions of God die.

The fact is, giving up out-dated notions of God is a natural process of growth and development. In our childhood, when we were growing up in and out of Gaia, our worship of the Goddess was natural and good. It was appropriate for that stage in our life. When we moved into adolescence, with an agenda of ego development, Father consciousness was appropriate. We left the Mother for what we needed to learn from the Father. That didn't make childhood, or Goddess worship bad, it simply represented a maturation.

In this dark night of the soul as people are becoming increasingly aware of the imbalance of our masculine ego, there is a lot of recognition of the limitations of father consciousness, and there is the desire to go back to the Goddess.

From the pen of the poet Robert Bly:

> Right now we long to say that father consciousness is bad, and mother consciousness is good. But we know it is father consciousness saying that; it insists on putting labels on things. They are both good. The Greeks and the Jews were right to pull away from the Mother and drive on into father consciousness; and their forward movement gave both cultures a marvelous luminosity. But now the turn has come.[19]

Growing Toward the Dawn

The wholeness we need at this time will not be found by going back but by growing forward. Mother consciousness was appropriate for our childhood and Father consciousness was appropriate for our adolescence. What is appropriate for our adulthood is neither one in isolation, but a new balance in a more mature spiritual wholeness.

A dark night of the soul always means our gods are too small, or that they have outlived their usefulness for this stage in our life. In this case, our dark night of the soul is telling us that it is time to mature beyond our adolescent notions of a masculine God. We have switched concepts of the Divine before, as well as the attendant value systems, and we can do it again.

For how much longer, you may be wondering, will we be in this miserable dark night of the soul? Frankly, I haven't a clue. I don't have a crystal ball with which to make any confident predictions regarding the length of time it will take us to move through this transition. We can say with confidence that everything is happening faster now, so chances are this transition will take place in decades rather than in millennia or centuries.

The full enlightenment of tomorrow is not yet visible. Nevertheless, for three decades now we have been growing toward the dawning light. With sacred eyes we can see, fairly accurately I believe, what the causes of our sicknesses are and what the new health, wholeness, and holiness will look like. We can see, for instance, that we must balance the physical and mental development of our past with spiritual development in our future.

Nature not only abhors a vacuum, it abhors lack of health and wholeness. We can be out of balance only so long before the forces of nature start balancing. We can repress pathologies and festering poisons below the surface only so long before nature's propensity for health cleans out the sores. And it seems like the more pathological or the more deeply repressed, the more violent the catharsis and the more eruptive the purging. Nature, including human nature, has a built-in bias for health and wholeness—although we don't talk about it much in these times, it is the spiritual in us that has to have a balancing.

Such dark nights of the soul are quite natural as means to move us along on our journey of growth and maturation. In the dark night we have both illness to purge and wellness to welcome. Both are occurring at the same time—evidence of what is not working, and evidence of what is more wholesome, more healthy, more in balance. We have sticks and carrots presented to us, and we can be scared out of hell, while at the same time we can find our energies being drawn to heaven as to a magnet. In the latter part of the twentieth century, we find ourselves being driven and attracted at the same time.

Take, for instance, America's space program of the 1960s. In many ways it was a brilliant supernova of the values of masculinity. An athletic male president challenged our competitive juices to beat our Russian enemies in a "space race" to the moon. Our dominant society looks at the moon as masculine—the "man in the moon"— in contrast to some Native Americans who from a more feminine perspective consider the moon to be "the old woman who never dies." The space program's goal was to put a "man" on the moon before the end of the 1960s, and our rockets—phallic symbols?— were the generative power to get us there and were named for Apollo, the male Greek god of rationality and emotional distance.

Yet, the space program gave us the picture of the Earth from outside—probably *the* catalytic image which put us on the path of the Gaian mythology, arguably the primary and guiding mythology for Epoch III.

Sometimes our pathologies erupt with a horrific juxtaposition of the old that is fading and the new which is emerging, such as in the assassinations of our hero's in the 1960s. Three of our male heroes— President Kennedy, Dr. King, and Senator Kennedy—were assassinated by three men using one of the favorite toys of our adolescence, guns, and punctuated the historical end of adolescent hero-worship. It may, however, take us several decades to grasp that maturation as we sing plaintively into the night, "Where have you gone, Joe DiMaggio? A nation turns its lonely eyes to you."

We are becoming increasingly aware of how we cannot continue down the same path of solving conflicts among nations through brute force. We now have weapons which, if used to their fullest extent, will kill us as well as them. We are forced to recognize that the same values of our past, in terms of dealing with nature, are simply not workable for a sustainable future. Nations all over the globe are facing the winds of change as people whose freedoms have been curtailed are expressing their demands for democratic empowerment.

There are hints all around us, and have been around us for more than three decades, that various pathologies and imbalances have to be dealt with, and that new health and wellness is emerging. Whether it was the civil rights movement that surprised us, or the resistance to the Viet Nam war, or the eruption of the women's movement and the ecology movement, there is a balancing taking place. Whether we get angry about our jobs being threatened by those "health nuts" who want us to stop smoking, or those radical animal rights people, or the Greenpeace radicals, there is a balancing taking place. Whether we think so or not, the recent attention to addictions, child abuse, battered women, "toxic parents," and the "child within," are simply different manifestations of the same demand—we know that freedom, empowerment, and a healthier future is emerging, and we want to do what we can to help usher it in. A marvelous new individual assertiveness for health and wholeness is taking place throughout our culture and it is one of the main Epoch III values that we will explore, in some detail, shortly.

The extent to which we are surprised by any of these movements only testifies to how sick we have been in the night, or how asleep we have been to the fact that we are in a dark night of the soul, or how unaware we have been of the impending dawn.

Crises as Natural Catalysts for Transformation

It is important for us to see that crises are natural catalysts for change, so that we can focus, not on resisting the change nor simply bewailing the chaos, but on welcoming the new health which is emerging. Mother Gaia provides an example of how crises have played natural roles in Her growth and development.

Gaia's life has not been one of steady progress and gradual

evolution. It has, rather, been a life of fluctuations between relative calm and violent crises. Her life has been periodically "punctuated" by cataclysmic change. "The history of life," writes Stephen Jay Gould, "is not a continuum of development, but a record punctuated by brief, sometimes geologically instantaneous, episodes of mass extinction and subsequent diversification."[20]

Such crises have aided the evolution of life. In Chapter Two we discussed the oxygen crisis, a crisis which threatened to end all life on Gaia. But life is a survivor, learned to breath the stuff, and set the stage for organisms like us. About 570 million years ago a mass extinction was the catalyst for what scientists call the "Cambrian explosion," or the first appearance of multicellular animals which left "hard" data for the fossil record. Some 225 million years ago Gaia experienced the loss of fully 96 percent of all marine species, which dramatically set the direction for later evolution. One of the most famous crises occurred about 65 million years ago when She lost about ten percent of Her "children," including the dinosaurs, which enabled the evolution of large mammals, including ourselves. Gaia has experienced such catalytic "dark nights of the soul" about every 26 million years.

The point here is that crises are natural, and act as catalysts. As we move into reflective life, crises continue to play catalytic roles in our growth, evolution, maturation, and development. Humanity's unconscious has always known this, and many of our ancient myths reveal the role of catastrophes in our evolutionary process— floods, earthquakes, hurricanes, fire, ice, etc. We either have the entire history of Gaia buried deep in our unconscious which comes out in our myths, or we know at some deep level that such crises play an important role in our own growth and development. Perhaps both are the case.

If we are to learn from our dark nights of the soul, however, it would seem to depend on how our consciousness deals with the nature of crisis. I am told that the Chinese word for crisis is made up of two symbols—one meaning danger and the other meaning opportunity. The question is then—when we face a crisis, do we focus only on the danger, and circle the wagons, or do we recognize and take advantage of the opportunities, no matter how dangerous they may be? Crises, and the transitional times they provide, present us with both danger and opportunities.

The world's great religions—their exoteric above-ground manifestations, as well as their esoteric underground—have spoken to the value of crises and other transitional challenges. This is true of other symbol systems as well, since humankind has always known, at least in our depths, that the greatest lessons were frequently camouflaged in what we called a troubling time.

Astrology, for instance, is a symbol system which relates to our movement through a Great Year, and our transitions from one Great Month to another, each consisting of approximately two thousand years. In astrological terms we are right now in a transitional period—experiencing the dark night of the Piscean Age prior to the "dawning of the Age of Aquarius." It is not coincidental that the Piscean Age was symbolized by the fish, and coincides with the Christian era, whereas the Age of Aquarius is symbolized by the water carrier, with water being the larger substance within which the fish swims. It is a transition from loyalty to particular systems, to an understanding of the larger spiritual context.

This transition is symbolized by the planet Pluto moving into the constellation of Scorpio, indicating a process of elimination. It is a time of eliminating the superfluous elements which have been inhibiting our lives. It is a time for destroying our psychic prisons. Pluto represents the transformational process that is essential for our growth, the process of death and rebirth. Astrology recognizes these changes as organic and necessary for life to continue. If we cooperate with change we experience renewal, if we resist we experience turmoil.

It is interesting to note that astrology characterizes the Age of Aquarius as a time of: 1) a movement toward the whole; 2) an emphasis upon the evolution and fulfillment of humanity; 3) a synthesis of science and religion, matter and spirit; 4) a renewed concern for the environment, and; 5) a revolution in our way of worshipping God. Regardless of what we may think about astrology, I would submit that it has been very accurate in suggesting the emerging trends—astrology calls it moving into the Great Month of Aquarius, whereas I am calling it a movement from adolescence into adulthood, from Epoch II into Epoch III.

Jewish and Christian apocalyptic literature is another example of symbols for transitional times. About two thousand years ago, and a couple of hundred years on each side, the Judeo-Christian world was going through a major transformational time. A considerable literature expressed the intuitions of an ending time and a beginning time, a dying time and a birthing time.

Only one was accepted in the Christian bible, the final book of the New Testament, Revelation—frequently referred to as the Apocalypse of St. John. Today, two thousand years later and again in a transitional time, it is significant that the book of Revelation is gaining a lot of renewed attention. Unfortunately, most of the attention is by Christian fundamentalists who take the book literally and negatively. Thus they draw literal parallels of what is predicted in Revelation and today's crises, concluding that the world is coming to an end. (Incidentally, the same mistake made by many two thousand years ago.)

The fact is, the word apocalypse means revelation—disclosure, not closure. It is an attempt to reveal, in symbolic terms so that it is applicable to all people in every transitional time, the destruction of an old age and the envisioning of a new age.

Syracuse University professor David Miller observes that when we lack a vision, we begin to visualize the literal. "In a time of change and de-structuring," Miller suggests, "we all need a way of comprehending endings—Apocalypse gives us an imaginal way of doing that. Yet the problem is we have lost our sense of mythic endings; thus we take Revelation and its images of the end of the world literally."[21]

The final book of the Bible is not a literal picture of the end of the world, but an allegory of initiation, a means to a new beginning. The mythic imagery of death and rebirth are meant to show us the inner process to a new step in maturation, the birth of a new level of consciousness.

A key passage in Revelation has God saying, "Behold, I am making all things new." The contemporary interest in that final book of the Bible is because we sense a new-making taking place in our time. We feel an existential tug toward the symbols of death and rebirth, of transformation, of endings and new beginnings.

Prophetic Voices Heralding the Dawn

When we leave the ancient symbols or religious literature and listen to contemporary social analysts, we hear essentially the same thing. Consider just a few examples taken from leaders in a variety of fields:

Social analyst Alvin Toffler:

> We are the final generation of an old civilization and the first generation of a new one. And although a new civilization is emerging in our lives, blind men everywhere are trying to suppress it. . . . What is happening is not like a hurricane that

sweeps across the landscape, leaving the earth itself unchanged. It is more like the beginning of an earthquake. For the subterranean structure on which all our economics are based is now, itself, shifting, and cracking.[22]

Pollster Daniel Yankelovich:

Tomorrow is not going to look like yesterday. In fact, tomorrow—to the extent that research data can yield clues about it—is being shaped by a cultural revolution that is transforming the rules of American life and moving us into wholly uncharted territory, not back to the lifestyles of the past.[23]

Economist Paul Hawken:

We have entered a period between economies, or to be more precise, between economic structures. . . . Current economic problems are no more a sign of failure than adolescence is the failure of childhood. While coming of age may not be the most apt metaphor for our crisis, it at least expresses the trauma that can accompany rapid change when proper understanding is lacking.[24]

Jesuit priest and paleontologist Peirre Teilhard de Chardin:

Humanity has just entered what is probably the greatest transformation it has ever known. Something is happening in the structure of human consciousness. It is another species of life that is just beginning.[25]

Historian, physicist, and biologist Lancelot Law Whyte:

The human psyche is about to turn a corner and enjoy vistas never seen before, . . . a radical metamorphosis of the psyche already underway, particularly in the West.[26]

Professor of physics and research biophysics John Platt:

Our recent era of change may be converging within this generation to a unique historical transformation to a totally new kind of life.[27]

Professor of law Charles Reich:

There is a revolution coming. It will not be like revolutions of the past. It will originate with the individual and with culture, and it will change the political structure only as its final act. It will not require violence to succeed, and it cannot be successfully resisted by violence. It is now spreading with amazing rapidity, and already our laws, institutions and social structure are changing in consequence. It promises a higher reason, a more human community, and a new and liberated individual. Its ultimate creation will be a new and enduring wholeness and beauty—a renewed relationship of man to himself, and to other men, to society, to nature, and to the land.[28]

Professor of history Theodore Roszak:

> The environmental anguish of the earth has entered our lives as a radical transformation of human identity. The needs of the planet and the needs of the person have become one, and together they have begun to act upon the central institutions of our society with a force that is profoundly subversive, but which carries within it the promise of cultural renewal.[29]

Author and journalist George Leonard:

> The current period is indeed unique in history and... it represents the beginning of the most thorough-going change in the quality of human existence since the creation of an agricultural surplus brought about the birth of civilized states some five thousand years ago.[30]

President of the Institute of Noetic Sciences Willis Harman:

> This is a special moment in history. We are undergoing a period of fundamental transformation, the extent and meaning of which we who are living through it are only beginning to grasp. I believe future historians will note that sometime between 1960 and 2000 the modern world passed through one of the great watersheds of history.[31]

We could go on and on, for there are many prestigious scholars of history and observers of culture who recognize this as a profoundly transformational time. It is not just one day ending and a new one beginning, or a change of decades. Even the powerful symbol of the end of one millennium and the beginning of another does not do justice to the magnitude of this transition. In the largest view of human history, we are going through only the second great transformation—from mental development into spiritual development, from adolescence into adulthood, from Epoch II into Epoch III.

Crawling into Death or Flying into New Life

The metamorphosis of a caterpillar into a butterfly can be a useful metaphor in understanding this historical transformation. The butterfly is a universal symbol of transformation precisely because apparent death and chaos precede new life. When the caterpillar goes inside the cocoon it must feel like a dark night of the soul. Chaos reigns while total disorganization and disintegration are taking place. To the caterpillar it must seem like death. But the caterpillar does not—indeed cannot—go back regardless of how scary the night might seem.

The caterpillar part of ourselves is preoccupied with the dying, with how scary the loss of identity is, with the frightening chaos of disintegration. It is understandable that we would like to go back to the familiar identity of the caterpillar. It is understandable that, after all that time with our feet firmly on the ground, we have a fear of flying.

As Richard Bach put it: "What the caterpillar calls the end of the world, the rest of the world calls a butterfly." If we can look beyond the dread of the situation, we can see with sacred eyes the disorganization that always precedes reintegration, the destruction that always precedes restructuring, the breakdown that precedes breakthrough, the death that precedes rebirth, the endings that precede new beginnings, and the night that precedes the dawn of a new day. Similarly, adolescence precedes mature adulthood. It is natural. It is the way life works.

If we are to have integrity with our time, and if we are to have integrity within ourselves, we cannot keep projecting our dark side out onto others. We can find our way into wholeness, integrity, and a healthy future by owning both the caterpillar and the butterfly within ourselves, and by knowing that it is an apt metaphor precisely because it is all part of one life—the caterpillar becomes the butterfly, naturally. We can move from adolescence into adulthood, naturally.

There is value in having our feet on the ground, and there is value in being attracted to the heights. On the wall of my mother's apartment is a little plaque, unsigned, which reads, "There are only two lasting bequests we can give our children—one is roots, the other wings." Indeed. To be grounded and able to be appreciative of one's roots, and yet to be able to fly high and see a more heavenly human existence—that is a balanced and marvelously holy, healthy, and whole life.

Sunsets, as well as Son-sets, Must Precede the Dawn

Before we conclude the discussion of our dark night of the soul one more matter needs to be addressed. Logically, and naturally, the sun has to set before we can experience the new sunrise. When it comes to theories or concepts, scientists often refer to the "sunset phenomenon," meaning that there needs to be a natural ending to a theory, or whatever, before there can be a new beginning. The sunset is a symbol in nature of the natural process of endings preceding new beginnings.

It is not my intent to simply be shocking or controversial—although I am sure that what I am about to suggest will be just that for some people. But if we are to leave the past behind and welcome the dawn of a new and more mature day, we need not only sunsets, but also Son-sets. In one regard this has relevancy for Christians, in another for everybody.

Epoch II has been characterized, as we have stated before, by a projection of power—up into heaven, out onto an external notion of God, out onto a savior figure, out onto institutions or "outside experts," and out onto machines and technology. For many Christians this has been represented by an adolescent form of hero-worship—the worship of Jesus. In this respect we need a Son-set, an ending of hero-worship, so that we can fully empower the inner Christ. What was heresy in Epoch II will be spiritual creativity in Epoch III—the empowering of each person in their own special version of divinity. But for the enlightenment of that creative sunrise to occur, many Christians need a Son-set.

"Not only do I leave the door open for the Christian message," wrote Carl Jung, "but I consider it of central importance for Western man. It needs, however, to be seen in a new light, in accordance with the changes wrought by the contemporary spirit. Otherwise it stands apart from the times, and has no effect on man's wholeness."[32]

In a larger applicability, Epoch II cultures need a Son-set in terms of leaving behind adolescent patriarchy. The patriarchy of Epoch II has thought of power, when not projecting it, as power over something or someone—power over nature, animals, women, our bodies, and our instinctual nature—a power enforced with violence. Epoch III wholeness and empowerment (explored more fully in Chapters Eight and Nine) will be experienced in all their brilliance and magnificence, only after the Son-sets of hero-worship and adolescent patriarchy.

Ever since we entered the chrysalis period of humanity's transformation, starting in the 1960s, we have been going through the crises of initiation. To the caterpillar part of us it feels like a very dark night indeed. It has been a painful time, a confusing time, and a chaotic time. It has been a time of fluctuating emotions—despair, perhaps moments of hope, and back to despair and depression. It has been a particularly challenging time.

Nevertheless, that which is in our genetic code, the butterfly part of us, knows that we will soon experience the full brilliance of an awe-inspiring dawn. "In a dark time," wrote Theodore Roethke, "the eye begins to see." Sacred eyes can, indeed, penetrate the darkness of this soul-level crisis and see the respective faces of the past, present, and future. Sacred eyes can envision where we have been and where we are headed.

Before we turn to the content of that dawning epoch, the value system which will take us into the 21st century and beyond, we need to get personal. This book is not intended to be just a head-trip, a cool analysis of ideas, but rather a book about a soul-level spiritual transformation. The new spiritual maturity involves the whole person in every step. So we turn now to an exploration of how we, as persons, are dealing with the fact that we are living in this extraordinary time in history. How are we personally experiencing the dark night of the soul? How do we deal with being the dying caterpillar, as well as the emergent butterfly?

CHAPTER 7

ON HAVING
HISTORICAL INTEGRITY
WITH A DYING EPOCH II

The universe is story. . . . Each creature is a story. Each human enters this world and awakens to a simple truth: "I must find my own story within this great epic of being."
—PHYSICIST BRIAN SWIMME

People need a story that will bring personal meaning together with the grandeur and significance of the universe.
—THEOLOGIAN AND GEOLOGIST THOMAS BERRY

THIS IS WHERE WE PAUSE, in the midst of our look at the large sweep of the collective human journey, to get personal. We now shift from the objective to the subjective, from the detached to the attached, from humanity's story to our individual stories, from Biography to autobiography. It is time to explore our integrity with the time of our lives.

In other words, are our small stories on the same page as the big story? Is the music of our lives in tune with life's larger symphony? Do our individual threads coordinate with the collective pattern in the fabric of our times?

We are historical beings and how we relate to our history is a matter of spiritual significance. That you and I have certain gifts and that we are living at this particular time in history are not matters of accident, meaningless chance, or purposeless coincidence. There is meaning and purpose in searching for and in finding an integrity between our lives and the time of our lives, in finding an integrity

100

between our spirit, our body, our gifts, our journey, and the place in which we are doing it all. This is what I am calling historical integrity.

I am told that if you telephone a certain British philosopher and get his recording, you hear something akin to the following: "This is not an answering machine. It is, rather, a questioning machine. The applicable questions are: Who are you?—and—What do you want? And if you think those are simple questions, consider the fact that most of us go through our entire lives without ever answering them fully."

Our lives are, indeed, shaped by the questions we live and love. The quality of our quest is determined by the questions we ask. So, in addition to those two big questions, we begin our search into our own stories with some other questions.

Why me? Why now? Why here?

How do I understand my life's purpose for being here at this particular time?

In what way can my gifts and propensities contribute to a healthier world?

What is my special purpose and destiny?

Why do I have this particular body, with these particular tests?

How am I choosing to relate to the central challenges of this time in history?

Am I part of the problem or part of the solution?

What does it mean to be living in a transitional time? Am I aware of and sensitive to what is dying as well as to what is emerging?

How have I participated in, been conditioned by, or fought against, the adolescent value system of Epoch II?

At least some of the meaning in the symbol of the Incarnation is found in the issue of historical integrity. The Incarnation symbolizes Spirit being in the flesh of our bodies. Our bodies are historical—they are formed within time, live in and for a particular time, and die at given time. Spirit, in our particular incarnation of it, is time-specific. Our spiritual nature is Spirit in this body, this time. Our self is our particular version of Spirit. Historical integrity is, therefore, our search for and discovery of our particular at-one-ment with Spirit, matter, flesh, and time.

The Epoch II separation of body and soul led some religious people to consider the body to be a temporary prison for the soul. They considered Spirit as totally separate and distinct from matter and, therefore, the body as an impairment to spiritual growth and development. At the same time, Epoch II materialism led others to totally discount spirituality altogether and consider the body as the only important arena. Both positions considered matter and spirit to be mutually exclusive. I am suggesting something quite to the contrary, and the symbol of the Incarnation points to the synthesis, the integration, the integrity of body and soul, matter and spirit, human and divine. I am suggesting that the body is a very important spiritual context.

The subject of spiritualized matter and materialized spirit will be explored in greater detail in Chapter Eight. Nevertheless, we touch on it here because of the way in which it speaks to our search for historical integrity. Our bodies are at least one way we can look for our particular meaning in this time in history. Our bodies are one very specific way in which we are historical beings. It is not by accident, nor an intended punishment, to have the opportunity to learn from Spirit being materialized in the universe, this planet, this body, and this time. There is a cosmological theology, a geological theology, and a biological theology—all part of our spiritual search for meaning.

As with so many other things, the subject of historical integrity needs a "but, on the other hand. . . ." Nothing is quite as simplistic as we always want to make it. I am trying to emphasize the meaning and purpose of our experience of the physical world at this particular time in history. But, on the other hand, Spirit is not limited to the physical and material world. Spirit is in matter, in fact the very essence of matter, but it is more than matter. Accepting the "more than" of transcendence, my interest at this point is to explore the here and now of immanence.

"Arise and drink your bliss," wrote William Blake, "for everything that lives is holy." You are alive and, therefore, you are holy. And the purpose of this chapter is to encourage you to drink your bliss, to explore the integration and the integrity of the holiness within you and the holiness within this time in history.

Perhaps taking his clue from Blake, Joseph Campbell, one of our time's most magnificent beacons illuminating the dawn of Epoch III, talked a lot about "following our bliss." "I'm not superstitious," he said, "but I do believe in spiritual magic, you might say. I feel that if one follows what I call one's 'bliss'—the thing that really gets you deep in the gut and that you feel is your life—doors will open up."[1]

I agree with Campbell. For our purposes here, however, I want to make a slight alteration in Campbell's words. One way to discover our historical integrity, I would suggest, is to "follow our bless/ings." If we look to the ways in which we have been blessed, and follow those blessings into their depths and breadths, we will be led to find our unique meaning and purpose in this life. If we follow our blessings we will discover our historical integrity.

When I have examined my blessings I have found, first of all, the cause for gratitude—an emotion, as well as an intellectual stance, in which there is to be found a great deal of spiritual health. Secondly, in my blessings I have found my "call to ministry"—insight regarding the meaning and purpose of my life. And, thirdly, it has been in following my blessings that I have experienced both the joys and the sorrows of life, the highs and the lows, the brilliant sunlight and the darkest shadow—in short, following my blessings has provided the unique texture of my life's journey.

Those three—gratitude, one's "call," and the complete journey—provide the balance, the integrity, and the diversity of life. Life can never be in balance if one does not have a large dose of gratitude—an awareness and appreciation of one's blessings. Life gains integrity when one hears and responds to one's unique and special call to service. And a thoughtful and sensitive life will inevitably experience the rich diversity inherent in the full life.

You and I are living during a marvelously active and special time in history, the dying of one large epoch of humanity's journey and the emergence of another. We have the extraordinary privilege to be living at the time when humanity moves from adolescence into adulthood; at the time when, having developed physically and mentally, humanity now moves into a time of spiritual development.

So we pause, after considering history to this point in time, and address the issue of our individual integrity with a dying Epoch II. I'll share some of my own attempts at following my blessings into historical integrity as a way of encouraging you, the reader, to explore your own. And then again, in Chapter Twelve, after considering the emerging spirituality of Epoch III, we will explore our personal integrity with those emergent themes.

I. Following My Blessings
Regarding Epoch II Social Injustice

It was somewhere around my eighth or ninth year of life. It was a clear, sunny, Saturday morning—the kind of day when fathers like mine, in towns like Des Moines, Iowa, took their sons with them to do some physical project. A sort of initiation rite in manly physical labor. We were at work spreading gravel on the parking lot of a gas station my father had just purchased. It was a Norman Rockwell scene—the ramshackle little office building, the antique gas pumps, the father and son working together, and the 1940s gas truck we called "Old Mable," because part of the warning sign "FLAMMABLE" painted on the rear of the truck was worn off leaving only the letters, "——MABLE."

All of a sudden, from around the corner building came a black man, screaming and running full tilt, being chased by a white man with a club in his hand. The image of unfairness took over my whole being—blacks were the underclass, this man was running scared, and the white man had a club. Without a moment's hesitation, and to the horror of my father, I grabbed a handful of gravel and started chasing the white man, throwing rocks at him as I ran, yelling at him to leave the other man alone.

The chase ended—I don't even remember how—and my father was nonplused at my behavior. "You don't know what preceded the chase," he said. "You reacted impulsively to a situation that had nothing to do with you. You were lucky he didn't use the club on you." All of my father's protestations had a ring of truth. Yet for some reason I felt compelled to try to even the odds for the unfortunate one who didn't have a club.

The Epoch II adolescent value system has entire groups of people with clubs, so to speak, and whole groups being chased at a disadvantage. As a child I felt the unfairness. As an adult, I can recognize the systemic injustice, prejudice, and oppression.

In a multitude of ways our Epoch II adolescent values favor certain persons while thrusting certain others out into disfavor. It's junior high revisited. We have divided the human family up into the good guys and the bad guys, "in" groups and "out" groups, us and them. We have gained our emotional security by being in the "in" clique vis-a-vis those defined as outsiders. And unfortunately, we tend to assign divine sanction to our side of the equation—we are favored by God and our country is a nation under God, while "they" are cohorts of Satan and their country, as President Reagan piously announced regarding Russia, is an "evil empire."

I grew up on the favored side of most Epoch II divisions. I am a white, heterosexual male, born and raised in a loving, solid, relatively affluent Christian family. And I was gifted with athletic ability. In Epoch II America you can hardly get any more favored than that.

Unless one is sleep-walking through the latter half of the twentieth century, it should be quite evident that people of black, red, yellow, or brown skin endure widespread subtle, as well as overt, prejudice. The same with Jews and other religious minorities. Only relatively recently have heterosexuals become aware of the homophobic culture in which gays and lesbians have to live. Women, in a patriarchal Epoch II, in spite of actually being in the majority, have had to endure the limitations of a minority. And a great deal of attention is now being directed to the lingering pathologies of people who, as children, experienced abuse from unhealthy parents.

The spiritual search for historical integrity, however, forces those of us who happen to be on the favored side of the equations to ask some questions. Are we favored by God over other people?—don't be ridiculous. Should we feel guilty for being white, male, etc.?—it doesn't make sense to feel guilty about things over which we had no control. Should we constantly try to understand how Epoch II favors some people over others?—of course. Should we try to be fair and just in our dealings with every person, regardless of where they fall in those racial or cultural divisions?—naturally. And should we try to bring greater justice and compassion into society's structures?—now we're talking.

As part of my attempt to understand my life's story, I have wondered what it was in that young boy that was instantly triggered when he saw a white man with a club chasing a black man. Was it an innate sense of fairness? Was it a family environment that tried to broaden my horizons about diversity and injustice?

In the matter of following our blessings, I certainly do not believe that it was God favoring me and disfavoring others—how can one believe that kind of rubbish? That would be such a small, immature, God—a God too small to inspire the highest and best in us. The quality divisions of humanity are clearly our own creations—Epoch II adolescent constructions—not an innate, divinely ordained, structure of reality. No, my blessings were that I had parents who helped me become aware of diversity without drawing quality judgments. The spiritual heredity of my family was to be aware of and celebrate human differences, a divine creation, while at the same time being aware of how the injustice and unfairness in our social systems are human creations.

Growing up in Des Moines, Iowa, in the 1940s and 1950s, one didn't have a lot of natural exposure to diversity, pluralism, or the injustices suffered by minorities. There were not aggressive confrontations by minorities to force an expansion of our narrow parochial consciousness. And, interestingly enough, I don't recall explicit "lessons" from my parents regarding prejudice. We were just a rather normal, middle-American family, living within the typical day-to-day process of school, work, and family activities. My parents certainly would not have been characterized as political or social activists, rebels, or mavericks. They were just good, solid, church-going, community-oriented citizens.

Yet, behind my memories of childhood ordinariness and normalcy lie some intriguing recollections of what seems like intentional exposure to magnanimity on the part of my parents. I remember, as a very young child, having a black doll among my playthings—I doubt that was an ordinary occurrence in middle-class, middle-American homes in towns with a single-digit black population restricted to living in a ghetto. I also remember being taken to the Jewish Community Center to learn swimming, instead of to the YMCA where my family was quite active. And as a young boy I took tap-dancing lessons from a Russian Jewish immigrant. Exposure to minorities did not come easily or naturally in Des Moines in those years—there must have been some intention on the part of my parents.

The challenges for those growing up on the dis-favored side of the Epoch II equations are substantial—how to deal with being the brunt of injustice and inequality, prejudice and bigotry, without simply getting angry at life, or without accepting the second-class self-image being projected on one. Yet, although quite different, there are challenges for those of us on the favored side. How can we be insightful enough, and courageous enough, to see through the prejudicial structures and concepts and challenge them? How can we rise above simple personal favor, to be sensitive to others disfavor? It takes even greater sensitivity to challenge the structures that favor you and to perceive their inherent unfairness to others. Such sensitivity was a blessing I received from my parents.

My adult life, in part, has attempted to follow that blessing and to contribute, whenever and wherever possible, to a diminishment of social injustice and the oppression of minorities. And when it came time for us to take our role as parents, Lee and I were thoughtful about increasing those sensitivities among our children. As social activists, we tried to alert our communities to fairness and justice issues and to work to change structures wherever possible.

Social injustice is one consequence of our Epoch II adolescent immaturity. It has been an area in which, by following my blessings, I have been active throughout my adult life.

Another interesting arena of Epoch II immaturity is how we deal with money—the role it plays in our lives, how it stands in our list of priorities, and how it affects our relationship with other people. Here, too, I received some blessings which, when followed, led to some of the particular texture of my experience with Epoch II.

In an overt sense, my family was comfortable financially but certainly not wealthy. It is from the subtleties, however, that one learns the most important lessons. And with any family, financial subtleties were evident everywhere in the home in which I was growing up. In balance, they constituted an enormous blessing. Not because I inherited a fortune—I didn't. Not because I learned how to make a lot of money—I haven't. And not because money was seen as the be-all and end-all—it wasn't. Precisely the opposite. In a family that was relatively affluent, I was blessed with a mature and spiritual perspective of money and material possessions.

My father, the sole provider of income, never finished high school, did not inherit any money, and had worked very hard his entire adult life. He started as a truck driver and, through a natural entrepreneurial propensity, started buying trucks, hiring additional drivers, and developing other businesses. Eventually he owned a rather substantial truck line, several gas stations, and quite a few parking lots.

That is the starting point for any number of financial attitudes and messages passed on to the children in that family. It could have been, "I worked hard for every penny and I am going to hoard every penny for my own benefit." It could have been, "Having 'made it' I can see that those who don't have money are clearly lazy good-for-nothings." It could have been, "Since providing a comfortable standard of living has been my primary preoccupation, you kids had better have it as your top value going into adult life." It could have been any number of scenarios that made the almighty dollar the object of worship. It could have been, but it wasn't.

The primary value that came through was that financial resources are simply a means to a higher end—quality of life for us and for anyone else within our scope of influence. That quality of life did not include country club memberships nor ostentatious material possessions, but it did include education, culture, family activities, and giving to others. I learned—usually inadvertently, for I never heard my father bragging about this—how frequently my parents gave money to worthy causes and to persons less fortunate. In a time when there was no legal obligation to do so, I learned that my father had committed himself to paying for the college education of the children of one of his truck drivers who was killed in an accident. And I saw my father lose money in business decisions precisely because of his primary concern for the people involved.

The circumstances surrounding the financing of my college education provided a particularly dramatic and vivid learning experience for me. I had been a highly publicized athlete in high school, and that provided two different challenges. One was that the New York Yankees baseball organization wanted me to bypass college and start playing professional baseball in their organization at age eighteen. So the matter was presented in terms of choosing financial reward now, or going to college. That challenge was taken care of rather quickly. The family's value system was clearly on the side of a college education. Professional baseball, if it were ever to be an option, would have to wait until after college.

The second challenge, how to pay for my college education, was the one that turned out to be most interesting, and the most revealing. I was receiving many lucrative scholarship offers from large universities, but they all wanted me to concentrate on one sport. I, however, loved football, basketball, and baseball equally, had demonstrated enough skill in each to compete at the college level, and wanted to continue playing all three. Consequently, I was looking more at smaller colleges where I could get a quality education and, at the same time, play all three sports.

Athletic scholarship monies, however, were not as plentiful at the smaller schools as they were at the large universities. That was a non-issue, I thought, since my athletic skills enabled me to receive even the rare scholarship offers. But that is where the process got interesting. For, to my mother, it did matter that if I accepted a scholarship it meant that someone else could not. A debate emerged within the family—basically, my father and I arguing on one side and my mother on the other. The odds, as I was to learn, did not favor my father and me.

My father and I assumed such athletic scholarships were just part of the ball game, so to speak, and that there was no question about accepting such financial aid. After all, instead of having a part-time job while I was in high school and saving money to help pay for my college education, I had been playing athletics—every day, all year—moving rapidly from football to basketball to baseball, and back to football.

Our argument made sense. It seemed like a reasonable return for that "investment," as well as the consideration that, as a college athlete, my athletic performance would help bring spectator dollars into the school's athletic coffers. It was reasonable. It was normal. It was accepted in the mainstream as the way athletes paid for their education.

What the mainstream considered reasonable or normal, however, did not necessarily dictate our course of action as far as my mother was concerned. My mother made the simple and straightforward point that our family could afford to send me to college, and she did not want someone else to be deprived of an education because the scholarship monies were spent on people like me. Although there was long discussion and heated debate, a unanimous decision was reached and there was no further grumbling. My family paid for my college education. I continued to play athletics. And I learned something about having a sense of ethics, undiluted by the economic consequences.

I was blessed with loving, ethically sensitive, and magnanimously spirited parents. In a culture which often assumes money, and particularly the selfish use of money, determines a person's worth, I learned from my parents that there were higher values. It is a matter of historical integrity to decide how one is going to deal with monetary resources, and how one's own choices affect other people. It is a central matter of spiritual maturation as we move out of a very materialistic age into one of greater balance.

In following that blessing, I did not take a vow of poverty, although I respect greatly those who choose that particular witness. I have had a comfortable life materialistically. I have not chosen any radical extreme on the matter. But in a rather common mainstream way I have tried to follow that blessing in the day-to-day ethical choices, as well as in the big life-direction choices. At several critical life-path decisions, I have chosen the path that led to greater service to humanity, rather than the path with the greatest financial reward. It's of no great consequence, and certainly does not compare with the great sacrifices some others make, but it has simply been my way of following my blessings regarding social and ethical sensitivity.

II. FOLLOWING MY BLESSINGS
REGARDING THE EPOCH II MIND-BODY SEPARATION:

The one other example I will share regarding my attempt at following my blessings into historical integrity has to do with the Epoch II medical separation of mind and body regarding health and illness issues. The blessing started with mountain-top experiences in athletics, took me into the "valley of the shadow of death," the death of a self-image through a medical emergency, the experience of a so-called "miracle," discovery of a "call to ministry" for a significant portion of my adult life, and a personal and professional historical integrity with a dying Epoch II notion of mind-body separation.

First of all, the blessing. Unless one has been there, it may be hard to perceive the incredible feeling of at-one-ment, the unity of body-mind-spirit, that can be experienced in athletic coordination. I was blessed with it. I experienced it early in life and I followed it with total commitment and zest. Nothing else in my growing-up years could compare with this feeling. I grew up knowing, not just believing in, the essential wholeness of body-mind-spirit—I *knew*, because I had experienced it. I lived it, and I loved it.

In the spring and summer I lived for baseball, when I could get on the pitcher's mound and throw the ball as hard and as accurately as possible. It was usually hard and fast but not very accurate. The feeling of throwing, however, was magnificent—it was a physical sense of letting spirit fly—and I experienced the innate connection between mental focus, the imagery of what I wanted to accomplish, and the results I achieved.

When summer faded into fall, it took me all of about three seconds to switch incarnations—from baseball player to football player. I now lived for football and the thrill of being a quarterback—out-thinking and out-strategizing the defense, faking a run to hold the defensive backfield, and then lofting a long pass to the streaking receiver down the sidelines. My spirit soared with every pass—the longer the better. Again, there was an attunement and at-one-ment between the mental processes, the spiritual feelings, and the physical expression.

There was something innately grace-full and forgiving to be able to put this week's game behind—win or lose—and focus on a new week, a new opposition, a new defense to dissect. There were lessons to be learned from both the victories and the defeats—

learning to leave behind either the pride and press-clippings or the guilt and disappointment and to focus on the new challenge and the fresh opportunities. There is a pragmatism in feeling the flow of time and the changes of experience in athletics.

Basketball season usually overlapped with football, at least as far as preseason basketball was concerned, so it was again a rapid transformation. I fell in love all over again. Basketball was different from football—more games, a faster pace, quicker results. I especially loved the coordination of dribbling the ball, daring anyone to take it away, creating a flow, and either creating a shot or drawing additional defenders to me and then passing off to an open team-mate. The one thing about basketball that was missing in football or baseball was the energy transfer one gets from the closeness of the cheering crowd and the blaring pep-band—when we would first come onto the floor with the band playing, I could feel the spirit of Super-jock coursing through my soul.

This experience of body-mind-spirit coordination, of the whole-ness of this personage, and of the joy of expression dominated my life up through college. Although my family's value system put a heavy emphasis on academics, I can't say I truly accepted that until I got to graduate school. All the way through high school and college, athletic expression was my experience of soul and I was committed to it all the way. I loved it, I lived it, and I planned it to be my professional path for "making a living."

(For the rest of this story to make sense, I need to add a paren-thetical explanation of what happened to my professional direction after college, although I don't want to get bogged down in that discussion right here. I was about to graduate from college, consid-ering a variety of professional athletic offers, when Spirit upset all my well-made plans. A powerful mystical experience instantly, and completely, turned my life around. Literally, at one moment I was planning to be a professional athlete, the next moment I was dedicating my life to the service of humanity. So, to the surprise of everyone who knew me, I passed up professional athletics and went to graduate school to prepare for the professional ministry, what seemed at the time the logical path for "service to humanity." I'll share more about that experience of transformation in Chapter Twelve. Incidentally, since that experience I have been fascinated by the variety of so-called "intellectuals" who denigrate mystical experiences. Throughout academic experience and throughout academic literature, one encounters many minds who, in one way or another, discount anything mystical. I can only believe those who discount such occurrences simply have never experienced such an event themselves. In other words, they don't know what they are talking about.

Before I leave this, I can't help but share one cute little exchange between my young son and me regarding my choice to enter the ministry rather than professional football. It occurred several years later when Jim was old enough to be getting enamored with sports in general and with star athletes in particular. And he was getting a bit nosy about my past. One day he was digging through an old box in the basement which contained some of my high school and college press-clippings. After discovering that I could have given professional football a try with the (then) Baltimore Colts, Jim could not hide his outrage. "You mean," he asked, with his voice escalating shrilly, "you mean that I could have been the son of a pro football player, instead of being the son of a minister?" It actually was not so much of a question as it was a loud disgusting protest regarding his fate. "Well," I said, trying to bring some humor into a discussion I knew I was destined to lose, "I was just trying to be a nice guy. After all, I didn't want to make Johnny Unitas sit on the bench his entire career."

My perspicacious young son, however, would have none of that kind of political double-talk. He not only knew that Johnny Unitas was one of the best, if not *the* best, quarterbacks of all time. He knew that Unitas was the Colt quarterback at precisely the time when I would have been competing for the job. He also knew that the Colt backup quarterback was Earl Morrell.

After a long thoughtful pause, Jim decided he had it all figured out. "Naw," he said. "You couldn't have beaten out Unitas for the starting job. Maybe, just maybe, you could have beaten out Earl Morrell for the backup position." End of discussion.)

The point here is that for the formative years of my life—up to age twenty-two—athletic interest, skill, and exuberance were at the core of my life. They defined my image of reality and, more importantly, my self-image. The self-image that was developed during those years, and that was to play an important role later on, had two particular components—first of all, a deep knowing of body-mind-spirit unity and, secondly, a deep confidence in the ability to tap vast resources when the pressure was on. It was also a profound experience of joy, as well as lessons in disappointment. All in all, it was an incredible blessing.

Secondly, the blessing led to a personal dark night of the soul. Dante was thirty-five years of age when he wrote in his *Divine Comedy:*

Midway this way of life we're bound upon,
I woke to find myself in a dark wood,
Where the right road was wholly lost and gone.[2]

I was also thirty-five when I found myself in a very "dark wood"—my first really deep dark night of the soul. It was severe chronic back pain and the resulting emotional depression that caused the darkness and the despair. It was also to be the catalyst for one of the most significant transformations in my life. It was that blessing of experiencing body-mind-spirit unity that first contributed joy and meaning and that then led me into a dark night of the soul.

"You've just got to accept your fate, Bob," the physician counseled. "There is nothing more that can be done medically or surgically, and I don't want to give you false hope. You just have to come to terms with the fact that you will spend the rest of your life in severe pain and confined to a wheelchair. We will give you the strongest drugs we can for managing the pain, but that's the best we can do."

The experience of joy that I had known in physical expression was gone. My body, rather than being the source of exhilaration, was now the source of pain and confusion. My physical and athletic self-image was dying. The "I" that I had known was getting lost in a deep "dark wood." What I was to learn much later was that a transformation was incubating in my soul.

Pain became my constant companion—at first with the face of a monster, eventually to be transformed into a spiritual guide. Actually the pain had been building for some years, but I had managed to keep it secondary. It was the accumulation and combination of several things: polio, when I was a growing young teenager, left me with one leg shorter than the other, as well as with frequent and severe muscle cramping. Then I had my back broken—in two places—with follow-up surgery inserting four large screws to rigidify my back from the sacrum up through the fourth lumbar vertebra. Throughout my early adult years arthritis and sclerosis developed in my spine and sent me into a downward spiral of increasingly severe pain, stronger and stronger drugs being prescribed by my physicians, and substantial crippling. Only much later was I to understand how a very stressful marriage contributed to the physical pain as well.

The darkest of my dark night came in the years when the pain was so unbearable, in spite of the strong narcotics being prescribed, that I could hardly relate to people or to life itself. I could only stand for about five minutes at a time; medical experts predicted—at age thirty-five—that I would soon spend the rest of my life in a wheel-chair, with no significant relief in sight from the pain and the drugs. There was a total absence of hope coming from them.

I was already becoming a lousy husband and a distant and impatient father, and was barely coping with my professional life. But in the darkest of a dark night the unconscious can see very clearly—it is accustomed to seeing in the dark—and it tries to communicate to us in our dreams. Dreams are a powerful night form of vision. Dreams provide in-sight. And in the midst of my darkest night came a dream—a dream that foresaw a "miracle."

Thirdly, in this progression of following my blessing, I was led into the "miracle" healing. Although I will discuss "miracles" more in depth in the next chapter, suffice it here to say that I don't think they are intrusions into normalcy by some outside divine element playing favorites. Since we have not understood some healings, due largely to our Epoch II mentality of dividing matter and spirit, we have labeled what we could not understand as "miracles."

The unconscious, however, is not limited to our narrow conscious paradigm regarding what is possible and what is impossible. Dreams, therefore, can be a source of insight which transcends popularly accepted beliefs.

In this particular dream I was sick and stayed home. I began to hear voices in the basement, however, and went to investigate. To my surprise I discovered an architect's office in my basement. In discussion with the architect, he revealed to me that he not only designed homes in general, but that he was the designer of my home in particular. The architect gave me a tour of my home, showing me room after room of which I had been totally unaware. The dream ended with my becoming so fascinated with this incredible house that, first of all, I got well and, secondly, instead of going back to my old job I began giving tours of the house.

One does not need to be a professional psychologist to see the symbolism in that dream—symbolism, incidentally, which pre-dicted quite accurately what was to happen to me over several subsequent months and years. It was, indeed, the discovery of previously unknown capacities of human potential that enabled a dramatic healing. And those discoveries led to changes in my professional career.

In discovering "rooms" of the self which the medical profession never considered relevant, I found a healing which has enabled me to manage pain, to get off all medication, to discover a happy and fruitful life, and to resume my involvement in and love for sports—

albeit under some restrictions. Those discoveries have totally transformed my life.

What happened, in essence, was that my unconscious led me out of the darkness of Epoch II, in terms of the body-mind separation, and into the dawn of Epoch III. We will take a closer look at that new light in Chapters Eight, Nine, and Ten. And I will address my healing more specifically in Chapter Twelve.

The point here is that the blessing of a self-image honed by athletic achievement made the back pain and physical crippling a very deep dark night of the soul. The self-image of the first half of my life was dying. The medical profession was doing its best to create a new self-image for me, that of a drugged-up cripple in pain. But the joyful blessing of having experienced body-mind-spirit wholeness then having gone through a breakdown was also what led to a breakthrough—personal healing that manifested in social contribution.

After long reflection on why I was able to experience the dawn of healing when all the experts said it was impossible, I find myself constantly moving back behind all the new fields of knowledge in human potential and the powerful mind-body skills to the essential ingredient of a powerful, positive, and confident self-image. It was a self-image blessed by athletic ability and honed on the experiences of being able to accomplish things in the face of predictions to the contrary. Many times, in the face of "expert" analysis regarding what was "possible" or "impossible" athletically, I had said down deep in my soul, "You wanna bet?" And many times I had experienced my ability to defy the odds and prove the "experts" wrong.

It was that experience of belief in a deep underlying power of self that emerged to give me the rebellious strength to say to the physician's dire predictions for the rest of my life, and against the almost overwhelming tide of a cultural belief in medical expertise, "You wanna bet?"

It may have been fourth down and a mile to go—but, you know, "It ain't over 'till it's over." My life was not over. Not yet. In spite of how much statistical research lay behind the doctor's predictions, in spite of how many other people with backs like mine experienced total crippling, in spite of any rationalization on the part of the experts—no one had the right to be so arrogant as to predict the rest of my life. From deep down within my soul came shouts of protest—"I am not helpless. Nobody is going to predict my future without my having something to say about it. I *will not* be a victim."

We will return to the themes of wholeness and empowerment

throughout the rest of this book, for they are central to the Epoch III paradigm and the value system that will take us into the 21st century and beyond. Here it is sufficient to say that it was in following my blessings of athletic experience that led first to the heights, then to the depths, and eventually to the breakthrough against all odds. In following my blessings I saw a clear image of Epoch II dying and of the marvelous impending birth of Epoch III.

Fourthly, following my blessings led to a "call" of historical integrity. I found, after the miraculous breakthrough from the pain and crippling, I could simply not return to ministry-as-usual. On the one hand, I was intellectually fascinated with the limits of the medical paradigm which said such a healing was impossible. On the other hand, I was spiritually stimulated by the fact that many persons were suffering severe chronic pain unnecessarily because of the limits of Epoch II thinking. I was blessed with a breakthrough, a "miracle." I had to do what I could to share that blessing with others.

So I followed that blessing into and through professional changes. Because of the dramatic nature of my healing, several publishers asked me to write a book about it. Although I had absolutely no self-image of being a writer, I eventually made the attempt. Then Hartley Productions made a film on the book.[3] Between the book and the film I was catapulted onto the speaker's circuit where I had the opportunity to articulate a dying Epoch II and an emerging Epoch III, particularly regarding pain management. I was then invited onto the faculty of the Ohio State University Medical School for the purpose of examining the role of mind and spirit in cancer prevention and treatment.

It became evident that for this new ministry in the field of health and wellness I needed a more credible degree than the master's degree in theology. So I went on for a Ph.D., helped launch several holistic health centers, and started what turned out to be a long and rewarding consulting career in corporate wellness—assisting companies to promote health and well-being while reducing illness, absenteeism, and medical costs.

It has been twenty years of attempted historical integrity—following my blessings as a way of helping our culture move out of the inadequacies of Epoch II regarding the limited and disempowering notions of body-mind-spirit separations, and into a liberating and empowering Epoch III. Gradually that entire picture has enlarged so that I now see the important transformation being not only in health and illness but in the larger scope represented by this book.

And What is Your Historical Integrity With a Dying Epoch II?

What have been (are) your blessings? If you follow them, where do they lead you? How do they increase your sense of gratitude? How do they provide your unique path into historical integrity?

How does your story fit within the larger story unfolding in our time? Have you had the challenges of being on the favored or disfavored side of the Epoch II equations? How have you dealt with those challenges? In what ways are you contributing to the elimination of the problems of Epoch II and the emergence of a healthier Epoch III? Do you contribute to the immaturities of our collective adolescence, or do you contribute to a coming of age for humanity into a more mature adulthood?

What has been your experience of pain? What did you learn from the pain? In other words, have your painful monsters been transformed into spiritual guides? If so, where and to what did they guide you? What has been your particular experience of body-mind-spirit pain and joy?

As we discussed near the end of Chapter Six, we not only have "caterpillar" and "butterfly" individuals in our culture at such a transitional time, but each of us has those opposing forces within. What in you is like the caterpillar who finds the transition stage primarily a time of dying? What do you fear losing? And, conversely, what in you resonates with the butterfly energy? What do you welcome in the form of new life? How do you feel about flying high in the heavens?

What has been the nature of your special historical integrity? Why you? Why here? Why now?

EPOCH III

COMING OF AGE INTO ADULT MATURITY

Spiritual Development

EPOCH III INTRODUCTION

*We stand on the brink of a new age: the age of an open world and
of a self capable of playing its part in that larger sphere, . . . a higher
trajectory for life as a whole, . . . a fresh release of spiritual energy that
will unveil new potentialities, no more visible in the human self today
than radium was in the physical world a century ago, though always
present.*

—HISTORIAN LEWIS MUMFORD

THE PRESTIGIOUS HISTORIAN LEWIS MUMFORD could hardly have been
considered a "New Ager," at least as that term has been used in
recent years. Mumford was an extraordinary historian, combining
vast and scholarly knowledge of the past with intuitive and visionary sensibilities.

Mumford wrote the above statement in the mid-1950s, before
most of us were seeing the overt evidence of a dying Epoch II or an
emerging Epoch III. It took a remarkable mind to perceive the
coming transformation that early in the process. Nevertheless,
observing the large flow of human history and looking with sacred
eyes into the soul of the twentieth century, he was able to see what
is now becoming more evident with each passing decade. He saw
that we are in the process of entering a new age, a new era, a new
epoch in human development. He predicted our experience of a
new world opening up and a new experience of self at "a higher
trajectory." Even more to the point, Mumford was a secular and
academic historian suggesting that this new age will be characterized by a fresh release of spiritual energy.

That is precisely the central premise of this book—for which all
of the previous chapters have been setting the stage—and the
matter to which we now turn. After a childhood of physical development, and an adolescence of ego and mental development, we
are now moving on to the next phase of our maturation, that of

spiritual development. As we get our body, mind, and spirit working together at "a higher trajectory," we will indeed experience a new self and a new world. Such is the exciting promise of Epoch III.

Before we get to that, however, it might be helpful to be explicit about something which has only been implicit throughout this entire discussion—that religion and spirituality are not necessarily synonymous. If we are going to explore the "fresh release of spiritual energy" that Mumford predicted, it will help to be clear how spirituality differs from the institutionalized religion of a culture.

Religion is manifested in a culture through institutional forms and traditions on the surface landscape, as it were, just as are science, education, politics, economics, health care, etc. Spirituality, on the other hand, is all-pervasive. It is the underground river which nourishes the *entire* landscape. Spirituality is that which emerges from our soul. It both stimulates our questions regarding meaning and purpose and guides us toward answers. The spirituality that is the organic outcome of the deep soul-level value system precedes and informs all religions on the surface, just as it precedes and informs all the other institutions and traditions in our culture.

Religion, if it is doing its job, gives more intentionality than other institutions to providing a well, as it were, for access to the underground river of soul. Ideally, that is the special role of religion in a culture. The root of the word religion is *religare* which means "to bind back," or "to re-connect." Religion, if it is true to the name, assists us in re-connecting with our soul.

Religion fulfilling that function, however, is not a given in times of great transition. In radically transformative times one underground river dries up while a new one begins to flow—a fundamental, deep value, soul-level change. Religion, however, can be so preoccupied with the past that it is out of touch with the present. It can be so totally consumed with the superficial structure, policy, dogma, bureaucracy, and the protection of power, authority, and professional turf that was developed when drinking from the *former* underground river that it may not be aware that the river has gone dry.

If an old institution is to tap into the new soul-river, it must be courageous enough to dig a new well. If religious institutions are not up to that transformative task, they will eventually fail to serve as a re-connecting force for their people, will lose legitimacy, and will eventually die. Unfortunately, there has been a great deal of evidence over the past three decades, of just such a massive loss of legitimacy on the part of mainstream religion. It is a time of crisis for religion—grow into Epoch III or die off.

And it is not an easy challenge for religion, for two reasons. First of all, religions tend to focus primarily, if not exclusively, on the past. They often see their "reason for being" as that of preserving a particular history, a form of revelation, and the traditions of the institution. They often see their primary task as articulating past dogma and gaining recruits for that dogma.

The late British economist E. F. Schumacher told of a visit to Leningrad some years ago. He was in the midst of studying a map to clarify his location.

> From where I stood I could see several enormous churches, yet there was no trace of them on my map. When finally an interpreter came to help me, he said: "We don't show churches on our maps." Contradicting him, I pointed to one that was very clearly marked. "That is a museum," he said, "not what we call a living church. It is only the living churches we don't show."[1]

If religion does not respond to the soul-level transformation that is ushering in Epoch III their churches, even in countries who pride themselves on being "under God," will become museums rather than "living" institutions.

Secondly, the arrogance of believing you have *the* well, the one and only direct line to Truth, sets one up for intransigence and spiritual tyranny. This is particularly the case for those religious people who think they have side-stepped pride and arrogance by believing that they have a book—i.e., the Bible—in which God is speaking Truth to us directly, literally, without human filters and without interpretation or translation. That is not exactly the optimal condition for a humility that is open to major changes in values, or in recognizing new revelation, or the need for new institutional forms.

My point here is that religion, like all institutions, is distinct from the spirituality which emerges from the underground soul. Consequently, *all* of human endeavor is influenced and informed by the changes taking place in the soul of our time. The Epoch III transformation of deep values will change business, politics, economics, education—*everything* that continues to survive and thrive on humanity's landscape. Any and all human activity will change or it will die—such are the consequences of an epoch-sized transformation.

What follows in the rest of our discussion is a general synthesis, an overview, and not a specialized analysis of any one institution or any one area of human experience. There are, or will be, books detailing the changes taking place in politics or economics, but that is not my purpose here. I am greatly tempted to discuss the Epoch III implications for the institution of the family, for they are many and substantial and there may not be any institution more important to a healthy future. Similarly, I am tempted to write about the implications of Epoch III for educational reform. Certainly, education is a crucial institution in our culture and will play an important role in either our dying or in our discovery of new life. And I have had past experiences of trying to awaken education to a new era, some successful and some quite frustrating. Nevertheless, to draw out all the implications for any one institution, or one specific area of human endeavor, would make this book far too long. This is a general look at the forces influencing all institutions and all human experience. Detailed application of this emerging spirituality awaits other authors or, at least in my case, other books.

Although not attempting to cover them in extensive detail I will, however, use science, medicine, and religion as examples to illustrate a waning Epoch II and an emerging Epoch III. Examples from science are used for three reasons. First of all, we come out of a four hundred year period in which science has been the primary frame of reference for what is legitimate. Science has been the dominant religion in our recent past. This is not to suggest that Epoch III spirituality gets its legitimacy from science. Rather, it is only to use science as a springboard for talking about, and as an apt illustration of, this epochal transition.

Secondly, science has been a dramatic example of the spiritual transformation taking place, with an early tap into the fundamental shift from an Epoch II soul to an Epoch III soul. The revolutions in the various sciences, of course, do not speak explicitly of a soul-level transformation—they talk, rather, of paradigm shifts and changes in world-view. However, just because science has not used conventional theological language does not mean it has not perceived the soul-level changes. The marvelous thing about spirituality, in contrast to any one religion, is that it can be spoken of in many different "languages."

Thirdly, in Epoch III we will experience a dynamic synthesis and a new partnership between science and religion, albeit at "a higher trajectory" than we had in Epoch II.

Medicine will also be a field from which I will draw examples. Because of what has just been said about science, medicine is an important example since it considers itself to be a scientific discipline. Medicine also impacts a great number of human lives, for better or for worse. Understanding how we think about health and illness, and the actions derived from such thinking, were the matters on which I did my doctoral work and in which I have both personal experience and professional expertise.

Religion, as with health and illness, represents a field in which I have both a graduate academic degree as well as professional experience. Beyond that, the transformation of religion, as mentioned above, is both crucially important and very difficult. With the major agenda of Epoch III being spiritual maturation, and the appropriate role of religion is to be an effective conduit of the Spirit from the soul to the surface, we desperately need vibrant, up-to-date, religions to facilitate the human journey. It is going to be a tough challenge, for as I have already stated, religion may have the hardest time of all institutions, in recognizing soul-level changes.

Although examples will be used from science, medicine, and religion, I want to state again for emphasis—we are essentially talking about soul-level stuff, a spirituality which cannot be identified with any one institution, yet which informs and influences all of them. All human institutions, all fields of thought, will be transformed as we enter Epoch III, or they will pass away. They will either become living dynamic conduits of Epoch III spiritual energy, or they will become dead Epoch II historical relics.

Let us now set sail on an oceanic view of Epoch III, exploring the five primary spiritual values that will nourish our journey into the future. Bon voyage.

CHAPTER 8

GETTING OUR
ACT TOGETHER

I. THE CONSEQUENCES OF EPOCH II
REDUCTIONISM: "FAULTS,"
"EARTHQUAKES," ILLUSIONS, ARROGANCE
AND A POVERTY OF CREATIVITY

The essential new quality implied by the quantum theory is. . . that a system cannot be analyzed into parts. This leads to the radically new notion of unbroken wholeness of the entire universe. You cannot take it apart. For if you do, what you end up with is not contained within the original whole. It is created by the act of analysis.
—THEORETICAL PHYSICIST DAVID BOHM

IN ORDER TO FULLY UNDERSTAND the emergent Epoch III wholeness, it may be helpful to see it in contrast to the problems created by Epoch II reductionism. As stated before, the primary agenda for our adolescence was that of ego and mental development. Developing the ego must, by necessity, start with making distinctions between the self and the other. Also, as stated before, the important first step in this process was taken about 8000 B.C. when we separated ourselves from nature through the domestication of plants and animals. We broke up a previous whole and created parts. We changed a cooperative and mutual relationship with nature to one of dominance, control, and manipulation. We created the illusion of separation. It was what science writer Morris Berman called the "basic fault."

I am not suggesting that adolescence is a failure, a mistake, or an error. So I am not speaking of a human fault in that sense. Adolescence is a natural stage in human maturation. That does not mean, however, that adolescence does not have its problems. The original meaning of the Latin root for fault is "to deceive," and that is precisely what our ego development did. The basic fault of our adolescence—namely, the illusion of our separation from nature— deceived us in a very basic way. It is this meaning of fault that I am emphasizing here, as well as to use the geological meaning of the word as a metaphor. In geology, a fault is a fracture in the earth's surface, and an earthquake is a violent dislocation that takes place along these faults.

Our developing ego created fault lines all across the landscape of human experience—separating heaven and earth, divine and human, matter and spirit, good and evil, the individual body-mind-spirit, humans from the rest of nature, one group of humans from other groups, etc., etc., etc. At the end of Epoch II, and as we begin to glimpse the dawn of Epoch III, we are becoming aware of the deceptions and illusions involved in these separations. Our dark night of the soul has us experiencing many earthquakes, or dislocations, across the landscape of humanity.

The problems associated with hierarchy are also the results of this ego development, with its faults and earthquakes. Because of the adolescent ego's need to be higher than, better than, and on top of the separated other, earthquakes taking place across the human landscape resulted in one turf being placed on top of another turf. Heaven was seen as higher than earth, divine as higher than human, spirit (until we ignored it altogether) higher than matter, humans higher than the earth or the animals, man higher than woman, and our religion or nation closer to God than theirs.

One metaphor that helps us consider the ego and the mental development of our adolescence is the so-called "split-brain" metaphor. In case you are not aware of its origin, although as a metaphor it has come into wide and popular use in recent years, neurosurgeons attempted to help severe epileptic patients by cutting the corpus callosum, the connective tissue between the left and right hemispheres of the brain. Subsequent research revealed that, when severed, the two hemispheres of the brain appear to function in very different ways and with very different skills.

The split-brain provides a good metaphor for several reasons. It created a fault line in our use of mental abilities, between left and right brain, as well as creating a hierarchy, left brain over right. In Epoch II we have clearly given priority to the left-brain functions—reading, writing, arithmetic, logical and rational thinking, analysis, as well as verbal skills. Consider our educational systems and how these talents have been given priority over the right-brain functions of perceiving patterns and wholes, creativity, intuition, instinctual knowing, etc.

The quote used in opening this chapter was from David Bohm, Professor of Physics at Birkbeck College in London, a protégé of Albert Einstein and one who many consider to be among the leading scientists in the world today. It is taken from his important book *Wholeness and the Implicate Order*. In it Bohm speaks directly to one of our favorite Epoch II mental skills, that of analysis—literally, the separation of wholes into parts. He then goes on to say that the fragmentation created by analysis leads us into illusions—illusions of separation and distinction that "cannot do other than lead to endless conflict and confusion."[1]

In the following, my attempt is not to cover every fault and illusion comprehensively, nor to illustrate them extensively. That would simply make this discussion much too long. My purpose is primarily to provide an integrating overview, brief identification of the faults of Epoch II and the contrasting wholeness of Epoch III, which should be sufficient to allow us to see the large picture of this transformational time.

The Fault of the Dis-Spirited Materialists

In Chapter Five we examined in some detail how Epoch II science divided the human being up into parts, starting with the "Cartesian reductionism" of the 17th century, initially giving the psyche (mind and soul) to the Church while giving the soma (body) to science. This started a binge of specialization, categorization, and compartmentalization—faults and fractures that have characterized the human landscape ever since. It also started the arrogance of scientific materialism—a world-view that thought it was above the need to include anything spiritual. In the example of medicine, for instance, priority was given to matter, to that which is measurable and quantifiable, while considering mental, emotional, and spiritual matters as secondary, at best, and irrelevant, at worst.

It is important to understand, however, that this is not really a case of mind versus body. It is not that the dis-spirited materialists, in the example of medicine, trust the body and not the mind. Quite the contrary, it is a *mental concept* that has drawn the distinction between soma and psyche and a *belief system* that has the loyalty of the dis-spirited materialists. It is not that medical people trust the "wisdom of the body" so much as that they trust the dominant concept *about* the body. And the Epoch II dis-spirited materialism thinks that mental, emotional, and spiritual issues have little or no effect on the body. It is quite understandable, therefore, that the metaphor of the machine was used to understand this dis-spirited materialistic world.

Deluded and deceived by the dis-spirited materialistic faults, we ignored vast areas of evidence that could have helped us understand health and illness far more quickly and far more thoroughly. The following evidence, for instance, has been with us for a long time—often within the medical field itself—yet it has had little impact on our overall mindset regarding health and illness. In spite of all this evidence, we have continued throughout Epoch II to act as if physical illness were strictly a matter of biological and physical factors.

(A) PLACEBO RESEARCH

The placebo, a "sugar pill" or an inert substance, is used widely in medical research to measure a drug's effectiveness. Everyone in a research project is told they are receiving the drug, but some are given only a placebo. The researchers then measure the difference between the two groups. The attention, however, is almost exclusively on the effectiveness of the drug, rather than on the other matter that is revealed—namely, the power of belief and expectation. The field is rich with evidence that the mind has enormous power. In one experiment having to do with chemotherapy, one-third of those receiving only a placebo lost their hair. In another, placebos were found to be 77% as effective as morphine in reducing pain. The placebo—the power of belief and expectation—has also been shown to change body chemistry such as the amount of fat or protein in the blood, blood-cell count, hypertension, and a myriad of other phenomena.[2]

(B) CANCER RESEARCH

Although the Epoch II dis-spirited materialistic mind continues to consider cancer as strictly a biological disease, there is considerable evidence that other factors are involved as well. Severely psychotic people almost never develop cancer. Women with breast cancer who receive group therapy and lessons in self-hypnosis live, on average, twice as long as those receiving only conventional medical treatment. Assertive breast cancer patients live longer than their passive peers. Among medical students followed over many years, the psychological profile of those who developed cancer was very similar to those who committed suicide. Other research found a strong link between a person's loss of their "reason for being" and the subsequent development of cancer. Dr. Karl Menninger, familiar with this and other evidence of mental, emotional, and spiritual roles in cancer, said:

> One of these days the cancer research people who have had such enormous financial support and who have worked so frantically and intensively on the problem for the past thirty years will wake up to the fact that *psychology has an influence on tissue cells*, a proposition which they have consistently regarded even until now as a preposterous heresy.[3]

These, and a great many other examples from the cancer research literature, reveal the primary illusion of Epoch II regarding this terrible disease—the separation of mind and body. I have no doubt that as we get our act together we will find the breakthroughs that have eluded us so far.[4]

(c) Multiple Personality Disorder

In people with Multiple Personality Disorder (MPD), the various personalities frequently have different physical phenomena. One personality may be right-handed, another left- handed. One personality needs glasses, the others don't. Different personalities have had different eye color. And different personalities within the one body suffer from different allergies. In one case, a female MPD was tortured as a child by both her mother and brother putting out lighted cigarettes on her skin. When she would shift, as an adult, into the personality that had received the burns, "the burn marks would reappear on her skin and last for 6-10 hours."[5]

(d) Medical Hypnosis Research

Medical hypnosis is a particularly interesting case, for evidence of profound mind-body interaction has been researched for many years within this medical field. The fact that it has had such little impact on the overall medical mindset is testimony to the tenacity of the dis-spirited materialistic paradigm. The British Medical Journal reported a case involving a sixteen-year-old London boy with advanced Brocq's disease. Brocq's disease is a congenital disease under the control of a particular gene, a terrible genetic defect resulting in the growth over the skin of a dark horny substance which hardens like a fingernail. It is a totally disfiguring condition. The young boy was covered with a horrible crust over his entire body except for his head. "To the touch," the medical report said, "the skin felt as hard as normal fingernail, and was so inelastic that any attempt at bending resulted in a crack in the surface, which would then ooze blood-stained serum." The boy's situation was declared medically hopeless. As a last resort the boy was taken to a skilled hypnotherapist, A. A. Mason, at Queen Victoria Hospital. Mason tried what according to medical orthodoxy would be totally irrelevant and unproductive—he worked with the boy's unconscious mind through the use of hypnotic imagery. The mind cannot affect a genetic disease—right? Well, read on.

In the first session they directed the imagery to the boy's left arm, and five days later the dark, horny layer fell away leaving soft, normal skin. Within ten days the arm was totally clear from the shoulder to the wrist. Working gradually with various parts of the boy's body a total cure was achieved within several months. A five year follow-up examination showed that the boy remained totally free of the genetic disease.[6]

"I'll believe it when I see it," says the realist, asking for evidence before believing some preposterous claim. The familiar twist on that phrase, which is particularly applicable in this mind-body area is, "I'll see it when I believe it." The fact is, there has been plenty of evidence of mind-body wholeness all around us during Epoch II, but our faults have deluded us, our paradigms have blinded us. When we start believing in wholeness, we will begin to see vast new worlds of connections and vast new realms of creative solutions.

Basically, what it comes down to is this. Unless one is prepared to directly challenge one of the fundamental tenets of quantum theory—the unbroken wholeness of the entire universe—and prove it wrong, one must face the question of what deception is perpetrated, what illusion is created, and what arrogance is revealed by any thinking that presumes separation and isolation—i.e., physical disease being only physical in origin or cure.

The Fault of the Dis-Embodied Spiritualists

The separation of ego-self from our instinctual-self started, as we have seen, some 10,000 years ago. As we separated ourselves from the plants and animals, we started the process which led inevitably to the "theology" of demeaning nature, women, our bodies, and the instincts. We moved into the left-brain concepts about spiritual life which left us dis-embodied. As Morris Berman put it, "instinctual repression is not merely unhealthy, but productive of a world view that is factually inaccurate."[7]

Plato, in the fifth century B.C., split spiritual love from vulgar or bodily love. The Stoics', in the forth century B.C., defined virtue as freedom from all passions. And then Augustine, in the late fourth and early fifth century A.D., influenced many subsequent centuries of Christianity by identifying sex and semen as a disease.

One of the most insightful scholars of early Christianity is professor Elaine Pagels of Princeton University. She points out that although the Bible speaks of God making the world and then calling it good, "when you look at the early Christian movement, it's striking in what negative terms many of the early Christians talk about sexuality."[8]

St. Augustine was perhaps the most influential voice in fathering the dis-embodied spiritualists among Christians. Instead of emphasizing human dignity, Augustine focused on our enslavement to sin and suggested that we were irreparably damaged by The Fall.

> Augustine developed an ingenious theory that this moral disease that Adam generated was sexually transmitted through semen. Jesus was the only person not 'infected' because he was presumably conceived without human semen. But the rest of us, conceived in the usual, depraved way, were infected by Adam's sin. So this moral problem, which he felt was endemic to our condition, is described in sexual terms.[9]

You can see how, in one of the most influential movements of our adolescence, we not only separated spirit and body but added a hierarchy of value judgment. The realm of spirit is pure and good whereas the body is a depraved prison for the soul and, therefore, bad. No way around it, in our adolescent illusions sex was seen as dirty.

It is little wonder that in the 1960s, as our repressed unconscious erupted sending us into our dark night of the soul, the liberation and affirmation of sex played such a central role. It was simply the first move into a more mature and balanced role of the body and sexuality in a whole, holy, and healthy life.

The dis-embodied spiritualists were an inevitable consequence of our adolescent illusions of separation and hierarchy, as were the dis-spirited materialists. It was, however, simply an immature stage of life beyond which we are now ready to grow.

Although it doesn't fit exclusively within this section, one further thing needs discussion—the reductionism of some so-called "New Age-er's." Although most of what has passed as "New Age" correctly points to the essential issue of wholeness and of the primacy of spirituality, there has been a huge participation in the faults of reductionism. As some well-meaning people tried to move out beyond the narrow specialities of the mainstream, they fell into the same reductionistic trap by believing that their alternative was the total answer.

In the health and illness arena, for instance, medical authorities frequently resisted the so-called "holistic health" movement out of their dis-spirited materialistic paradigm. At the same time, many of the self-proclaimed holistic health practitioners simply replaced one tunnel vision with another. Consequently, we have experienced a plethora of New Age tunnel-visioned, single-issued, narrow-minded evangelists for this or that alternative. "It's *all* in what you eat," some would proclaim. Others said it was "mind over matter," or that "It's *all* in the mind." There are other evangelists proclaiming that everything goes back to past lives. And many others saying, in their various ways, "If you simply believe right— [read: *our way*]—you will be saved."

Unfortunately, during the early years of this transition from Epoch II into Epoch III, the general public had to choose between some simplistic "alternative" or the equally simplistic knee-jerk negative reaction of the establishment. Reductionism, whether it be from the establishment or from some "New Age" alternative, is still an Epoch II illusion.

The Fault Between Illness and Wellness

There have, in fact, been three faults in this area—separating illness from wellness, the attempt to isolate a single cause of disease, and the almost exclusive focus on one diseased part of the person, rather than on the entire human being. For our purposes here, however, let's consider them all simply as representing the fault between illness and wellness.

Our primary "health" professionals are not schooled in health or well-being, but in disease and pathology. This is not an argument against such expertise—we need knowledge and expertise in the illness side of the spectrum, but studying cadavers, sick people, and laboratory animals are not the way to learn about health, well-being, spiritualized matter, and self-actualizing human beings. The fact is, the wellness side of the spectrum also has a great deal to teach us about how people get sick and how they can cure disease.

A Dallas internist, Dr. Larry Dossey, has been one of the increasing number of physicians who, although trained in Epoch II, perceive the limitations of that paradigm and are heralding the dawn of Epoch III.

"Our orthodox models in medicine," Dossey writes, "have come to the same fate as the models of the first scientific revolution: they are sadly inappropriate to studies of the living."[10]

The psychologist Abraham Maslow once said that if the only tool you have is a hammer, you tend to treat everything as if it were a nail. If the medical "tool" is single causation of pathology in exclusively physical terms, everything that falls within the so-called "health" arena will be treated as if it were that kind of nail. It creates, frankly, gross illusions and deceptions, and the people who are dislocated along those faults suffer earthquakes in the terra firma of their lives.

The Numerous Faults of the Categorical Mind

Ever since we separated from nature and started this adolescent ego development we created, as we discussed before, a need for control. Our rejection of our instinctual nature separated us from our bodies, and we went on a several thousand year long head-trip—actually, a half-brained head-trip. The need to find security in control was manifested in two ways—analysis and hierarchical arrogance.

We tried to control our world by understanding it with concepts, and the easiest way to do that was to break it down into small pieces—pieces small enough for us to get our mind around. This led inevitably to the fault of thinking that the little piece on which we were knowledgeable was all that really mattered.

Two brief additional comments, without developing them at length. One is that although I don't know of any research that verifies this particular point, I strongly suspect that our need to control and the fear that we are losing control plays a major role in the development of *many* disease processes. This is particularly true, I think, with coronary heart disease, but is also a contributing factor in the development of cancer, arthritis, and perhaps many others.

The second, which is related to the first, is that our need to control is a major reason we resist, and are fearful of, change. I'll develop this idea more in Chapter Ten.

With security and control related to analysis and hierarchy it was natural that in our Epoch II patriarchy the left-brain became associated with masculinity and the right-brain with femininity. To be a "real man" was perceived as being intellectual, analytical, verbal, and definitely in control. Women were viewed in quite different ways. Intuition, for instance, was always preceded by the prefix "woman's," until just recently. "Why," Epoch II men would ask, "why can't women be more reasonable."

"I am far from wishing to belittle the divine gift of reason," wrote Carl Jung, "but in the role of absolute tyrant it has no meaning—no more than light would have in a world where its counterpart, darkness, was absent."[11]

And speaking of darkness, that points to another fault of the categorical mind—the division between daytime and nighttime consciousness. Daytime rational consciousness has been seen as good, nighttime unconscious as bad or irrelevant. Some religious people have identified the unconscious as the "realm of the devil," while most secular people have simply ignored it. Consequently, dreams and those aspects of our life that are—well, the name says it all—*unconscious* are ignored as playing any role in health and well-being and in every-day affairs. The devaluation of the unconscious and of spirituality go hand-in-hand. It is a devaluation which carries a cost the Epoch II mind cannot even fathom.

One loss, when we devalue the unconscious, is in human relationships. An author profoundly insightful regarding our depths is Helen Luke. She writes regarding unconscious projection of one's own stuff out onto someone else:

> If you find you hate a person or that there is something that makes you absolutely furious, you may be perfectly sure that it is a part of yourself that is projected there—no matter how true it may be that the other person is behaving badly. . . . If you

are projecting you are incapable of compassion, you are incapable of understanding that this person is behaving in this way for reasons that you cannot see, from problems that you know nothing about.[12]

Jungian author Lucindi Frances Mooney takes a similar tack as does Morris Berman in suggesting that our separation from nature is what got us out of touch with our natural depths, our unconscious. "Our degree of alienation from nature," she writes, "is directly proportionate to the degree that we are isolated within the confines of blind rationalism, egocentricity that denies the unconscious."[13]

The Numerous Faults Between Groups of Humans

There are at least three levels of adolescent ego development that allow us to fall into these faults.

The first is, of course, the very root of ego development itself, namely, emphasizing the distinction between ourselves and others. Consider, in contrast, how within our own bodies many different types of cells—liver, heart, blood, brain, etc.—all work cooperatively together within the same sense of "self." The very function of our immune system distinguishes self from non-self, but includes within the definition of self many different types of cells. In contrast, rather than perceiving all the variations of human beings as within one family, our adolescent ego has chosen to consider as "other" anyone who looks, acts, talks, or believes differently, or those who happen to be born in a different country. It is an illusion of separation simply based on differences.

The second level is ideological. As we have suggested before, our ego development emphasized left-brain intellectual constructs and separated ourselves from our bodies. "When you've lost your body," writes Morris Berman, "you need an ism. From there it is a short step to seeing other isms as life-threatening, and to seeing the Other as an enemy." Berman reports a conversation he once had with a friend, having asked the friend what he had gotten out of studying the Feldenkrais method of body therapy: "Hard to say," replied the friend, "except that after a while I began to notice that it became less and less important for me to win an argument."[14]

The third level is what we do after we have identified someone as the enemy. In order to perpetuate our separation, fear, and hatred of the enemy, we go through what has historically been a rather predictable process of dehumanization. Sam Keen has written a brilliant analysis of how we create and deal with enemies. "In the beginning we create the enemy by projecting our own fears, inadequacies, and self-hatred onto others. Before the weapon comes the image. We think others to death and then invent the battle-axe or the ballistic missile with which to actually kill them. Propaganda precedes technology."[15] Keen also says, "As a rule, human beings do not kill other human beings. Before we enter into warfare or genocide, we first dehumanize those we mean to 'eliminate.'"[16]

The "Basic Fault" Between Humans and Nature

As mentioned earlier, this is what Berman called the "basic fault"—namely, the separation of humans from nature. In a very real sense, all other faults are the consequence of this one.

The Judeo-Christian tradition gave it theological and biblical sanction, and so we came to see ourselves as having dominion over the earth and the animals. All of nature, we came to believe, was created to serve us. And as we explored at some length in Chapter Five, the fathers of modern science continued the illusion by despiritualizing nature. Such illusions have now led, in our dark night of the soul, to widespread ecological disaster, on the one hand, and increasing ecological sensitivity, on the other.

The Resulting Poverty of Creativity

When one has seen the light, the temptation is to curse the darkness. Or, to put it another way, when one has seen the expansive view from the top of the mountain, it is easy to condemn the restricted view of the valley.

As we begin to glimpse the promise of Epoch III it is natural to be particularly critical of the limitations of Epoch II. Harsh condemnation, the arrogance of 20/20 hindsight, or implying that we should feel guilt or shame regarding our past is not very productive, however, nor my purpose in this discussion. We do begin to see, though, how much we have been missing regarding creative solutions to the problems that continue to cause us much suffering.

My heart aches for those in severe pain who have been shackled within the narrow confines of the Epoch II medical paradigm regarding chronic pain. My mind wonders why more medical professionals do not consider the hints all around them that mind and spirit play such strong roles in the pain experience, and we could expand that circle of concern to every person suffering from any disease.

There is the oft-used story of the man down on his hands and knees looking carefully all around the ground underneath a street light. Another man came along and asked him what he was doing. "I'm looking for a key I lost," replied the first man. "How do you know," asked the second, "that you lost it right here? "I don't," replied the first, "but this is where the light is."

The paradigmatic light, for the medical establishment, shines only on the physical aspects of health and illness, and a great deal of creative solutions go wanting because that is the only place they're looking. The same, of course, can be said for any speciality, not only medicine. In the reductionism of Epoch II, the spotlight shines on a very narrow piece of the human landscape. Creativity is thus, by its very nature, severely restricted. Having spent all our lives within these restrictions, it is hard for us to realize how poverty-stricken we have been or how many creative solutions await us in Epoch III.

II. IN CONTRAST, THE HOLISTIC AND ECOLOGICAL LANDSCAPE OF EPOCH III

> *Holistic society is thus coming upon us from a variety of sources that cut across the traditional left-right political axis. Feminism, ecology, ethnicity, and transcendentalism (religious renewal), which ostensibly have nothing in common politically, may be converging toward a common goal. . . . They represent the repressed 'shadows' of industrial civilization: the feminine, the wilderness, the child, the body, the creative mind and heart, the occult, and the peoples of the non-urban regional peripheries of Europe and North America; . . . it is the notion of recovery. Their goal is the recovery of our bodies, our health, our sexuality, our natural environment, our archaic traditions, our unconscious mind, our rootedness in the land, our sense of community and connectedness to one another."*
> —HISTORIAN OF SCIENCE MORRIS BERMAN

The dawning light of Epoch III holism, in contrast to the narrow spotlight of Epoch II, throws light on the entire landscape. It exposes material that we previously thought irrelevant. It exposes the faults, the deceptions and illusions that previously dominated the scene; and it will reveal a wealth of creative solutions to previously intractable problems.

The use of the word ecology is for very intentional reasons. Ecology has to do with diverse elements sharing an interdependent relationship in which every part has its important and unique role. An ecology is unavoidably holistic. An ecology also rules out any notion of isolation or hierarchical arrogance. It is the living, natural, organic form of cooperation and synergy.

An Ecology of the Whole Person

Perhaps only those who have gone through the investment of time, money, sweat and tears of a doctoral program will fully understand the huge temptation I am faced with here. When one starts to write about one's field of expertise, and the one in which one did doctoral research, there is a tremendous temptation to dump the entire load on the reader, so to speak.

I have amassed a great deal of evidence regarding the interaction of body, mind, spirit, and environment, in creating one's state of health or illness. Were I to share all that in this chapter, it would be too long; in addition, it would be redundant with what is already published and, most importantly, you would be bored out of your mind. Consequently, I'll spare you all that and simply suggest that my notes and/or the "suggested reading" can direct anyone who wants to go deeper into, or check the research verification pertaining to, the issues I discuss.

In Epoch III we will begin to thoroughly explore how we as living beings are spiritualized biology, or to put it another way, how we are materialized spirit. We are spirit incarnate. We are bodies manifesting spirit, and our spirituality is lived out biologically, albeit usually incognito.

In many respects, Teilhard de Chardin of France and Aurobindo of India were Epoch III prophets pointing to this kind of physical-spiritual wholeness. Both spoke often of Spirit being the "within-ness" of matter and how, in concert with physical evolution, there is a spiritual evolution.

This "within-ness" of matter, the Spirit incarnate, is constantly communicating with the "outside." It speaks to us first through our dreams, but most of us don't pay attention. If we don't get an important message that way, it then communicates to us in physical metaphors, either in our bodies or in our life's circumstances.

It was this spiritual "within-ness" of life that Carl Jung was getting at when he suggested "the psychological rule says that when an inner situation is not made conscious, it happens outside, as fate."[17]

In our holistic universe everything is interrelated, including our unconscious and our body, as well as our unconscious and the world. In this transitional time, in the move from reductionism to holism, we can only begin to imagine how thoroughly our inner life is manifested in our physical and circumstantial "fate." We can start by paying attention to our dreams, and by learning their symbolic language. If we don't speak the language, we won't hear the message.

This issue, like all others, can also be over-simplified. But the fact that it can be trivialized does not discount its validity. It only means that we must work to become more knowledgeable and more sophisticated in understanding how we can listen better, and sooner, and how we can thus prevent and treat disease, and/or generally enhance the quality of our life.

The familiar tag in this transitional time, "holistic health," is actually a redundancy. The word "health" shares the same root as does "whole" and "holy." True to the word, therefore, concepts of health should automatically include wholeness and holiness. "Holistic health" has been a necessary redundancy precisely because of our Epoch II materialism and the fact that we have so distorted the word health to mean simply the absence of illness. Nevertheless, the word health actually includes all the spirituality and wholeness necessary to describe Epoch III.

In Epoch III we will grow into the maturity which will be able to transcend small ego over-simplifications and arrogant hierarchical arrangements. We will be mature enough to look with sacred eyes, think with open minds, and feel with soft hearts how to utilize all of our capacities for health and well-being—for our capabilities are legion.

We have focused for so long on the body, that which is visible and gross, that we have missed crucial aspects that participate in determining health or illness—the psyche, the invisible, and the subtle.

> The physician should speak of that which is invisible. What is visible should belong to his knowledge, and he should recognize the illnesses, just as everybody else, who is not a physician, can recognize them by their symptoms. But this is far from making him a physician; he becomes a physician only when he knows that which is unnamed, invisible and immaterial, yet efficacious.[18]

One might expect such a quote to come from one of the "New Age" physicians of today. In fact, it was one of the "founding fathers" of modern medicine, Paracelsus, the incomparable sixteenth century physician and alchemist. And I use it simply to illustrate that the Epoch III ideas have been around for a long time. We have been blind to them, however, because of our Epoch II adolescent reductionistic and materialistic eyes. The fact is, there have been physicians ever since Paracelsus' time—delightfully, a number that is increasing as we move through this transition—who have approached health and illness in holistic and comprehensive ways.

A common illustration that shows how simplistic we are in a given area is the fact that Eskimos have many words for what we simply call snow—many words because they understand many different forms, types, and textures of snow. The same point could be made, at this early stage of the emerging Epoch III, regarding our understanding that stress plays a significant role in health and illness.

Hans Selye, the father of stress research, said that stress plays a role in *every* disease. But the fact that we continue to have one word—stress—to describe such a multitude of conditions is indicative of how simplistic our understanding is of the psychological, emotional, and spiritual components of health and illness. There is the stress of loud noise, of over-crowding, of negative expectations, of cigarette smoking, of the death of a spouse, of financial disaster or the threat of financial disaster, and the presence or lack of meaning and purpose in our life, etc., etc., etc. I am convinced that, as we begin to understand the subtle nuances of stress and the many different forms of stress, we will begin to understand the profundity of Dr. Selye's words.

An Ecology of a Whole Mind

Although becoming fascinated with the split-brain metaphor was helpful in some ways, and certainly symbolic of our Epoch II illusions of categorizations, the fact is most of us have our corpus callosum intact. In other words, we have a whole brain not a split-brain. In Epoch III we will begin to explore the vast capabilities that we have once we stop being half-brained and start discovering an ecology of the whole brain.

If you think we have come a long way in Epoch II, just wait until you see what we are capable of when we fully actualize our intuition as well as our intellect, our unconscious as well as our conscious mind, our nighttime dreams as well as our daytime aspirations. A new trajectory of human achievement will indeed be on the horizon when we learn to see the valuable riches in symbolic language, as well as the growth possibilities in myths and metaphors.

Anyone studying the vast creativity literature can see the enormous testimony to the value of dreams, visualizations, guided imagery, and intuition. As Jung put it, "Great innovations. . . come invariably from below, just as trees (grow). . . upward from the earth."[19]

An Ecology of Humanity

Epoch III maturation will also bring about a different quality of dealing with humanity's diversity.

First of all, we have long been able to include diversity within our circle of friends when we perceived that we had the same interest. Epoch III will help enlarge our imagination so that we can perceive the common linkage and the common interest we have with all life on planet Earth.

Secondly, we will gain a new appreciation of how diversity enriches all of the parts. Take religions, for instance. Instead of the adolescent ego need, so prevalent throughout Epoch II, to make exclusive claims to Truth, we will explore a divine symphony with each "instrument" providing its invaluable contribution. There will be an appreciation of each "instrument," yet the discovery that the music is so much better when we play our heavenly song together.

Epoch II religions were founded around a particular man's spiritual experience. Enormous effort was expended to preserve and protect that man's experience and to secure singular loyalty on the part of followers. Notre Dame theologian John S. Dunne had a glimpse of Epoch III, however, when he wrote:

> The holy man of our time, it seems, is not a figure like Gautama or Jesus or Mohammed, a man who could found a world religion, but a figure like Gandhi, a man who passes over by sympathetic understanding from his own religion to other religions and comes back again with new insight to his own. Passing over and coming back, it seems, is the spiritual adventure of our time.[20]

This approach to an ecology of human experience does not eliminate or demean specific traditions. Nor does it call for a singular world religion. Quite the contrary, an ecology affirms the specific contributions while opening us to wider enrichment through holistic cooperation. "It may well be," said Ewert Cousins, sensing the same spirit as did Dunne, "that the meeting of spiritual paths— the assimilation not only of one's own spiritual heritage but that of the human community as a whole—is the distinctive spiritual journey of our time."[21]

The same ecological approach will be true in Epoch III regarding all the rich pluralism of the human family. It is not accidental that a new level of cross-cultural enrichment and understanding is occurring throughout our culture in this transitional time.

An Ecology in Nature

It may sound rather simple at first blush, but we humans are part of nature, in spite of how we have thought and acted over the past several thousand years. We were born out of Gaia's womb, interact constantly with nature in quite profound ways, and have, unfortunately, been living within an illusion of separation for a long time.

The spirituality emerging in Epoch III will help us recover that innate connection. We will begin to feel at home again in nature. We will gain a more mature appreciation for Gaia's tremendous wisdom regarding ecological balance and integration. She has been doing a remarkable job of creative parenting for a long time now, and if she can just get her adolescent children—who arrogantly dubbed themselves as doubly wise, Homo Sapiens Sapiens—to grow up before they ruin the home planet/parent.

We Americans had a precious opportunity, when we first came to this continent, to learn from those already here. The Native Americans, in contrast to the Christianity we brought from Europe, had a spirituality based on their mutually dependent relationship with the earth.

Instead, consistent with our comments earlier in this chapter, we were still too deep into our adolescence, and we labeled them "savages." That, of course, justified not only our killing them, but also made it absurd to learn anything from them about religion or spirituality. Instead, we considered ourselves missionaries to those "savages," bringing them a "civilized" religion.

It is significant that there is a coincidental timing between the emerging decades of Epoch III and a renewed interest in Native Americans. There has been a substantial increase in our openness to learn from their earth-based spirituality. It is, however, one of the tragedies of our adolescence that we so decimated their people and their culture before we grew up and became a little wiser and a little more mature.

As Epoch III spiritual development brings a greater maturity, perhaps we can grow into the holistic wisdom uttered by the Suquamish Indian chief Seattle on his death-bed: "All things are connected, like the blood which unites one family. It is all like one family, I tell you."[22]

As we re-member our innate connection with nature, and re-unite with our native soul, we will embrace a spirituality with no hierarchy, no faults, and fewer illusions. We will celebrate all people, all aspects of nature, and not have to say one is right and one is wrong. "One cannot say that the ocean is right and the continent is wrong," says William Irwin Thompson. In this new spirituality we will move, again in Thompson's words, "from ideology to an ecology of consciousness."

The Anticipated Riches of Epoch III Creativity

The rich expansion of creativity awaiting us in Epoch III will be, in part, connected to a change in the way we deal with the subjects of the "possible" and the "impossible." Neat, easy, and simple definitions of what is possible and what is thought to be impossible are major hindrances to creativity. Much of our narrow definitions of what is considered "possible" is the result of Epoch II reductionism. Conversely, Epoch III wholeness will release our minds, our bodies, and our spirits to experience creative solutions to problems previously considered to be intractable.

Perhaps you can understand my strong feelings about this subject since I was told for so long that it was impossible for me to manage severe chronic pain without drugs and that it was impossible for me to expect a life without major crippling. Such pronouncements closed the door, at least for a while, to a creative solution to the medical problem that was ruining my life. If I had continued to accept the predictions of the "experts," I would still be in severe pain, taking strong narcotics, and confined to a wheelchair.

After I discovered that there was, in fact, a creative solution to the severe chronic pain and the crippling, I became fascinated with creativity in general and pronouncements of impossibility in particular. We don't have room here for me to list the many expert pronouncements that I have gathered regarding perceived impossibilities, pronouncements soon thereafter were proven wrong. Suffice it to say, the list is long. It would seem that if anyone read just a little history beforehand a bit of humility would be in order in making such pronouncements.

I don't know where I heard the following, but it has stuck with me.

> Don't say the thing's impossible, chances are, you'll rue it.
> For some fool who didn't know, will come along and do it.

"There is no use trying," said Alice in Lewis Carroll's *Through The Looking Glass*, "One can't believe impossible things." "I dare say you haven't had much practice," replied the Queen. "When I was your age, I always did it for half an hour a day. Why, sometimes I've believed as many as six impossible things before breakfast."

The creativity in Epoch III will be so much greater than we have experienced to date, in part because we will practice exploring the impossible. Einstein, when asked how he discovered the theory of relativity, is reported to have said, "I challenged an axiom." Axioms tend to define what is possible and what is impossible.

The poet Theodore Roethke was pointing toward Epoch III when he said, "What we need is more people who specialize in the impossible."[23] And the same spirit is found in a passage in one of Schumann's piano sonatas where it is marked, "As fast as possible," followed a few bars later with "Faster."[24]

To point out that the same letters make up the words "impossible" and "I'm possible," is to point out that a big difference is created in how you look at those same letters. It is, perhaps, a bit corny, but that corn has a kernel of truth in it—actually, quite a powerful kernel of truth. The strong belief in the innate human potential can overcome many small-minded proclamations that something is impossible.

The point here is that definitions of possible and impossible have been made during Epoch II from within the narrow confines of specialities and categories. Because Epoch III will look more at the interaction between categories, it brings new players into the creative mix. The result is that much of what has been impossible in the past will become possible in the holistic playground of creativity in Epoch III.

It is safe to say that when we heal the fractures we have created in our Epoch II reductionism, when we overcome the deceptions and illusions of separation and categorization, we will discover a richness of creativity that we cannot now imagine. The Epoch II mind is, literally, unable to imagine what will be possible in Epoch III.

We are not talking about utopia, which literally means "no place," and which was an imaginary island made famous in a book written by Sir Thomas More in 1516. We are talking about a very real place, very real people, and real time—this place, you and me, today, or at least by tomorrow. We are talking about what Lewis Mumford saw as he looked into the future. Let's consider again his words, since they are so powerful. We will experience, he said, "a higher trajectory for life as a whole, . . . a fresh release of spiritual energy that will unveil new potentialities, no more visible in the human self today than radium was in the physical world a century ago, though always present."

"Miracle," "impossible," "idealistic," and "utopian"—words frequently used when the imagination fails to see beyond what we are capable of at this particular moment. Sacred eyes can see the image of tomorrow, and it is a new and different form of human life. Sacred eyes see holistic interaction that creates a whole new level of creativity.

One of the words that will play a dramatic role in increasing our creativity, a word that will guide us into discoveries that Epoch II would have considered impossible, is "synergy."

III. THE EPOCH III "MIRACLES" OF SYNERGY

In order to be able to understand the great complexity of life and to understand what the universe is doing, the first word to learn is synergy.
—SCIENTIST, ARCHITECT, AND PHILOSOPHER, BUCKMINSTER FULLER

Although we may be more familiar with Bucky Fuller's use of the word, it was actually Ruth Benedict, professor of anthropology at Columbia University in the first half of this century, who invented and developed the concept of synergy. And it is probably significant that it was a woman whose main interest was in Native Americans who was the one to come up with this enriched concept of wholeness and cooperation.

Synergy has two primary meanings:

1. The whole is more than the sum of its parts.

2. No part can be fully understood separate from the whole.

Let your mind absorb the rich meaning in those definitions, and you will begin to see what a revolution we have in store.

Synergy, as you can see, is what gives wholeness its texture and its character. Synergy is what saves our concept of wholeness from slipping into a fuzzy minded, bland, homogeneity. Synergy is what keeps us from taking all the rich colors of life's rainbow and, in a misinterpretation of wholeness, creating a dull gray.

Synergy affirms the unique contribution and power of each color and paints a picture of life with rich texture and contrasts. In other words, synergy affirms the unique value of each part, while drawing us into the grand potential of the whole being more than simply the addition of the parts. It is the "more than" that will open up the surge of creativity in Epoch III.

In this time of maturation, the time of a growth spurt from adolescence into adulthood, synergy is the concept that can affirm the grand achievements of Epoch II—the value and dignity of the individual person, and the individual area of specialization—while moving us beyond the tunnel-vision and arrogant diminution of life's diversity which often resulted in Epoch II. Synergy affirms the part while drawing us to the "more than" promised in the whole.

To take a closer look at the implications of synergy, let's again turn to the field of health and illness. When people are very sick with a serious disease and get well—particularly, suddenly—without any conventional medical intervention, we don't know what to do with it. It lies outside our Epoch II definitions of the possible, the normal, and the natural human experience with health or illness. We don't have a category for it. What just happened was impossible.

Our practice, when something happens that we consider to be impossible, is to put a label on it that categorizes it but does not explain it. For the general public, the category for the inexplicable and the impossible is "miracle." For the medical profession, it is "spontaneous remission." First, let's deal with miracles.

Ever since we divided heaven from earth, and divine from human, we explained anything that did not fall within our definition of normal humanity as coming from outside divine intervention— e.g., a miraculous healing. If it is impossible within our understanding of *natural* human capabilities, it must be *supernatural*.

Miracles in Epoch II, however, are just the preview of the synergistic "more than" of human potential in Epoch III. St. Augustine had it right, I believe, a long time ago: "Miracles do not happen in contradiction to nature, but in contradiction to that which is known to us of nature."[25] The higher trajectory of life that is coming in Epoch III, when we get our act together, will have us redefining miracles and experiencing dramatic healings as a natural process.

The reason we have had so few miracles in Epoch II, and the reason why we have thought they must be initiated from some outside non-human divinity, is that we have been living a diminished life within narrow categories. It is the wholeness of Epoch III, informed by the concept of synergy, that will introduce us to the naturalness of miracles and of their much more frequent availability. They are simply the "more than" that we will discover in the synergy of Epoch III spiritual maturation.

Although there are many miraculous healings to choose from, it might be helpful if we look at the experiences at Lourdes, in France, where an apparition of the Virgin Mary appeared in 1858. Anecdotal stories are interesting and certainly provide direction of what should be investigated, but they are not convincing evidence, per se. At Lourdes, however, there has been a process of extraordinarily rigorous investigation and documentation. All in all, there have been about six thousand claims of miraculous healings among the people who visited Lourdes. Of that number only sixty-four have made it through the narrow gate of credibility set up by the International Medical Commission.

Sixty-four well-documented cases of miraculous healing, however, is ample evidence to suggest that other factors are at work in healing than are included in our conventional medical theories. Let's take a brief look at just one example.

The official report of the Medical Commission tells the story of a man admitted to the Military Hospital of Verona in Italy with a large tumor in the hip. The cancer had dislocated his hip and x-rays showed massive destruction of the pelvic bone. "He was literally falling apart," the report stated; "the leg was being separated, this mass was growing, and the actual bone of the pelvis was disintegrating."

The man, instead of receiving any medical treatment, chose to visit Lourdes to be bathed in the spring. Immediately after the bathing he reported a sudden sensation of heat moving throughout his body. Before Lourdes he could not eat and had lost a great amount of weight. After Lourdes he had an immediate return of his appetite. He gained weight and appeared to be getting so much better that his doctors, after a month, decided to take new x-rays. They discovered that the tumor had totally disappeared. But perhaps even more remarkable was that his disintegrated bone grew back. From the Medical Commission report:

> The x-rays. . . confirm categorically and without doubt that an unforeseen and even overwhelming bone reconstruction has taken place of a type unknown in the annals of world medicine. We ourselves, during a university and hospital career of over 45 years spent largely in the study of tumors and neoplasms of all kinds of bone structures and having ourselves treated hundreds of such cases, have never encountered a single spontaneous bone reconstruction of such a nature." The report concluded by saying, "the prognosis is indisputable, the patient is alive and in a flourishing state of health nine years after his return from Lourdes.[26]

Or consider stigmata. Stigmata is a phenomenon, in one sense, just the opposite of miracle healing—it is a miracle wounding. Stigmata is where a person has a spontaneous, literal, and empathic experience of the crucifixion wounds of Christ. There are over 300 documented cases where, in various degrees, people have a spontaneous appearance of wounds and bleeding. In every case it is a person of strong religious belief. There is an interesting seven to one ratio of women to men. And most stigmatics are cloistered nuns or priests.

Medical specialists, many profoundly skeptical, have been called in to witness the phenomenon. It simply defies conventional medical explanation. One such stigmatic had continuous bleeding from the holes in his hands for fifty-five years, day and night, without remission, resisting every attempt to heal or cure them, and never became infected.[27]

The point is that miracle cures and miracle woundings are not, as we thought in Epoch II, an external divine intervention into natural laws. They represent, rather, a synergy of factors—particularly the power of belief and imagery—previously thought to have little or no effect on the body. In Epoch III sacred eyes will see this "more than" of untapped human potential. As we learn to understand this power of synergy and learn how to harness that power, miracles will become commonplace.

Medical professionals have generally been somewhat skittish about the word *miracle*. The mainstream of medicine thinks it is not appropriate to speak of an external divine force when discussing healing. It is not considered scientific, for as we have already discussed, the "priests" of science and those who have worshiped at the altar of materialism have eliminated God from their worldview. The term preferred is "spontaneous remission." It is a euphemism for—"We don't have the foggiest idea as to why that person got well."

If there is no evidence that the healing took place *because of medical intervention*, Epoch II medicine doesn't know how to explain it. And because medical professionals are trained to treat pathology rather than to understand health, they generally turn their back on spontaneous remissions and return to treating sick people. At first blush, it is a compassionate act on the part of the physician. And certainly the sick people appreciate it very much. But since this process ignores valuable evidence regarding how people get well, it does not serve us well in the long run.

There has been tragically little medical attention given to spontaneous remissions. In fact, after an extensive search for such evidence the Institute of Noetic Sciences published a special report indicating that "there are no existing texts on the subject. Remission simply is not a subject a physician or a researcher can look up in the library." There are only two books on the subject, both out of print, and two of the three authors are deceased.[28]

Spontaneous remissions are simply inexplicable from a disspirited materialistic perspective—in other words, the current medical paradigm—precisely because they involve a synergy with non-material factors. It takes a courageous, creative, and curious professional to be able to transcend narrow training and paradigmatic borders.

Dr. Deepak Chopra is just such a physician. A specialist in endocrinology, Dr. Chopra has also been the chief of staff at New England Memorial Hospital. He was originally from India and studied the ancient holistic healing techniques of Ayurvedic medicine, which is probably why he has been able to look outside the conventional medical paradigm. He has looked, for instance, at the spontaneous remission of cancer—over four hundred cases—with an eye on what could be learned.

"Research on spontaneous cures of cancer. . . has shown that just before the cure appears almost every patient experiences a dramatic shift in awareness. He knows that he will be healed, and he feels that the force responsible is inside himself but not limited to him—it extends beyond his personal boundaries, throughout all of nature."[29] In Epoch III we will give more attention to what a "shift of awareness" is, and how people can be enabled to harness that power.

In addition to medical examples, one general thing that must be said about synergy is that it moves us beyond the self-limiting and self-defeating nature of competition and takes us to the "more than" of the self-enhancing and win-win nature of cooperation.

Competition has been one of our favored concepts in Epoch II— understandable during a time when we were trying to develop our ego strength. But we justified competition by trying to convince ourselves that it is the most natural way to relate. We convinced ourselves that nature is fierce, competitive, dog-eat-dog, and naturally aggressive.

Nature, however, is much more varied that we gave her credit for, much more pluralistic, and has many different things that are "natural." In Epoch II we chose the evidence for competition and blew it up to banner, and gospel, proportions. It is thus heresy to suggest that competition is not all that it's cracked up to be.

Nevertheless, as we near Epoch III, there is a growing body of research which suggests that cooperation is just as prevalent in nature as is competition, and in fact may be the dominant quality. We talked in Chapter Two about how biologists are discovering that it was through ingeniously cooperative networking, rather than a competitive "survival of the fittest" action that nature progressed on its evolutionary ascent.

Nature, it seems, had this wisdom from the start—we progress further and faster if we cooperate with one another. Competition separates and divides—cooperation re-joins. "The equation of competition with success in natural selection," as Stephen Jay Gould put it, "is merely a cultural prejudice."[30]

Consider, for instance, the implications for our educational systems. In many subtle ways, and many not so subtle, we have competition permeating our learning environments. Consider how much "more than" children could learn if they really were exposed to synergy, networking, and cooperation. Instead of learning that other people are obstacles to our own achievement, our children might learn that working together they could learn much more and everybody would progress much further—not to mention having more fun doing it. And consider the educational implications of a competition that divides, analysis that separates, and Bohm's statement that such reductionism leads only to confusion and illusions. Are we literally educating our children in illusions?

Both competition and cooperation are natural parts of life. It is the either/or mentality of Epoch II that wants to pick one and eliminate the other. Personally, I have had a great deal of enjoyment out of athletic competition. In many respects, friendly competition can play a helpful role in pushing one to discover one's untapped potential. If you are forced, through the cooperation of friendly competition, to push yourself in ways that you would not do alone, you can discover realms of capability previously unknown. There is substantial value in that. As I mentioned earlier, I credit this very experience in athletics with enabling me to challenge the experts' predictions of what I was capable of in pain management. But make no mistake about it, when we paint our entire life with the competitive brush we miss a great deal of additional enrichment.

Consequently, I am not suggesting that we consider anything competitive as wrong and everything cooperative as right. That would be the either/or Epoch II mentality talking. The point is that we have *over-emphasized* competition in Epoch II, and Epoch III will usher in a new appreciation for the role of cooperation and synergy. Because of our adolescent ego need, we have misinterpreted "nature" and over-emphasized competition—the result of which is a poverty of life in general and of creativity in particular.

Synergy is the concept, as we come of age into adult maturity, that will lead us into a higher trajectory of life—one that affirms the unique contribution of the part, yet leads us to the "more than" of cooperation. And it is the power of love that both drives the re-uniting of that which has been torn asunder and heals that which has been fractured. It is the power of love that makes synergy and cooperation "more than" singular individualism. But it is a new and more powerful understanding of love, and it is that to which we now turn.

IV. THE EPOCH III DISCOVERY OF LOVE AS THE ESSENTIAL POWER OF WHOLENESS

A fresh interpretation of love is needed. . . that shows that love is basically not an emotional but an ontological power, that it is the essence of life itself, namely, the dynamic reunion of that which is separated.

—THEOLOGIAN AND PHILOSOPHER, PAUL TILLICH

Unless one spends time within philosophical, theological, or metaphysical jargon, one might not be familiar with the word "ontological." Basically, it points to what is essential in reality, as opposed to what is peripheral or superficial. Tillich here is calling for the realization that love is not just something superficial, emotional, or sentimental. Love, rather, is at the very core and essence of life. *Love is fundamental to everything that is.*

It is not that we might *like* love to be central, or that we would *wish* it were more important. It is not that *if* we could design the perfect world we would put love at the center. The suggestion here is that love *is* the essential energy of the universe—we just haven't fully appreciated that fact. In our collective adolescence, like young teenagers just getting a glimpse of love, we were first enamored with the emotional and physical aspects of love. We had a teenage crush level of understanding love. Our encounter with love was sentimental, infatuated with a superficial form of love.

As we move into Epoch III, however, spiritual maturity will open our eyes to the profoundly *essential* quality of love that permeates the universe. The challenge for us, and no small challenge at that, will be to think in new ways about love.

Because we have so worshiped science in our late adolescence, perhaps it would be helpful to lay the groundwork of our understanding of love with a look at the scientific revolution that took place during this century. We can get a better sense of the ontological nature of love, perhaps, if we take the scientific journey in understanding matter—a journey from the atom to love.

The Scientific Journey from Solid, Dis-spirited Matter, to the Loving "Allurement" that is the Essential Universe

We came to the brink of the twentieth century thinking in mechanistic terms. The "basic building block" of matter, we thought, was the atom. And we thought the atom was solid—the word literally means indivisible.

About the turn of the century, however, we discovered that the atom *was* divisible—in fact, there were many smaller particles whizzing around inside the atom. We discovered that matter was, in fact, pent up energy.

Dramatic and revolutionary changes continued, in the name of relativity and quantum physics. Physicists started describing that pent up energy in strangely non-materialistic ways—a "web of relations," and "dancing energy." Perhaps the most revolutionary discovery was that our mind is profoundly interconnected with sub-atomic reality. "It will remain remarkable," writes physicist Eugene Wigner, "that the very study of the external world led to the conclusion that the content of consciousness is the ultimate reality."[31]

David Bohm, summing up the vast evidence of the way mind and consciousness penetrate all of matter, says that it is now clear that consciousness is not just a product of higher animals, recently created in the long evolutionary journey. Consciousness is, rather, woven implicitly into all matter, and *matter emerges out of consciousness.* "There is mind even down at the quantum level," says Bohm.[32]

In the span of a century we have moved from understanding matter as a dis-spirited world made up of solid, inert, "building blocks," to the idea that mind and consciousness are at the core of reality. Those still uncomfortable with religious language speak not of God but of the "Universal Mind" or "Cosmic Consciousness." But let's face it: those terms, as well as the various symbolic terms referring to God, are all attempts at describing that which is most basic in the universe, that which is the "within-ness" of creation, and that which drives and directs the evolutionary process.

It is not a big step, therefore, to suggest that the quality of that consciousness is spiritual in general, and love in particular. In one sense, we can see a microcosmic journey in this century, regarding our understanding of matter, parallel to the fifteen billion year macrocosmic journey of humanity—we saw matter as essentially physical (our childhood agenda), then as consciousness (our adolescent agenda), and what is emerging now is the recognition of matter as essentially spiritual (our adult agenda).

In this manner of speaking it is not mind that is at the center of the universe, so much as it is heart—albeit, a smart heart. A wise, pragmatic, ontological love that is the "within-ness" of matter, and that which is inside the evolutionary ascent of life drawing us into re-union and com-union with the divine creative energy.

The visionary paleontologist and Jesuit priest, Teilhard de Chardin, was one prestigious scientist who perceived, early in this century, that love is the fundamental power in the universe. Teilhard saw love as "a universal form of attraction linked to the inwardness of things."[33] He lamented the fact that modern philosophies— materialism and rationalism—discounted love as an essential power "but sooner or later we shall have to acknowledge that it is the fundamental impulse of Life. . . the blood of spiritual evolution."[34]

And at least two contemporary physicists have come to a similar interpretation of reality's essence. One, Fritjof Capra, sums up the evidence from 20th century physics and says, "the new vision of reality is a spiritual vision in its very essence."[35]

Another, Brian Swimme, is more explicit about that spiritual essence being love. Dr. Swimme, director of the Center for Science and Spirituality at the California Institute for Integral Studies, suggests that love begins as allurement, attraction, and that it is cosmic love that binds the universe together. Science has traditionally called this gravity, but:

> Gravity is the word used by scientists and the rest of us in the modern era to *point* to this primary attraction. We do not understand the attracting activity itself. . . . The attracting activity is a stupendous and mysterious fact of existence. Primal. We awake and discover that this alluring activity is *the* basic reality of the macrocosmic universe. . . . I'm speaking precisely of the basic binding energy found everywhere in reality. I'm speaking of the primary allurement that all galaxies experience for all other galaxies. . . . [This is] love in its cosmic dimension.[36]

Love is the cosmic quality of the Spirit that makes this a holistic universe. Everything is connected precisely because everything has the allurement of love as its most fundamental energy. And that is why our adolescent ego need to separate things has been, in one sense, unnatural and responsible for illusions, deceptions, fractures in the collective body, and faults along the human landscape.

There have been times in this discussion that I have been rather harsh on Christianity, as well as on the medical paradigm. I have tried to make it clear, however, that each has great complexity with pros as well as cons, great benefits as well as short-comings. I have identified primarily the shortcomings precisely because we must be clear about our adolescent immaturities if we are to grow into greater maturity.

The subject of love, however, is one in which we must give great credit to the Judeo-Christian tradition. In spite of its many short-comings and adolescent immaturities, followers of this tradition have made great contributions to our experience and knowledge of love. Jesus is the man around whose life and death Christianity is based, and he clearly had an ontological sense of love as the most essential element in reality. Love was at the very heart of Jesus' life, ministry, and message.

It is not surprising that since we had two thousand years left in our collective adolescence, followers of that man and the Christian Gospel frequently promoted division and faults rather than the uniting power of love. Nevertheless, there have also been many grand examples of love being manifest. And somehow, through it all, we have usually known that it was in living and manifesting love that we came closest to the life revealed in and the understanding of reality preached by Jesus of Nazareth.

The convergence of science and spirituality, such a crucial healing of an Epoch II fault and so central to Epoch III, leads us to see that love is the energy that makes this a holistic universe. That is the first realization about love—it's ontological nature. It has been traditionally phrased, simply—God is love. The second, to which we now turn, is that love is also the most fundamental power for healing and for the recovery of wholeness.

Love is the Spiritual Collagen that Heals our Brokenness

In a physical sense, collagen is found in our connective tissue. The word, in its Greek root, means *glue*. In a very real sense, collagen is the physical glue that holds our body together.

Love is the spiritual collagen that holds the entire universe together. It is the universal power that is available to us to heal the many fractures that our adolescence has created. In other words, the "within-ness" of the universe is not an inert or static entity. It is, rather, a power that reconciles, a power that heals, and a power that re-unites. It is a power inherent in every cell of the universe, and as close as our own being.

As an ontological power, love is fore-given. It is a given in the universe since its very beginning. It is a given before we came into being. But that fore-given love gains its specificity in our lives—its capacity to heal *our* life, and *our* relationships—when we utilize the power of love found in forgiveness. Love is the power, and forgiveness is the strategy to release and realize that power.

It is in forgiving ourselves that we access that core energy of the universe. It is in forgiving ourselves of our adolescent fractures that we are made whole, healthy, and holy. Many spiritual traditions have spoken to this very point. It is the grace that we need not earn— we simply accept its fundamental reality and its applicability in our lives. We can access forgiveness precisely because love is fore-given.

And it is armed with this power of loving forgiveness that we heal our separations from others. One of the illusions created by our adolescent ego development was that we would find security in separations and divisions—in our family, our tribe, our nation, our religion, etc. We have found, time and again, that such divisions do not lead to security. The Epoch III spirituality which focuses on love and forgiveness will help us realize that security is only found as we reconstitute the whole. We engage in whole-making by the power of forgiveness—living and sharing the love that is fore-given.

A typical phrase, dribbled almost unthinkingly across the lips, has been, "forgive and forget." But it is more insightful, empowering and liberating to "forgive and remember." It is in forgiving that we remember love is fore-given. It is in forgiving that we remember who we really are—beings of love, by love, and for love. And it is in forgiving that we re-member that which has been dis-membered—parts of ourselves and our innate connection with others and the world. Forgiveness *is* re-membering.

There are an increasing number of physicians who are growing beyond the materialistic and reductionistic past to realize that love and forgiveness are powerful forces in the healing of the physical body. One such physician is cancer surgeon, Dr. Bernie Siegel.

> I feel that all disease is ultimately related to a lack of love, or to love that is only conditional, for the exhaustion and depression of the immune system thus created leads to physical vulnerability. I also feel that all healing is related to the ability to give and accept unconditional love.[37]

Dr. Siegel, predictably, has received a great deal of criticism from the medical establishment. Many have considered his pronouncements regarding love to be overly simplistic, in terms of its impact upon disease, and cruel in terms of making cancer patients feel guilty. Is it possible, however, that what is simplistic is the medical establishment's understanding of love as a healing power? And is it possible that the greatest help for a cancer patient is to teach the enormous healing power of forgiveness?

In one very real sense, it is in healing the Epoch II faults between body, mind, and spirit—within oneself—through the power of the spiritual collagen of love that provides the most potent healing power for any specific illness of the body. Many "miracles" would be experienced if we could only learn to tap that essential power of healing that is fore-given.

Love is also the power to heal others. This is illustrated by a story about an autistic child, fractured from the relationship with the external world, cut off from normal relationships with others. Fortunately for their son, Barry and Suzi Kaufman did not accept the diagnosis of severe autism as an impossible situation, nor did they take on the role of helpless victims. Instead, they applied tough, tenacious, pragmatic love.

The Kaufmans' approach was one of total, unconditional love and acceptance. They were willing for their son *not* to change, if that turned out to be his choice. They lovingly entered his world, joining him in the seemingly bizarre behavior of spinning, chanting, and hand-flapping. They gave him intense attention and loved him just as he was, not as someone else expected him to be. The result was a miracle—more than anyone expected, and certainly more than the orthodox mainstream could handle.

The Kaufmans applied their loving, but unorthodox, technique on another boy, Robertito Soto. Robertito appeared to be a hopeless case of autism. At five and a half he was little more than a vegetable. His IQ was almost non-existent, measuring between seven and fourteen points, and he had negligible activity in the left hemisphere of his brain. He was unresponsive to external stimuli, including peope, and received a diagnosis from one neuropsychologist as "the lowest functioning child I've ever seen." Another diagnosis labeled Robertito as having "a severely incapacitating lifelong developmental disability."

Within a year and a half the Kaufmans, joined in the therapy by their own son, had transformed Robertito "from a vegetable into a lively, loving child." He was able to speak in sentences, complete

complex puzzles, roller skate, ride a bicycle and express spontaneous affection for his friends and family.[38]

The Kaufmans reportedly have been criticized by the National
Society for Autistic Children, and by other professinals, because:
"1) it has no theoretical basis, and 2) it makes other parents feel
guilty for not having committed themselves to a similar seven-
days-a-week marathon." They tried to get a grant to work with
autistic children, but were reportedly turned down because their
methods were considered inefficient.[39]

Inefficient. Made others feel guilty for not doing the same thing.
No theoretical basis. No grants.

No comment.

The point here is not that unconditional love is only available to
those who are fortunate enough to have loving parents or friends.
That helps make it more obvious and the absence of loving support
clearly sets up barriers to love's appropriation. But the point is that
the ontological nature of love means that it is available, unconditionally, to everyone. Love is available because we participate in a
loving universe. We only have to accept it, realize it, receive it. We
only have to open the doors and windows of our soul, take a deep
breath, and be inspired by the loving energy that is at the core of
reality. It is grace unconditionally given.

Easier said than done, you say? True. I was blessed by loving
parents and a loving family, so it was easy for me to experience love
as ontological. Many have not been so blessed. It certainly must be
harder for them. I can only say that, to the best of my ability, I try to
be a carrier of that love, in very pragmatic ways, to anyone my life
touches. That, it seems to me, is a given for any of us who have been
blessed by knowing and experiencing love.

It is marvelous to see the increased emphasis by therapists,
public speakers, and various groups in helping people recover from
the wounds inflicted by the lack of love early in one's life. Those
emphases are evidence that we are feeling the emerging light of love
coming from the soul of our time. We are beginning to feel the
essential ontological nature of love. The recent increase of interest
in the many forms of child abuse is an important and healthy
awakening. We are beginning to tap a sensitivity about which Sam
Keen spoke so poetically:

> A child is the form in which the flesh brings forth its promise.
> Eros in bud. Every child has an inalienable right to be bonded
> in welcoming arms, kindly initiated into a caring culture,
> allowed to play freely in the realms of the senses and

imagination. As the seed is betrothed to fertile soil, sun, and rain, the child bears an organic right to nurture.[40]

As mentioned back in the introduction to Epoch III, what the Bible purports to be the very beginning of the human journey on earth—the fall from grace in the Garden of Eden—was actually the symbolic representation of our transition from our collective childhood into adolescence. Collectively, therefore, we did not have an abused childhood. We were loved and nurtured by Father Sky and Mother Earth. Our childhood was one of experiencing love, organically and ontologically. We knew love because we grew up in it.

Collectively, therefore, we are not "adult children" of abusive parents. The abuses and illusions from which we suffer are the result of our natural ego development as we grew through adolescence. That makes it a very different picture regarding our future. We fell from the grace of love, not as abused children but as "prodigal sons"—rebellious adolescents reaching for independence. But the ontological grace and love that we experienced in our childhood is still there in our depths. For a healthy maturity we need only to tap back into our collective soul, find that ontological love that our cosmic "parents" ordained us with from the very beginning, and grow on into a healthy, whole, and holy future. That is part of the reason why the major agenda of our adulthood is spiritual development—rediscovering the love in our soul. As prodigal sons we need only return "home" to the realization that love has been in us from the very beginning.

For it is love that can and will put us back together again. It is love that can heal us and make us whole. It is love that enables us to discover that which is fore-given—a love that expresses its power in forgiveness, a love that can reconcile our estrangements, re-unite our separations, re-member our dismemberment, and heal the faults and fractures of our adolescence.

CHAPTER 9

EMPOWERMENT:
A Holy Ambition
Invading Our Souls

It is not only a change that is happening—it is the change. . . . The very blueprints of what it means to be human are changing. . . . We are becoming a much less limited species.
—AUTHOR GARY ZUKAV

We can discern. . . a transformation of human personality in progress which is of evolutionary proportions, a shift of consciousness fully as epoch-making as the appearance of speech or of the tool-making talents in our cultural repertory.
—HISTORY PROFESSOR THEODORE ROSZAK

YOU HAVE HEARD IT SAID MANY TIMES that at any given moment we are utilizing only a small percent of our abilities. When lecturing or conducting a seminar, I will often ask the audience to identify the percent of our abilities that they think we are generally using. Never has anyone picked 50% or above. Some guess we might be using 25% or 30%, with the majority estimating between 10% and 20%, and some suggesting that we are utilizing only about 3% of our abilities. The results of this informal poll have been similar regardless of the audience—business or professional group; various educational levels; diverse racial, cultural or sexual identity. It would seem that we all share a belief that we are tapping only a small portion of our abilities and that our personal resources are grossly under-utilized.

But consider this. For us to guess *any* percent—3%, 10%, 20% or whatever—would presume we know what constitutes 100%. Do we? No. We simply do not know what a 100% human effort would consist of or look like. We just plain do not know the upper limit of human capabilities; we only know that we haven't begun to approach it. Just imagine what exciting discoveries await us in Epoch III as we take the leap of growth from adolescence into adult maturity, as we get our act together in the synergy of body, mind and spirit, and as we become more fully empowered.

The illusions of Epoch II had a great deal to do with keeping us far below our maximum capabilities. Simply consider the consequences of dividing body and mind as it relates to peak athletic performance. Until relatively recently only the body was trained for athletic performance, and even the way the mind is currently "trained" will be shown in Epoch III to be amazingly primitive in terms of utilizing whole person capabilities.

Consider, as another example, "physical education" in our schools. How many elementary schools are teaching children that they do, in fact, have the ability to alter blood-flow in order to avoid a migraine headache or to aid the healing of a wound? Does physical education include the knowledge and skills of controlling muscle tension or of avoiding tension headaches or fatigue? We could go on and on. The point is that our divisions and separations in Epoch II have kept us constricted within illusions—illusions about our full capabilities. Consequently, we have a truncated notion about individual power, about education, religion, health care and creativity.

As Epoch II adolescents we acquired a fascination with power, but it was a power projected onto externals rather than owned internally. In addition, in the hierarchies of Epoch II power was seen as power over other people. The power brokers in religion ran the institutions that controlled the "keys to the kingdom" and the spiritual destiny of the participants. The power brokers in business ran the companies that controlled the economic destinies of their participants. The power brokers in medicine controlled how health and illness were thought of and dealt with, as well as which interventions were considered legitimate and could receive third-party pay.

Our notion of power in Epoch II had to do with having considerable money and/or prestige, having control over other people, or projecting power out onto other people, gods, devils, or machines. Our fascination with technology is one of the most prevalent and current projections and, indeed, our mental development has given us an extraordinary capacity to develop machines that are quite fascinating. But the point is that in our constant projection of power we have disempowered ourselves.

Institutions and concepts that put the power in the hands of the few, while disempowering and "taking care of" the many, has been the hallmark of Epoch II. The emerging spiritual maturity, however, will be quite different. While affirming the mental development and resulting technological advancement that took place in Epoch II, we will be more discerning regarding the impact that any theology, philosophy, institution, or technology has on personal affirmation, freedom of self determination and empowerment.

If we return to the original meaning of the word "power" we find that it means "to be able." It is not "to have" or "to acquire" or "to control other people." Power as able-ness points to an inner power, whereas the way we have used the term power in Epoch II points to externals. The coming spiritual maturation will liberate the concept of power from the superficialities and return it to the essentials—a discovery of the deep well of power inside each and every person. A major agenda for Epoch III will be the empowerment of persons "at a higher trajectory" than we have known to date.

We have developed a love of power precisely because we are meant to be powerful. It is not the fascination with power that has been our difficulty, only the projection, misinterpretation, and misuse of power.

Our Epoch III understanding of empowerment starts, in fact, with the topic of the last chapter—wholeness. Just as disempowerment is a result of separation, division, and projection, so also is empowerment the result of wholeness, integration, and the discovery of our own taproot to the power of the universe. Epoch II was divide and conquer—Epoch III will be integrity and empowerment. The science of reductionism disempowered us and made us feel insignificant in the universe—a diminution of our role and innate capabilities. The science of wholeness, in contrast, empowers us to play out our destiny—a powerful co-creator role in the evolution of life.

As we discussed in the last chapter, we will discover love to be ontological, an essential core of reality. In like manner, Epoch III empowerment will lead us into the realization of the ontological nature of power.

"Classical science," writes Nobel laureate Ilya Prigogine, "made us feel that we were helpless witnesses to Newton's clockwork world."[1] But science in the twentieth century has brought us a view of "a universal order that includes us in a very special way. . . . In other words, ultimately and fundamentally we affect the universe."[2]

David Bohm, the theoretical physicist, has suggested a metaphor, the hologram, that can help us begin to understand the nature of our power.

"A hologram," explains science writer John Briggs,

> is a photographic image produced by laser light. The image is stored on the holographic plate, then retrieved by shining a laser beam through the plate to create a three-dimensional projection. Curiously, if a piece of the holographic plate is broken off and the laser beam is passed through it, the whole image still appears, though it is somewhat fuzzy. In other words, each "part" has implicitly retained information about the whole.[3]

Bohm uses this metaphor to explain how he believes that quantum physics suggests that we live in a completely holistic universe, everything connected and every piece containing the image of the whole. In other words, he is saying that we humans, as individual pieces of a holistic universe, contain the information *and the power* of the whole—only in a slightly fuzzy form.

The point in using this metaphor is to suggest that in exploring our inner nature we can access the essential power of the universe, and by empowering our self we empower the piece of the universe over which we have responsibility. We are individually unique yet contain the image of the whole. Empowerment, therefore, is our birthright. Empowerment helps us discover our uniqueness, while at the same time helps us discover the nature of the universe.

We can also use the metaphor of the hologram to speak explicitly about the spiritual rationale for empowerment. The world was created, as religions have stated in their various ways, "in the image of God." In all languages, God is the symbol for the whole of, and the essential power in, reality. We are individual pieces of that divine whole, whether we speak of it as the Goddess, God, Spirit, or whatever. Love is the laser beam of light, in this holographic metaphor, that illuminates the divine power within each of us. When the laser beam of love is shone through our unique piece of that whole an image of the whole is seen albeit in somewhat fuzzy form.

We are individually created in the image of the divine, and we reveal that image when we let love shine through us. Love can penetrate the opaqueness of the human version of materialized

Spirit. To empower our piece of the whole is, therefore, our spiritual task. Our maturation spiritually creates a sharper image of our uniqueness, while at the same time creating a sharper image of the whole for others to see and experience. That's the power of personal integrity and example.

It is with ourselves, therefore, that the process of empowerment starts. It is not, however, where we stop. We start with the individual but don't stop with individualism. We empower ourselves in order to become the best image of the divine of which we are capable, but individual empowerment does not happen in isolation. As individuals we are never fully empowered until we are in healthy and holy, synergistic relationships—with other people, with nature, with the whole of reality.

We will get to this relational aspect a bit later. First, however, we need to focus on the empowerment of the individual. It is only an empowered individual who can bring substantial empowerment to others. It is only after self-love has healed the internal fractures and empowered our own unique piece of reality that other-love is healthy, effective, and empowering.

We will look, first of all, at pro-active empowerment—strategies for taking responsibility for our own empowerment. Secondly, we will examine re-active empowerment—strategies in how to react to crises so that they empower rather than disempower us. If pro-active empowerment is taking responsibility for our lives, re-active empowerment is taking charge of our response-ability—the ability, the able-ness, the power we have to choose our response to the various challenges that confront us. Thirdly, we will discuss how an empowered person enters into synergistic relationships—becoming more empowered while empowering others. And finally, we will touch on the courage which fuels our search for inner power.

I. PRO-ACTIVE EMPOWERMENT

Jesus said: "If you bring forth what is within you, what you bring forth will save you. If you do not bring forth what is within you, what you do not bring forth will destroy you."
—THE GOSPEL ACCORDING TO THOMAS

Becoming a Virgin: On Loving Our Uniqueness

Hold on, it's not what you think! Before you slam the book shut, hear me out!

In spite of our preoccupation with a sexual meaning to the word, the fact is that "virgin" originally meant "belonging to no man." It had nothing to do with sex and everything to do with being true to oneself. So, to be a virgin means to be true to one's own nature and not be controlled by or conformed to someone else's opinion of you. It is the same sense as when we speak of a virgin forest—we're not talking about sex, but of a forest that has not been exploited or ruined by somebody from outside the forest. A virgin forest is natural, instinctual in its living, and not dominated by "man." The same is true with a person who is of virgin nature.

The symbol of the Virgin Birth has been used by various religions to refer to the original Earth Mother, or to claim uniqueness for a savior or primary prophet. The symbol points to the quality of being special and extraordinary.

In the Christian tradition, the Virgin Mary gave birth—i.e., a Virgin Birth—to the central figure of the religion, Jesus. As noted earlier, this emphasis upon the Virgin Birth of Jesus, however, was not in the first Christian writings. Neither Paul, whose writings date at about 50 A.D., nor the Gospel of Mark, written in about 70 A.D., mention anything about the Virgin Birth. It was in the Gospels of Matthew and Luke, both written down about 85 A.D., that this symbol first appears.

The point, however, is not to get bogged down in historical literalism regarding one person, but to grasp the symbolic significance of a virgin birth for every person. If and when Christians transcend the one-person focus they will have access to a rich symbolism that can assist spiritual empowerment.

This challenge—moving beyond the projection of power to personal empowerment—is, as we have stated before, one of the most crucial challenges of our collective maturation from adolescence to adulthood. In Epoch II our attention was on how the symbol spoke to someone else's specialness, someone else's uniqueness. Someone else was impregnated with the Holy Spirit.

Now, however, comes the time for integration and wholeness, a time for owning our own responsibility for spiritual growth and transformation. In Epoch III we will realize that *everyone* is impregnated with the spirit of the holy, the spirit of wholeness, and the spirit of health. In Epoch III we will claim our own virgin birth—or a virgin re-birth in which we are born anew into our own uniqueness, our own special individual version of Soul.

Another term pointing to much the same reality, although this time from a more secular lexicon, is the word "maverick." The word comes from a story about a real-life Texas cattle rancher named Samuel Maverick. It seems that Samuel Maverick chose not to brand his cattle, contrary to the custom of all the other cattle ranchers. So, when his cattle would get mixed up with other neighboring cattle, the ranchers could always tell when one was a "maverick"—it was not branded. Today, to be a maverick is to be one who refuses to be branded by stereotypic "labels." A maverick, like a virgin, is one's own person, not simply following a group, a dogma, or projecting power onto someone else.

Jesus might very well have been speaking to this point—realizing that followers would simply project their spiritual power out onto him—when he said, "It is expedient for you that I go away. For if I go not away the Holy Spirit will not come unto you."[4] If we continue to worship him, Jesus was saying, we will never know, personally and internally, our own version of the Holy Spirit. *He* must go away—and he can't go away unless we release him from our adolescent hero-worship—so that *we* can grow into a mature incarnation of the Holy Spirit.

There is a statement attributed to Jesus, in the Gospel of John, that speaks to our empowerment as we move from Epoch II into Epoch III. It is a statement, however, that you rarely hear quoted by adolescent Christian hero-worshipers, in spite of their frequent Bible quoting:

> In truth, in very truth I tell you, he who has faith in me will
> *do what I am doing; and he will do greater things still* because I am
> going to the Father."[5] (emphasis added)

Some Christians have been so involved in hero-worship that to suggest that one might do and even surpass the miracles Jesus performed would quickly label one a heretic. The heretic in this passage is Jesus himself.

In similar fashion, the Buddha told his disciples to quit the unproductive hero-worshiping and to move on in their journey of personal empowerment. He said that his teachings are "like a raft which they are using to cross a river: once they have reached the other side of the river, it would be foolish to lift up the raft and carry it away on their shoulders out of gratitude for its aid in crossing."[6] Rather, they are told, they should leave the raft on the riverbank and proceed on their journey. Carrying the raft would only be a burden and hold them back. Giving emphasis to this theme of empowerment, Buddha, as he was dying, is reported to have said to his disciples, "Walk on."[7]

Ultimately the spiritual journey has to be that of a virgin or a maverick. It cannot be done by proxy, absorbed by osmosis, or experienced vicariously. It is, by necessity, a solitary process. Even when considering the role of relationships and community, which we will do shortly, the responsibility ultimately has to rest with the individual. We are born alone, die alone, and must be reborn alone—whether we are talking physically or spiritually. It cannot be done as a group. It cannot be done for you by someone else. It cannot be done for you by an institution. The spiritual task of empowerment is to find your own unique relationship with Spirit and to discover and live your own special version of Spirit incarnate.

Your power. *Your* soul's version of Soul. Not your parents.' Not your peers.' Not an institution's version. And not some hero onto which you project your power. Your own virgin and maverick nature, unique and special, is what you are called to empower. In our adolescent immaturity we defined ourselves in contrast to or in conformity with others. But in the coming maturity our task will be to find and empower our own unique virginity.

There is, of course, value in learning from others and in having teachers. But, again, the responsibility and capability for growth and transformation is ours and ours alone. Another form of spiritual projection has been in seeking and/or following a guru. But as Jeffrey Masson put it, "There are no experts in loving, no scholars of living, no doctors of the human emotions and no gurus of the soul."[8]

The starting point for empowerment is to spell the word "guru," slowly, and with emphasis—"Gee, U R U." Indeed, you are the only you that has ever been or ever will be. You are a special version of Spirit incarnate and have the special opportunity to empower that uniqueness. You have the spiritual responsibility to empower that piece of creation which you and only you have the capacity to empower. The famous Protestant theologian, Paul Tillich, put it boldly when he said, "The submissive self is the opposite of the self-affirming self, even if it is submissive to a God."[9]

The spiritual virgins and mavericks are the grass-root architects of a new spiritual democracy. Kings, saviors, gurus, and institutional tyranny represented the hierarchies and external power of Epoch II. But it is the democratization of spirituality that is part and parcel of the coming maturity.

Krishnamurti could be considered a twentieth century prophet of Epoch III spiritual democracy. He not only had this at the center of his own message but lived it in an extraordinarily courageous way.

As a child early in the twentieth century, Krishnamurti was tabbed as the new Messiah by the Theosophical Society. He was taken into training and prepared to live out the privileged and venerated life of a guru. But in an exemplary act of courage and perspective in 1929 at age thirty-four, following a powerful spiritual experience, he severed himself from the Theosophical Society, renounced his role as the coming Messiah, turned his back on all the personal veneration, wealth and privilege, and spent the next sixty years proclaiming individual spiritual empowerment.

The Webster definition of democracy is "a government in which the supreme power is vested in the people and exercised directly by them." It is appropriate, I think, in a time of reuniting heaven and earth, divine and human, the sacred and the profane, to use this political term to refer to the coming spiritual empowerment of Epoch III. The supreme power is, indeed, vested in every one of us—it only remains for us to welcome it, come to know it intimately, and to exercise the use of it.

No more secret knowledge held and protected by a privileged priesthood—we can simply look within ourselves, and in the "in-between-ness" of our relationships, and we can see and know the divine. No more institutional imperialism presuming to be exclusive conduits to divine authority—we are all unique and special incarnations of Spirit with the ability to find our own virgin re-birth. No more spiritual hierarchy, as if a self-proclaimed guru or a hero-worshiped savior were closer to the divine than we are. We can't be "given" this kind of knowledge; we can't be "saved" by proxy. We need only cultivate sacred eyes to see it within us, between us, and in the ground on which we are standing—right here, right now.

If and when we do become aware of the heaven within us, between us, and all around us—Spirit incarnated within every cell of our minds and bodies—there will be no more problems of self-esteem and self-worth. How could we not then love ourselves? How could we not love others? We will become human beings living fully empowered lives of love and service.

To linger on that point for another moment, it is a misunderstanding of Epoch III empowerment to think that it leads to egotism. Egotism is an adolescent, immature, distorted and small notion of empowerment. The empowerment of spiritual maturity is to know that we did not create this universal love-power, and we do not have exclusive use of it. Rather, we are individual "special case" incarnations of the power that permeates and evolves the universe. It is an incredible blessing that, if followed, is awesome in its capacity to empower us, yet connects us with the cosmos at large—a humbling realization, indeed.

Each person is a piece of the spiritual hologram. Each person is a particular image of the divine Soul. And with the laser beam of love each person will become empowered to reveal their own unique version of Soul. The result will be a whole Soul that is more than the sum of the parts.

Go to Hell: On Loving our Depths

Jesus Christ, a powerful symbol of the empowered individual, is said to have descended into hell before he ascended into heaven. A similar journey for ourselves is an absolutely necessary part of the maturation process. We become whole, healthy, and holy only if we are willing to descend into hell and then ascend into heaven.

In Epoch II we divided heaven and hell, as well as good and evil, and made everyone fit into one category or the other. It was a time of either/or—either you are in heaven or you are in hell; either you are good or you are evil. It was a time of immature oversimplification, a time of illusions about the nature of wholeness. It led to disowning parts of ourselves and projecting them externally. If we were good, all evil was "out there." If we were bad, all good was "up there."

We do not become whole, healthy, and holy, however, until we become lovers of our darkness, healers of our deep fractures, and integrators of our disparate parts. Joseph Campbell pointed out that to see something you have to have shadow. This is true in the external world as well as in the internal world. Sacred eyes that want to see into our soul do not deny our "shadow," nor project it externally onto someone else. Empowerment can only come when we are willing, with eyes wide open, to see our personal devils and lovingly integrate them into a whole, healthy and holy self.

If you do not know your demons, if you do not know your devils and if you cannot recognize your hell, just pay attention. Pay attention to your dreams, particularly your nightmares. Pay attention to where things are not going well for you in life. Pay attention to the people who make you really angry, for in them lie clues regarding your shadow. Pay attention to your dis-ease, as well as your disease. Hidden within those sometimes dark, ragged, hellish pieces of coal is your sparkling diamond of a heaven.

Hell without heaven, or heaven without hell, is only half a truth and, more importantly, only half a life. We cannot be healthy or holy without being whole, and to be whole is to integrate our heaven and our hell.

Campbell also pointed out that mythology is constantly telling us that where we stumble is where we find our treasure. In other words, if we find and pay attention to our hell, we will find our path to heaven. In *The Arabian Nights*, as Campbell told it:

> Someone is plowing a field, and his plow gets caught. He digs down to see what it is and discovers a ring of some kind. When he hoists the ring, he finds a cave with all of the jewels in it.[10]

In Epoch II we have projected hell down deep in the earth. Down below the surface. Down in the realms of demons and monsters. Down in the house of the Devil. Down, out of sight. Down, in the unconscious. And in Epoch II we certainly did not want to dig around down there, for it was forbidden and scary territory. In our adolescent and categorical mind, if you wanted to go to heaven you certainly did not fool around in hell. If you wanted to commune with God you certainly did not court the Devil. And if you wanted to be a "nice" person you certainly did not confront your demons.

Jesus, however, did precisely the opposite of what we adopted as an Epoch II religious life. He went into the wilderness and confronted the Devil, he spent time with the outcasts of society, he directly challenged the religious authorities, and he went into hell before ascending into heaven. He was a radical and a heretic, a virgin and a maverick.

By the very nature of a holistic universe we have our depths as well as our heights, our hell as well as our heaven, our dark as well as our light, and our evil as well as our good. We are holistic beings, encompassing all aspects of the world—we are piece-images of the holographic universe.

The suggestion of going to hell before one can ascend into heaven relates back to the quote by Jesus taken from the Gospel of Thomas and used to introduce this section—namely, that the integration and bringing forth of that which is within will mean health, whereas the failure to do so will mean disease and death. It also touches back into the quote from Carl Jung in which he stated that the psychological rule is that if an inner situation is not made conscious, it will happen outside as fate. If we don't become empowered by going into our hell and loving, healing and integrating our dark side, we will experience hell in a lot of unexpected and disempowering ways in our life's circumstances and in our relationships.

Reach for the Stars: On Loving our Heights

If the first step in empowerment is to love our uniqueness, and the second is to love our depths, the third is to love our heights and reach for the stars. These three stages integrate the three vertical levels of a holistic holiness.

The original root of the word "disaster" meant to be out of touch with the stars. It may be that at least part of the solution to the many disasters dotting the transitional landscape in the late 20th century would be to reclaim our astronomical heritage and get back in touch with the stars.

In Epoch II we thought we lived only in the middle territory of the "earth plane," projecting heaven above and hell below. We divided our reality between the positive and the negative. In our adolescence, characterized by pessimism and cynicism, we have preferred negative thinking to positive thinking, calling the former realistic and the latter idealistic or naive. We preferred pessimism to optimism, cynicism to idealism, and the spiritual gutter to spiritual heights. Many have considered humanity to be thoroughly depraved creatures, victims of Original Sin.

The same preference for the negative was lived out when we switched our worship from God to science. As we discussed earlier, the idea of change was introduced in the nineteenth century both in physics as entropy and in biology as evolution. The point at issue was the *direction* of change, and collectively we preferred the pessimistic message of entropy over the optimistic message of evolution. Instead of a collective philosophy which viewed life as a living evolutionary ascent, we cast our lot with the idea of a universe, a world and life itself as a machine running down. We took our mental, physical, emotional and spiritual stance firmly in "Murphy's Law" and assumed that if anything could go wrong it would. Consequently, Epoch II has been a profoundly paranoid time—our collective expectation has been that the world was out to do us harm.

In contrast, the emerging empowerment of Epoch III recovers, rediscovers, and reaffirms the positive side of the various spectra. Recognizing our previous paranoia as illusion, Epoch III brings us back to the hope that is at the core of the universe. Epoch III spiritual prophets like Matthew Fox remind us that "original blessing" preceded the notion of original sin in Christianity. God created the world and proclaimed it good long before St. Augustine decided that humanity, through that dastardly semen, became totally depraved. And in contrast to Epoch II pessimism, history professor Theodore Roszak sees an emerging optimism that knows "a whole and healthy nature at the core of us; not an original sin, but an original splendor which aspires to transcendence."[11]

Epoch II religious paranoids anticipate the "Rapture" and the end of the world. Epoch II scientific and secular paranoids see only the continuation of technological trends until we are dehumanized by computers, totally overwhelmed by rapidly escalating change and "techno-stress," and are eventually done in by other such entropic scenarios. Epoch II paranoids, whether religious or secular, see nothing but impending disaster.

Regarding our ultimate fate, the religious paranoids, as the televangelists tell us with emotional fervor, believe that everything will end up just fine for those who believe in the party line. However, for the spiritual virgins and mavericks—well, we're in deep trouble. The secular paranoids, in contrast, don't have a similar escape-clause for conformists—we're *all* in deep trouble.

In contrast, Epoch III will reveal a larger picture of possibilities. Certainly we face crises, but there are opportunities just as there are dangers. In Epoch III we will be more creative, knowing the organic fact that endings mean new beginnings, destruction precedes reconstruction, disorganization precedes reorganization. In Epoch III we will discover the joy of a reverse paranoia—the belief that the universe is out to do us good. With love as the essential energy at the core of the universe, we are fundamentally accepted and affirmed.

One of the ways we can access that reverse paranoia is to reach for the stars. We are star children and participate in an evolutionary ascent back to our genetic heights. This path into Epoch III was, in fact, anticipated by Pico della Mirandola in the fifteenth century when he wrote so poetically:

> Let a certain holy ambition invade our souls, so that, not content with the mediocre, we shall pant after the highest, and—since we may if we wish—toil with all our strength to obtain it.[12]

Epoch II paranoids have spiritual acrophobia—a fear of the heavenly heights. But in the emerging spiritual maturity we will be fearlessly reaching for the stars with that "holy ambition." It is, indeed, a holy ambition that emanates from our very souls because reaching for the stars is our genetic predisposition. We are physically made of star-stuff. The heights are where we came from, and we yearn to return "home." We are, physically and spiritually, children of Father Sky and Mother Earth. Reaching for the stars is simply reaching for our natural inheritance. Epoch III will be the time to put the small notions of humanity behind us, to cast off the paranoia and to leave the fear of heights in our past. As Marilyn Ferguson put it:

> Our past is not our potential. In any hour, with all the stubborn teachers and healers of history who called us to our best selves, we can liberate the future. One by one, we can re-choose—to awaken. To leave the prison of our conditioning, to love, to turn homeward. To conspire with and for each other. Awakening brings its own assignments, unique to each of us, chosen by each of us. Whatever you may think about yourself, and however long you may have thought it, you are not just you. You are a seed, a silent promise.[13]

We *are* star-seed. We *are* the promise, a promise buried deep in our astronomical heritage, a promise of all that the universe has to offer. No matter how silent we have been to date we are a promise waiting to be empowered. If we love our heights, if we overcome our fears of cultivating the seed of divinity within us and if we reach for the stars, we will have the feeling of returning home. The highest and the holiest are inside us. We start discovering the kingdom of heaven by loving, affirming and empowering that part of the universe over which we have responsibility—ourselves.

To put it another way, we have been asleep to our divinity

throughout Epoch II. Epoch III is the time for awakening—awakening to who and what we really are. Star-stuff is in our bodies; heaven is in our soul. As Wordsworth put it in his poem, *Intimations of Immortality:*

> Our birth is but a sleep and a forgetting:
> The Soul that rises with us, our life's Star,
> Hath had elsewhere its setting,
> And cometh from afar.[14]

Jesus scoffed at those who projected a literal kingdom of heaven outside or out into the future. "If those who lead you say to you, 'Look, the Kingdom is in the sky,' then the birds will arrive there before you. If they say to you, 'It is in the sea,' then. . . the fish will arrive before you." Instead, Jesus spoke of a very holistic reality, saying "the Kingdom is inside you, and it is outside you." And then, pointing to self knowledge and empowerment, he said, "When you come to know yourselves, then you will be known. . . . But if you do not know yourselves, then you dwell in poverty, and it is you who are that poverty."[15]

If we get to know ourselves we discover not poverty but the vast riches of empowerment. And the process for mining those riches is first of all to become a virgin, secondly to go to hell, and thirdly to reach for the stars. When we discover our personal uniqueness and love, heal and integrate all dimensions of ourselves, then and only then are we empowered with star-power to reach for and experience the heavens.

II. RE-ACTIVE EMPOWERMENT

*The emergent theme of the age has been sounded, I believe, by those
who begin to see themselves as unfinished animals summoned to
unfold astonishing possibilities.*
        —HISTORY PROFESSOR THEODORE ROSZAK

Victim or Victor:
On Loving Our Freedom to Choose

If being pro-active has to do with taking responsibility to utilize empowering strategies in general, being re-active has to do with response-ability. In the face of a challenging disease or some other crisis we have abilities to respond in magnificent and heroic ways. We turn now to the matter of empowering those response-abilities; and it starts with a fundamental choice—do we want to be a victim or a victor?

In Epoch II, as we have seen both religiously and scientifically, we tended to see ourselves as victims. We were insignificant, if not good for nothing. We needed to be "saved" by external power—a God in his heaven, a savior playing the intermediary, the knowledge of an outside expert, or the appropriate technology. We were victims; and the victory, if there was to be one, could come only from the outside. In Epoch III we will discover an enormous inner power, the power to choose an inner posture of victor rather than that of victim.

This is not to say that we can always choose or determine the external outcome—say, of a disease. It is not so simplistic as to suggest that we have absolute control over life's circumstances. We must always start any discussion such as this with acknowledging the grand mystery in which we live, move, and have our being. The loving universe of which we are a part is so far beyond our comprehension that it takes an extremely small mind to hold the illusion that we can understand it, let alone manipulate and control it with absolute certainty.

That said, however, we must also add that we have a great deal more power to affect our lives and circumstances than we have been led to believe in Epoch II. We have been living within disempowering images of "human nature" for so long that we have yet to tap our full capacities. As we become virgins, go to hell, and then claim our heritage of the heavens, we will empower response-abilities that will "blow our socks off."

Any discussion of a person's role in the creation of an illness, or even in a person's ability to respond to the illness in substantial ways, usually raises the complaint that we are "blaming the victim." "How cruel," this thinking goes, "to blame the victim of a disease for causing it. They have enough burdens already without adding guilt."

We do need to recognize that such concerns usually arise out of well-meaning compassion. There is no need for the kind of rancorous debate that so often surrounds this subject. Let us presume that everyone approaching the subject has compassion for those who get sick and wants to be of maximum help to them. The point of debate should be—what approach, in fact, renders the most help?

In raising the issue of personal responsibility and response-ability in relation to health and illness, I certainly have no interest in blame, guilt, or condemnation. My interest here is in how we think about health and illness, as well as the empowering or disempowering results of such thinking. The fact is, we do more to liberate the potential power of a person by strategies that "empower a victor," rather than by being overly cautious out of fear of "blaming a victim." The key, obviously, is how to empower a sense of response-ability, while at the same time helping people choose a victor mentality rather than a victim mentality.

To illustrate this I want to return, briefly, to my own experience with severe chronic pain. Rather than pontificating about theories or assuming that my experience is applicable to everyone else, I want to simply share the way it worked for me.

For several years medical professionals, with great compassion and concern, tried to help me deal with the severe pain and the resulting crippling. Their paradigm, however, did not even consider how I might be participating in creating the pain experience. They only looked at the physical evidence of polio, of the broken back, the screws, the arthritis and sclerosis. They concluded that nothing could be done to help me, medically or surgically, and proceeded to treat the pain with stronger and stronger drugs. They certainly could not be accused of "blaming the victim." They didn't blame me for anything. But, and this is a crucial point, they also gave me no hope for a better future.

It was only going off on my own and exploring leading-edge research that I discovered that we *do* participate emotionally, psychologically and spiritually in the *experience* of pain and its *level* of severity. Once participation was established, I had to face a choice—a choice, literally, of which way to face.

I could face the past and wonder how I could be such a despicable person as to cause myself all that suffering—an atmosphere charged with blame, guilt, and self-condemnation. Or, I could face the future—a future which, starting from the point of participation, led to hope and an eventual "miracle."

If I participated in the creation of pain, it must mean I could choose to change my participation and, therefore, my experience of pain. For the first time, I could see a ray of hope for my future. That ray of hope illuminated an aggressive search for ways to tap my innate power to be a victor over rather than a victim of the pain and crippling. The result was not only enlightenment but a physical "miracle."

I'll deal with the details of that "miracle" in Chapter Twelve. Suffice it here to say that fear of "blaming the victim" kept the medical professionals from giving me hope, a hope which illuminated a path to a "miracle." I could have remained safely within the assumption that I did nothing to cause the problem and, consequently, could do nothing to solve it. That position of emotional safety would have resulted in my spending the rest of my life in pain and in a wheelchair—a victim for life or, to put it more accurately, a victim for the rest of a miserable life.

It was only in confronting my participation in the pain experience that I found the path to victory. It was only by descending into the hell of personal responsibility that I found a heaven of response-ability. Yes, there was a seemingly hard choice—would I face the past or would I face the future? The fact is, it was not that difficult a choice at all—I had (and have) a lot more energy for fashioning the quality of the rest of my life, than I did (and do) in rehashing the past.

If our interest is in judgment we can face the past and spend our time and effort condemning our shortcomings. If, however, our interest is in empowering our future we can choose to learn from the past and use that knowledge to transform a victim into a victor. A short-sighted compassion can be, in the long run, cruel. And empowerment, through knowledge and skills in response-ability, can occur in compassionate ways.

It is extremely important to be clear about the distinction between empowerment and neat, easy, simple guarantees. Epoch III will give much more attention to empowerment, exploring the vast resources that we have so grossly under-utilized in Epoch II. This does not mean life is so simple as to have a direct correlation between effort and results. A transformed victor may not get rid of all the pain, may not be cured of cancer, and surely all of the victors will eventually die. But a victor transforms the experience, in any case, whether that be a transformed quality of life or a transformed quality of dying. The transformation—from victim to victor—is absolutely incredible when experienced first-hand. The theoreticians and outside experts—needless to say, I have strong feelings on this matter—should either facilitate that transformation or get out of the way. At the least, stop telling people it can't be done.

In Epoch II we have been too cautious, too afraid to risk, and too familiar with playing the victim role. Our fear of potential disappointment has kept us from empowering, with vigor, the potential of high hopes. And we have not given enough attention to how fear, caution, and the victim role keep us from realizing our potential for health and wholeness.

Consider, for instance, the frequent practice of a physician giving a patient the most depressing prognosis possible—the physician might call it the most "realistic" prognosis, for fear of raising "false hopes." Such caution, however, does not adequately consider the costs of false despair and pessimism. The costs are considerable—unnecessary suffering, "miracles" that never happen, cures that are not realized, and happier and more fulfilling lives that never will be.

The late Norman Cousins, following his own dramatic experiences with illness, became very interested in how hope and optimism or, conversely, despair and pessimism, participate in the health/illness experience. In the ten years that Cousins was on the medical school faculty at UCLA he saw hundreds of patients, from whom he learned some important things about the role of the mind and emotions in the progress of disease.

He noticed that most patients experienced a worsening of their disease at the time of the diagnosis. He saw a panic and victim reaction to the diagnosis, the result of which was to make the disease worse. There was a passive compliance, a sense of hopelessness, a very child-like dependent relationship to the physician. These patients generally died quickly, and within the period of time the physician had predicted.

There was another group of people that Cousins studied while at UCLA, however—people who were just as sick and received just as dire diagnoses and prognoses. But, for some reason, these people

did not panic. They demonstrated a sense of personal determination—a defiant, independent, hope-filled determination. And they
had a very different experience with their disease—they lived
longer than the physicians predicted. They did not deny the diagnosis, Cousins points out, but they defied the verdict.

Cousins told about one particular patient, a woman in her late
70s. The woman had been given a diagnosis of terminal cancer and
the doctor told her she had four to six months to live. Cousins asked
the woman what she did then. The woman said, "I looked that
doctor in the eye and said—"You go straight to hell! God could give
me 4-6 months, but no other human being can predict my future.'"
Cousins asked her how long ago that conversation took place. "Six
years ago," the woman replied, "and I am still going strong."[16]

There is a great deal of evidence that suggests that a victim
attitude of hopelessness contributes greatly to the progress of
disease. In contrast, a victor attitude of hope and determination
contributes to health and well-being. Because of the Epoch II
emphasis on disease rather than on health, we have more research
on the former than on the latter.

Evidence linking a sense of hopelessness with the development
of cancer has been around a very long time. The second century
physician Galen observed that women who were depressed had
cancer more frequently than did women who were cheerful. In the
nineteenth century Dr. Walter Hyle Walsh examined a great amount
of evidence and wrote what has been called "an influential and
definitive book covering nearly all that was known about cancer at
that time." In it he stated:

> Much has been written on the influence of mental misery,
> sudden reverses of fortunes, and habitual gloominess of tem-
> per on the disposition of carcinomatous matter. . . . Facts of a
> very convincing character in respect to the agency of the mind
> in the production of this disease are frequently observed. I have
> myself met with cases in which the connection appeared so
> clear that. . . questioning its reality would have seemed a
> struggle against reason.[17]

We tend to be suspicious about knowledge of so long ago and
doubt the research validity, but moving into the twentieth century
we find one of the most thorough and long-term studies made by
Dr. Caroline Thomas of Johns Hopkins Medical Institutions in
Baltimore. Starting in the 1940s she collected psychological data on
seventeen successive classes of medical students—altogether some
1,337 healthy young adults. She followed those students over many

years to see what patterns emerged linking personality characteristics, early life events, habitual ways of dealing with stress, and their subsequent experience of health or illness.

At first Dr. Thomas thought she would find patterns that would inform our view about coronary heart disease, suicide, and other major health problems; she did not assume she would learn anything about cancer. She, up to that point, accepted the general medical paradigm that cancer was a disease unrelated to psychological factors. As the evidence began to accumulate, however, she had to confront a "striking and unexpected" finding—"the psychological profiles of those who have developed cancer (have) strong similarities to those who committed suicide."[18]

This startling observation is reinforced by the renowned New York psychiatrist Arnold Hutschnecker who writes:

> Cancer strikes me as a form of suicide in the unconscious of many people who, in reality, would never dare to express or to admit any thoughts on suicide, which they may reject for moral, religious, or other reasons.[19]

William Green, internist and professor of psychiatry at the University of Rochester, conducted research on leukemia and Hodgkin's disease patients and found that in 90% of the cases the disease started when the person was in emotional distress, feeling "helpless and hopeless."[20]

Later, at the same university, Arthur Schmale set up a project "to see if he could predict cancer through psychological means." Specifically looking for recent emotional losses and a sense of hopelessness, he correctly predicted in 36 cases out of 51 which persons would get cancer.[21]

Dr. Martin Seligman has devoted a career to studying the matters of helplessness and hopelessness versus a sense of control, of pessimism versus optimism, and their respective relationships with health and illness. He started out with laboratory mice and trained them in helplessness and hopelessness, not letting them escape electric shocks regardless of what they did—in other words, he trained them to feel like victims. He trained others in the experience of being able to help themselves, to master their circumstance—in other words, he trained them to feel like victors.

Dr. Seligman then injected both groups with cancer cells and gave them additional stress. The result was that 70% of the mice who had learned hopelessness developed tumors, whereas only 32% of those who had learned mastery did so.[22]

Dr. Seligman then moved his research to human beings. One study asked women, three months after having a mastectomy for breast cancer, what they thought about their disease and how they expected it to affect their lives. Five years later, 75% of those who expressed optimism and the belief that they could control their destiny were still alive. Only 35% of those who expressed feelings of pessimism and hopelessness were still alive.[23]

Seligman, through decades of research, has found that optimists (those with a victor mentality) are life's big winners. They succeed more often than the pessimists (those with a victim mentality) in school, in athletics, on the job, and in their personal health. Pessimists have weaker immune systems, get sick more often, suffer depression more often, and have many more major health problems after age 45.

The most important implication of Dr. Seligman's research, however, is that these respective attitudes are learned and can be unlearned, if we so desire. There would be little value in pointing up the connection of hopelessness and disease if it were not for the fact that we can do something about changing destructive attitudes and choosing more healthy ones.

As Marilyn Ferguson said, "our past is not our potential." Regardless of how we developed negative attitudes and a general sense of hopelessness and pessimism about our lives, we can change. Our future can, at least to a great extent, be what we choose it to be.

Dr. Seligman, in his most recent book *Learned Optimism*, shows the specific techniques he has used to cure people of "learned helplessness" and to foster a healthy optimism. He includes tests so that you can measure how pessimistic or optimistic your style is before you make whatever adjustments you want to make. He also shows the extensive research upon which his theories are based.[24]

Illness as Teacher:
On Loving Your Stumbling Blocks and Transforming them into Stepping Stones

Our Epoch II adolescence has been, increasingly, on a pill-popping, "cut it out," quick-fix, and instant gratification binge. We want quicker and quicker solutions until we ask, as Carrie Fisher did in *Postcards from the Edge*, "Why does instant gratification take so long?" We want freedom from pain and we want it now. We want the elimination of any symptom and will take any medicine or submit to any surgery to get it done. We watch the TV to see what medication acts the fastest and then rush out to get it. Symptomatic relief has been our adolescent code of action, and we don't much care if we get to the cause.

In Epoch III, however, we will take a more mature approach to such matters. We will give more attention to what we have always known at some level—that a symptom is just that, a symptom of something going wrong. By growing beyond the immature short-sightedness and desire for instant gratification we will begin to live into the larger and longer view that mature wisdom brings. We will start looking more at what the symptom can tell us about that which is going wrong. We will look at the symptom as a message, usually a symbolic message, regarding the more serious matters of our life. We will start exploring the spiritual metaphoric messages in how our materialized spirit is "speaking" to us.

What does your heart attack say about how you are choosing to live your life—physically, nutritionally, emotionally, or spiritually? What does your cancer say about how you are dealing with the stresses of life? What does your autoimmune disease say about how you feel about yourself? Etc., etc., etc.

Several cancer physicians have suggested a symbolic connection between a disease in which cell growth has gone wild and the stagnation of spiritual growth. Is there a symbolic message in stomach trouble regarding something in our life that we "can't stomach?" Does a "pain in the neck" symbolically refer to how we think about someone or something in our daily lives?

Pain in another part of the anatomy was the subject of a telephone call I received from a hospital bed in Indianapolis. "You don't know me," the caller started out, "but I just read your book, *The Spirit of Synergy*, and I feel like sharing with you what is going on in my life right now." The man explained to me that he was a clergyman and he was in the hospital recuperating from surgery for colon cancer.

With plenty of time to think the man said he began reflecting on possible symbolic meaning to his disease. He was inclined to think disease is never *only* a physical problem. After considerable soul-searching he had decided that, if he was really truthful with himself, he had to admit he didn't like being a minister. In fact, he considered his entire work, and particularly his parishioners, as just one big "pain in the ass." He told me his soul-searching led him to a very important conclusion—"I won't heal up *this* pain in the ass, until I resolve *that* pain in the ass." He continued his frank confession—"I have decided that essential to my healing process will be a search for another line of work."

It should be said that a story like this does not *prove* that being in the wrong profession caused the man's colon cancer, nor does it necessarily prove that a change will assure his healing. But it should also be said that "proof" is looking for answers, and we are dealing here more with questions. Could a deep feeling of being in the wrong line of work contribute to the body's rebellion? And could the process of getting your whole being aligned with what you feel best about contribute to healing? We might not, as yet, have all the medical proof to provide absolute answers, but there are an increasing number of us who believe in following the questions.

Symbols are a form of language that do more to raise pregnant questions than to provide neat simple answers. To glean the most out of "illness as teacher," to have the greatest chance of giving birth to a new and healthier life, we need to explore those questions. Although I doubt the poet R. M. Rilke was intending to speak to this particular issue, he hit the nail on the head when he wrote:

> Have patience with everything unresolved in your heart and try to love the *questions themselves* as if they were locked rooms or books written in a very foreign language. . . . Live the questions now. Perhaps then, someday far in the future, you will gradually, without even noticing it, live your way into the answers.[25]

Indeed. If we wait until we get medical proof for the symbolism in physical disease, we will continue to suffer with illness for a long time while the medical paradigm shifts. If we are interested in healing and well-being, we will not think in terms of answers but live and love the questions. As Rilke pointed out, they are written in a foreign language—foreign to our Epoch II literal minds because they are in a symbolic language.

III. Synergy Empowered Relationships

For one human being to love another human being: that is perhaps the most difficult task that has been entrusted to us, the ultimate task, the final test and proof, the work for which all other work is merely preparation. . . .

Loving does not at first mean merging, surrendering, and uniting with another person (for what would a union be of two people who are unclarified, unfinished, and still incoherent—?), it is a high inducement for the individual to ripen. . . it is a great, demanding claim. . . something that chooses (us) and calls (us) to vast distances.
                                                  —Rainer Maria Rilke

Just as we found the concept of synergy giving maturity and texture to holism, so also does synergy in relationships give maturity and fulfillment to the empowerment of the individual. Just as synergy keeps holism from drifting into a bland homogeneity, so also does relationship keep individual empowerment from getting stuck in a truncated individualism. Synergy gives holism the "more than"—a synergistic relationship gives individual empowerment the "more than."

We had to start with empowering the individual, for a relationship that will result in the "more than" cannot occur without empowered individuals coming together. As Paul Tillich put it, "The right self-love and the right love of others are interdependent, [just as] selfishness and the abuse of others are equally interdependent."[26] If we are to love others in a mature fashion, so that synergy is the result, we must first of all be empowered individuals. And much if not all the failure of relationships to be empowering is because the individuals are not whole, healthy, and holy to start with.

But, on the other hand, an individual is never fully empowered in isolation, and mature healthy relationships are an essential ingredient for full empowerment.

(This subject could, quite obviously, range across the broad spectrum of family relationships of parent-child, siblings, etc. It could include relationships of friends and/or colleagues. It could include relationships with other races, religions, and/or nationalities. Once again, however, this broad-scope discussion cannot cover all implications and must focus on one simply to illustrate the point. I am choosing to focus on the intimate, primary relationship of the man-woman partnership or marriage. This choice, however, is not to imply any judgment regarding homosexual relationships. I simply don't know that kind of relationship, so will leave its discussion to those who do. There are already too many heterosexuals pontificating about homosexuality—something about which they know little or nothing.)

Burning in a Transformational Flame: *the Epoch II "Filmstrip" on Men and Women:*

Epoch II has had a very influential and all-pervasive "filmstrip" of patriarchy projected onto the screen of our lives and culture. We have used the term "projection" before in referring to our failure to "own" our psychological and emotional stuff and the propensity to project it outside onto other people. John Welwood does as good a job as anyone in helping us understand the term "projection."

> Like a light that shines forth on the world around us, awareness usually passes through the 'filmstrip' of our stories. As a result, we project these stories, along with all the pre-assigned roles they contain, onto the world and other people. What we generally see, then, is the movie we are projecting rather than things as they are in themselves.[27]

The Epoch II film that has influenced our understanding of "woman" and "man," as well as the relationships between the two, has been that of an adolescent patriarchy. Therefore, empowering either men or women is a tricky and difficult task in and of itself as we attempt to move from Epoch II into Epoch III, let alone the complexity brought about in achieving the synergistic "more than" of healthy, whole, and holy relationships.

There is one kind of challenge for women who have been the dominated, and quite a different kind of challenge for men who have been the dominator. They are, perhaps, complementary paths toward wholeness, but different.

As is typical in social movements, the dominated are the first to recognize injustice and usually the first to take steps to correct it. The persecuted are, understandably, the first to demand change. The dominator and the persecutor are generally reactive rather than proactive. And they react in rather predictable ways.

From the time we entered our dark night of the soul in the 1960s it has been women who first fought against patriarchy. (There were women fighting this fight before the 1960s, but as a social movement that gained a "critical mass" it is appropriate to look to the recent two or three decades.) I don't need to belabor this point, for one would have to have been asleep or in a coma for at least twenty years to be unaware of the various aspects of this struggle. There is a vast and insightful literature of how women can burn the Epoch II "filmstrip" in the fire of transformation and how they can overcome the deep-seated wounds of millennia of patriarchy.

It is not simple or easy to transform one's own "minority" mentality, even though women are actually in the majority. It is not easy to stop being disempowered in almost every aspect of life, even when that disempowerment comes from being put on a protected pedestal. Nor is it easy to burn the "filmstrip" regarding the projection of wounds and anger onto men who are growing, or have grown, past male chauvinism. But frankly, and not surprisingly from an historical perspective, women are ahead of men, generally speaking, regarding this transformation. There is a vast literature of women (and some men) speaking to this liberation of women from Epoch II. There is a smaller but growing literature for liberating men from Epoch II.

Make no mistake about it, men need liberation from Epoch II if they are to mature beyond the adolescent notions of power and become internally empowered. Men need liberation from an adolescent notion of masculinity if they are to grow into a healthy and mature masculinity. And no matter how much women mature into Epoch III they will not find healthy, holy, synergistic heterosexual relationships if men remain stuck in adolescent Epoch II. It is, however, a very different kind of challenge that faces men in this transitional time.

For we men to make this transformation we must cultivate sacred eyes so as to perceive the soul-level immaturity of Epoch II, the soul-level transition that is taking place, and the soul-level new maturity emerging as we move into Epoch III.

There has tended to be a rather predictable pattern of reaction, when sacred vision is missing, for those who have been in a favored, dominator status. Generally, the first reaction has been to project the problem out onto those who confront us with our injustices. *They* are the problem, in this case the "radical feminists." We don't know why they are so disturbed—"After all, we have generally taken care of them, haven't we? Those 'women's lib-ers' are just trouble makers!"

The second reaction has typically been that of obstinacy—*they* are making life difficult. *They* are upsetting the status quo. So our job is to stand pat, resist in every way possible. When they persist, get angry. Some men take their stance of obstinacy firmly behind an Epoch II interpretation of the Bible and Christianity—"God is male, Jesus was male, so women were clearly meant to be second class. If God made it that way, who are we to challenge it?"

The third reaction has, at least for those men who were trying to be sensitive, included guilt, a loss of identity and mirroring what some women thought a man should be like. With at least some recognition of the rightfulness of the feminist perspective, some men acknowledged that there were major problems in the immaturity of the Epoch II patriarchy. But in giving up an immature notion of masculinity, they had no clue as to what a mature masculinity was like. And taking their clues from women they fashioned a notion of masculinity *defined by women.*

The point here is that women cannot receive an adequate definition and understanding of essential femininity from men and, conversely, men cannot receive an adequate definition and understanding of essential masculinity from women. The women's movement has contributed greatly to women becoming virgins, but masculine virginity has been a bit slower in coming. For much of the 1970s and '80s, men who were attempting to make the transition from Epoch II into Epoch III got their notion of masculinity from women.

None of the above reactions, in my opinion, are adequate for masculine empowerment—an empowerment that is necessary if healthy, mutually empowering relationships with women can take place. For both men and women, empowered individuality as well as empowered relationships come from burning the Epoch II "film-strip" and then rediscovering our true essential nature by going back again into the wilderness.

"I'll meet you in the wilderness."

Reiterating what we have said several times before, our adolescence started when we separated ourselves from nature. In doing so, we separated ourselves from our instinctual and "wild" inner nature, eventually taking on the "nice" and "tame" aspects of civilization. But more importantly for our discussion here, we adopted an adolescent patriarchy which, for millennia, distorted our notions of masculinity and femininity. What came to dominate us, as Robert Moore and Douglas Gillette term it, is a "boy psychology."

Epoch III is the maturation of "boy psychology" into fully empowered humanity—respectively, fully empowered femininity and masculinity. A crucial part of that maturation is the rediscovery of, a reunion of, and a communion with our wilderness. Getting back in touch with, as Robert Bly speaks of it, our "wild man," or "wild woman," gets us in touch with what we were meant to become—empowered men and empowered women who can then come together in synergistic relationships.

What we discover in the wilderness is who we innately are and not what the distortions of Epoch II have said we were. The first thing we discover is what power is all about.

In Epoch II we thought power, in relationship to others, was power over others. We had power to the extent that we could control others, or at least had more power (control, money, prestige) than others. Power, therefore, was a win-lose situation—to be empowered was to disempower others. So a man was powerful if he controlled others, usually with military might, monetary might, or position of authority. A woman was powerful if she controlled others by sex, cunning, or manipulation. But usually in Epoch II the primary systems and institutions have been controlled by men to empower men and to disempower women.

As we move into Epoch III those notions of power will increasingly be seen as immature and inadequate. Power will be seen as essentially internal—the extent to which a man or woman is empowered from the inside out. We will know a powerful person by the extent to which they are in touch with, at home in, their instinctual manliness or womanliness—in other words, their innate wilderness.

It is in the wilderness where a woman will find her unique version of feminine soul. It is in the wilderness where she will find an integrity and "at-home-ness" which knows, from the inside out, what femininity is in general and what her expression of that is in particular. In the same way, it is in the wilderness that a man will find what instinctual and natural masculinity is all about, not the "boy psychology" that has so dominated the recent five thousand years. In the wilderness we men will find our own special version of masculine soul and discover our integrity, our health and our holiness, to which we have so far been blind. Sacred eyes, masculine as well as feminine, gain their acuity in the wilderness.

Robert Bly is right when he rejects the notion of the "soft male" in favor of the man who has a "fierce tenderness." The men and women of Epoch III are not some fuzzy, murky, androgynous "person"—the word "person," incidentally, comes from "persona," meaning a mask. Rather than wearing a mask of "personhood," we will be fully empowered men relating to fully empowered women, and vice versa. That is where the health and wholeness is and that is where the sparks fly in a synergetic hot holiness.

Teilhard de Chardin often spoke of love as *the* inexhaustible source of energy, and he often likened its power to that of fire. Teilhardian scholar Ursula King writes that, "The symbol of fire, so frequent in his writings, stands for the warmth and radiance of love and light as well as for the fusion and transformation of the elements."[28] It is no coincidence that we are star-children discovering fire and light as we rediscover our able-ness inherent in our genetic star-power.

In this case, the power is found in the discovery of the fire and enlightenment of love. It is a discovery, in the wilderness of our essential nature, that can transform our Epoch II immaturity into Epoch III maturity.

The first transformation has to do with empowering our essential masculinity if we are male, or our essential femininity if we are female. The second transformation has to do with empowering our inner opposite—the minority feminine element within the masculine, and the minority masculine element within the feminine. And the third transformation has to do with the synergistic relationship, when two fully empowered people come together for the glorious "more than."

It is another confirmation that this is the time of transition from Epoch II into Epoch III that the women's movement emerged with a new energy in the 1970s, and that the men's movement started gaining attention in the 1980s. It is also verification of this maturation taking place that renewed attention has been given recently to the inner opposite.

Make no mistake about it, however, the notion that a mature man has an inner feminine element and that a mature woman has an inner masculine element is not a concoction of contemporary pop psychology or the human potential movement. It has been known at least as far back as the fifth century B.C. in Eastern philosophy, articulated in the *I Ching*, and was referred to as the yin (the feminine) and yang (the masculine) principles. Reality as a whole, and individuals in particular, are a flowing intercourse between the two principles.

This matter has been written about extensively in recent years, so I need not belabor the point here. It is sufficient, in our discussion of the wilderness, to affirm that such complexity of personality is natural and instinctual. It is what we discover in the wilderness. It is quite contrary to the immature notions of sexual identity that define themselves either in contrast to, or in conformity with, the other. t is also contrary to the homophobia—the fear of homosexuals—so prevalent in those trying desperately to hold onto a dying Epoch II, wherein one tries to define masculinity or femininity without a trace of the opposite.

When we experience the wilderness, and discover our own true nature, then we are ready for synergistic relationships. Then, and only then, do we have empowered men and empowered women coming together in a sexual intercourse—and I am not talking here about genital sex—the result of which is a conception of a new life. The new life that emerges is the synergistic "more than" the sum of the individuals involved. The possibilities inherent in relationships have been so distorted by "boy psychology" in Epoch II that our collective idea of relationship has been terribly truncated. The synergistic "more than" of a relationship between an empowered man and an empowered woman will show us, in Epoch III, a "higher trajectory" of possibilities.

I want to return, for just a moment, to the larger issue of relationships in all their varied guises—with parents, children, partners, friends, business associates, bosses, employees, other nationalities, races, religions, etc., etc., etc. All that I would convey, if I were to take considerably more time and space to discuss each of them, eventually sifts out to a "bottom line," as they say. And that "bottom line" consists of two questions: *Is what you are bringing to the relationship empowering the other? Is the relationship empowering you?*

If the answer to either question is "no," then the follow-up question is: *Do you have the courage to change it?* To change yourself so that you can empower others, and/or to change the relationship so that you are empowered—both sides of that are necessary if we are to experience the full glory of what is possible in Epoch III relationships.

IV. THE COURAGE TO BE EMPOWERED

Love has sacred power not because it makes us high, allowing us to rise above ordinary life on clouds of blissful glory, but because it helps us relax the struggle between self and other that is at the root of human suffering. . . . The profound question love poses is, "Can you face your life as it is; can you look at all the pain and darkness as well as the power and light in the human soul and still say yes?"
—PSYCHOTHERAPIST JOHN WELWOOD

The journey of trying to discover and integrate the essential power of the universe, love, takes courage. The way of getting to the ontological "yes" is sometimes long and difficult.

It takes courage because we are in a transitional time and have to leave the all-too-familiar Epoch II. It is easier to drift along with what-is than it is to reach out for the not-quite-yet. It is easier to turn a deaf ear and a blind eye to the immaturity of Epoch II than it is to co-create with Spirit the emerging Epoch III.

It takes courage because everything is changing so fast. We'll dig into that subject in the next chapter, but for now let's simply say that rapid change calls us to dig deep into our courageous reserves.

It takes courage because to become empowered you have to discover your virginity—and finding your uniqueness takes more courage than simply conforming to someone else's image of you.

It takes courage because to become empowered you have to descend into hell, and that can be one hell of a trip. It's easier to stay on the surface and project your dark side onto someone else.

It takes courage because to become empowered you have to ascend into heaven and reach for the heights. That takes courage because we don't always achieve the heights we reach for and discouragement is the result. It's easier to be a pessimist, to be cautious and to be content with mediocrity, than to face the inevitability of disappointment. The trouble, however, is that in expecting the worst so as to avoid disappointment, we tend to invite the worst.

It takes courage to be empowered in a relationship and to be empowering of the other, because in reaching out for that hot holiness you sometimes get burned. It takes courage to be vulnerable to burns and the attendant pain even though it may be the fire of transformation.

It takes courage, but make no mistake about it, it can happen. It can happen because our courage is supported at the deepest levels of reality with an ontological love and acceptance. And the rewards are so wonderful and so substantial that, once experienced, we would never return to the blandness and shallowness of living only on the surface.

Seligman said that "each of us carries a word in his (or her) heart, a 'no' or a 'yes.'"[29] He was referring to our personal tendency toward either pessimism or optimism. I agree but would like to take that to a deeper level. If we have in our heart an essential 'no' it is for one of three reasons—all illusions.

First of all, if we have a "no" in our heart it could be because we have accepted the Epoch II entropic illusions. The illusions of separation, of disempowerment, of separation of the divine and human, of the insignificance of humanity, and/or the illusions that the world is going to hell in a hand-basket. It's the "no" in Murphy's Law, another illusion of the Epoch II pessimists.

Secondly, if we have a "no" in our heart it could be because we have had our heart wounded or deformed by someone of Epoch II immaturity. It could be a father who, still in adolescent "boy psychology," was too immature to relate to a child in ways that communicated the innate, ontological, "yes" of love. Or it could have been a husband who, for the same reasons, was unprepared to be in an empowering marriage. Or a mother, wife, or lover who, out of her own woundedness continued the wounding. For these, and many other reasons, some people know only how to magnify their own heart-felt "no" and pass it on.

During a materialistic Epoch II we have spoken of genetic inheritance only in physical, biological terms, but in a holistic Epoch III we will recognize spiritual genetics. Spiritual inheritance has to do with passing on a "no" or a "yes."

As is often said in the recovery movement—the wounded heart feels that, rather than having *made* a mistake, I *am* a mistake. No wonder some persons feel an essential "no" in their heart—it is real for them, no question about it. But if we look into the Spirit at the core of the universe with sacred eyes we see an essential, cosmic "YES." Consequently, any "no" is fundamentally an illusion.

Thirdly, if we have a "no" in our heart it could be simply because we have not yet matured enough to get below or above the surface of life. If we never penetrate to the core of life or if we never reach the heights of life we may be deluded into thinking life is a "no."

But deep in the wilderness is a discovery, a discovery of our innate connection with affirming love. It is a "YES" that was spoken at the moment of creation and a "YES" that is repeated over and over if we are listening. It is the "YES" that fuels the evolutionary ascent. It is the "YES" of the "withinness" of matter. It is the "YES" that is the gravitational "allurement" of the cosmos. And it is the "YES" that will be proclaimed loud and clear during Epoch III.

Out of the wilderness comes a story that illustrates this point—an East Indian myth called "The Roar of Awakening." It is a story about a pregnant tigress who breaks her neck in a fall, but gives birth to a male cub as she dies.

A flock of goats grazing nearby found the cub, took him in and raised him as one of their own. The baby tiger learned the ways of the goats and adapted his voice to their gentle bleating, for the goats were the only world he knew.

One night, however, a fierce old male tiger came upon the goats, let out a mighty roar, and all the flock went scurrying off—save one, the baby tiger, who for some reason was transfixed with the sound of the old tiger. The old jungle tiger could not believe what he was seeing—a baby tiger among the goats bleating as if he were one of them.

"What," the old tiger roared, "are you doing here among these goats?" The cub just shrugged his shoulders and bleated, showing his total confusion. Whereupon the old tiger picked up the cub by the scruff of his neck, carried him to a nearby pond, and forced him to look at his reflection in the water.

"We look alike," he pointed out. "We both represent fine tiger nature. How, then, do you imagine yourself to be a goat, bleating in that funny tone?"

Gradually a transformation took place as the young tiger looked at his reflection and then at the old tiger and as he gradually remembered who he really was. Finally the young tiger cub "stretched out his paws, lashed his tail, and opened his mouth with a mighty yawn, as though he were awakening from a long, long sleep. Then he threw back his head and gave forth a powerful roar."[30]

When we go into our wilderness we get in touch with our instinctual nature. We then can discover who we really are, and find deep within our own soul our special roar of awakening. Our roar will be a resounding "YES," for that is our nature. When we rediscover our essence we learn again that we are affirmed, accepted, loved, supported, and sustained with a cosmic "YES."

The cosmos roars a "YES" to our virginity—an affirmation of our unique version of Soul. It is a "YES" that we can feel well up and burst forth in our liberating roar of awakening. It is a "YES" that we can shout from our mountain-tops until it reverberates in our valleys. It is a "YES" that comes from our heaven so that it is felt as a healing force in our hell.

As we accept and absorb that cosmic "YES" we will cultivate the sacred eyes that can see the fore-given love which predates Epoch II's negativity, sacred eyes that can see ourselves as piece-images of the sacred whole, and sacred eyes that can see us climbing a mountain-top and letting out with our own unique roar of awakening. Sacred eyes, perceiving the hidden yes within its own nature proclaims, with uproarious vigor, a Sacred EeeeeeYES.

CHAPTER 10

BECOMING USER FRIENDLY WITH CHANGE

Change is avalanching upon our heads and most people are grotesquely unprepared to cope with it.
—CULTURAL ANALYST ALVIN TOFFLER

I. WE LIVE AMIDST CHANGE

EVERYTHING IN THE UNIVERSE, AS FAR AS WE CAN TELL, is changing, evolving, transforming. Nothing is static. Nothing stands still. Our survey, throughout this book, of the evolutionary past has been about little else. Life on this planet is precisely the result of the changes Father Sky and Mother Earth went through to become fit parents. The evolutionary journey which has brought humanity to this point in our development is, obviously, the result of change. And the central premise of this book—that the late twentieth century is an epoch-sized transformational time—assumes, also quite obviously, the matter of change.

Because humanity has been receptive to understanding changes, by and large, we have changed our collective minds throughout history. At one time we thought we were an integral part of nature—then we changed our minds and thought we were different from, and above, nature. We thought the world was flat—then we changed our minds. We thought the earth was the center of the universe—then we changed our minds. We thought the cosmos was spiritual—then we changed our minds. We thought humanity was special—then we changed our minds. And now we are going through additional, and major, changes of mind. Some of us keep trying, however, to stop the world. Having a basic dislike or fear of change, we still have a "flat earth society." We still have in our midst "creationists" who want us to stop teaching evolution in our schools. We still have biblical literalists and others who would like to have static, certain, simple, and clear answers to all of life's challenges—and want those answers to stand still.

Others of us, perhaps less fundamentalistic, try subtler means to accomplish the same desire. "Life is just a perpetual deja vu," we say. Wrong. "There is nothing new under the sun," we say. Not true. "The more things change, the more they stay the same," we say. Not so. In spite of our mental and emotional gymnastics in trying to statisize the world, the world keeps changing. It keeps spinning at 1,000 miles per hour, circling the sun at 66,000 miles per hour, and along with the solar system we are zipping through space at many hundreds of thousand miles per hour. And all the time, life here on this planet keeps evolving, changing, and transforming. We may not like it, but it's happening.

And least we think that static-itis affects only small minds and hearts, consider Albert Einstein, for instance. Other scientists started realizing that Einstein's grand and revolutionary theories of relativity actually predicted an expanding universe. Einstein, however, was emotionally committed to the prevailing notion of a "steady state" universe. In his attempt to maintain his belief in a steady state universe, and to prove the other scientists wrong, Einstein made a mathematical error in his counter-argument. Later, Einstein said it was his most foolish mistake and was caused because of trying to maintain and protect his earlier belief.

We have already discussed how, in the nineteenth century, change and the direction of change came into the scientific picture. We cast our lot—emotionally, psychologically, and spiritually— with the most pessimistic notions of change and entropy rather than with evolution. (Actually, the spiritual propensity for this was laid at the beginning of our adolescence when we separated heaven and earth, divine and human, etc. Once having so separated reality and having projected all good up and out, humanity was left with being depraved and helpless, needing salvation to come from the outside. Consequently, we could do nothing but change for the worse— unless or until we received outside help.)

Back on the matter of science, however, the Epoch II dichotomy between the negative notion of entropy and the more positive notion of evolution remained until the Nobel Prize winning contribution of the Belgian chemist, Ilya Prigogine. Prigogine, in the spirit of Epoch III synthesis, showed how both entropy and evolution are true.

Entropy, Prigogine explains, is true only for what he calls "closed" systems. Closed systems are ones that have no internal transformation of energy and drift toward disorder. A machine is an example of a closed system. It is very significant that mechanical models of the universe and of human beings have been used during the last three hundred years of Epoch II as metaphors for our understanding of life.

"Open" systems, in contrast, are alive and in constant exchange of energy, internally and externally. These systems are always in process, always in a flow of energy, always in flux, and always experiencing some degree of stress. It is, in fact, the flow, flux, and stress that is the key to transformation. If stress is sufficient enough, it is the fuel for transformation, a reordering. Such is the nature of evolution.

Erich Jantsch, an interpreter of Prigogine's work, said that the most fundamental result of the Nobel laureate's insights is the resurrection of hope.

> [It is]. . . the hope associated with *life*, with the dynamic notions of continuity and transformability, of being embedded in a purpose and meaning transcending ourselves and the lives of our transitory systems, the hope inherent in the nondualistic experience of *being* the stream.[1]
>
> This new type of science. . . orients itself primarily at models of life, and not mechanical models. . . . The basic themes are. . . self-determination, self-organization and self-renewal. . . . We are not the helpless subjects of evolution—we *are* evolution.[2]

Prigogine offers scientific minds a new point of view, new because of looking at models of evolving life, rather than basing our notions of the universe by studying entropic machines. Epoch II looked at the universe as a machine and concluded that everything was running down. Prigogine looks at models of life and writes, "what we see here on Earth is just the opposite of entropy. With the paradigm of self-organization we see a transition from disorder to order."[3]

Positive results from any evolutionary change, however, are not automatic—possible but not assured. Humanity has arrived at such a position of power and influence that we can make our participation negative or positive, destructive or constructive. We can live out an entropic spirituality and create a negative self-fulfilling prophecy, or we can choose to resonate with the natural built-in bias of the universe to evolve. We can participate in the co-creation of a "higher trajectory" of life. We can develop an evolutionary and hopeful spirituality and participate in a positive self-fulfilling prophecy. In doing so we become participating prophets of a collective coming of age.

Also, one of the dominant realities experienced in the twentieth century, is the pace of change. No question about it, the rate of change is escalating. The future is avalanching down upon us, as Alvin Toffler put it, and what we feel is "future shock."

Remember our use of the "cosmic year" illustration in Chapter Three? When we compressed the entire history of the universe into a one-year span, we had not developed into human beings until late on December 31st, did not discover fire until 11:46 p.m., and were finally drawing on cave walls by 11:59 p.m.

We get some sense of how things are speeding up when we realize that with our entire evolutionary journey compressed into one year, the life of Jesus occurred just four seconds before the end of the year. Modern science, the crowning achievement of Epoch II, has been around only the last second, and all the technological advances of this century have occurred in the last quarter of a second of our cosmic year. No wonder it feels like everything is happening faster and faster—it is.

A group of scholars led by Robert Anton Wilson attempted to measure the rate at which human knowledge has grown. To figure this out, they decided to determine how much humanity knew as of 1 A.D., and then figure out how long it took to double that amount of knowledge, and how long it took to double it again, etc. As scientists are wont to do, they named their little project after a famous person living at that time, dubbing it the "Jumping Jesus Phenomenon."

Their research indicated that the quantity of human knowledge as of 1 A.D. doubled by 1500 A.D., took only an additional 250 years to double again, and then just 150 years to double yet again. So, we had "one Jesus" in 1 A.D., "two Jesus" in 1500 A.D., "four Jesus" in 1750 A.D., and "eight Jesus" in 1900 A.D. By 1950 we were at "sixteen Jesus," and then only ten more years to double again. By 1988 we were doubling our amount of knowledge every year, so that by 1992 we had 65,536 times the amount of knowledge as humanity did in 1 A.D.

Other groups of scholars differ—some suggesting that our knowledge is doubling every eighteen months, some put it at every two years. Any such attempt is open for considerable controversy. The point, however—and who can argue with the essential message—

is that life is speeding up. The challenge to "keep up" gets tougher and tougher every year.

Social change was so slow up until the twentieth century, points out scientist and novelist C. P. Snow, "that it would pass unnoticed in one person's lifetime. That is no longer so. The rate of change has increased so much that our imagination can't keep up."[4]

Social psychologist Warren Bennis elaborates the same point by saying, "no exaggeration, no hyperbole, no outrage can realistically describe the extent and pace of change. . . In fact, only the *exaggerations* appear to be true."[5] (emphasis added)

"If it ain't broke, don't fix it," has been a favorite cliche in mainstream society which, by implication, assumes that things can stay the same and work very well. Increasingly, people responding to a world of rapidly escalating change have been changing that old cliche to: "If it ain't broke, fix it anyway." Business guru Tom Peters has his own version, emphasizing the pace of change: "If you don't think it's broke, you ain't looked."

Alice, in *Through the Looking Glass*, must have thought the whole world was broken when, after running very fast for a very long time with the White Queen, she still found herself at the same place.

> "Why, I do believe we've been under the tree the whole time," exclaimed Alice. "Everything's just as it was."
> "Of course it is," said the Queen. "What would you have it?"
> "Well, in *our* country," said Alice, still panting a little, "you'd generally get to somewhere else—if you ran very fast for a long time as we've been doing."
> "A slow sort of country," said the Queen. "Now, *here*, you see, it takes all the running you can do, to keep in the same place. If you want to get somewhere else, you must run at least twice as fast as that."[6]

What really grabs us is the *personal* impact of living in a world of rapidly escalating change. And all of us know that impact is substantial. There is increasing evidence that many of us are feeling the stress of not knowing how to keep up, let alone get ahead. It makes life seem like a race—rat or otherwise—and we are not sure we want to keep running as fast as we have been, let alone twice as fast. Sometimes we just feel sick and tired of being sick and tired of changes. We want to stop the world and get off.

There is a great deal of evidence from many different corners of medical research that suggests that a large amount of our disease is the result of not dealing effectively with changes in our lives.

As we discussed earlier, the bio-mechanical model of Epoch II medicine has looked for the causes of disease only where the light of their paradigm shines—namely, on physiological evidence. But as we become more holistic in Epoch III, we will surely come to discover that causes of illness come far more from the psyche than we have previously thought. And my strong suspicion is that we will discover that the deep spiritual issues in dealing with changes in our lives play significant roles.

If that suspicion proves to be right, the chronic diseases of our time will never be "cured" until we learn to integrate spiritual and physical matters of health and illness. And how we deal with change may prove a, if not *the*, central issue.

Like it or not, we are not going to stop the world from changing. So we have a choice: to either continue living uncomfortably in fear of and resistance to change, or to find a way to live creatively in and through change. Our primary choice at the end of the twentieth century apears to be choosing between dis-ease and disease resulting from discomfort with change, or health and wholeness through effective resonance with change.

II. THE STRATEGY FOR BECOMING USER-FRIENDLY WITH CHANGE

> *To put it bluntly, we need a different kind of human being. . . [one who is] able to live in a world which changes perpetually, which doesn't stand still. . . [We need] to make ourselves over into people who don't need to staticize the world, who don't need to freeze it and to make it stable, who don't need to do what their daddies did, who are able confidently to face tomorrow not knowing what's going to come. . . and who can improvise in that situation which has never existed before.*
>
> —PSYCHOLOGIST ABRAHAM MASLOW

In a world in which everything is changing, and changing faster and faster, the skills with which to deal with change effectively and productively are invaluable. We need a strategy to become user-friendly with change.

No one's life can have a sense of well-being without an effective strategy for dealing with the escalating rate of change. And no religion can effectively facilitate spiritual growth without making a central issue of how the phenomenon of change, unique in its nature to *our* time, participates in the life of the spirit.

We need a strategy that can help us transform our experience of change from victim to victor. We need a strategy that can transform our fear of and resistance to change into an opportunity for healthy growth and development.

Ironically, the strategy effective for this new time is not a new invention. It is not some brand new insight from late-twentieth century pop psychology, from some esoteric New Age spiritual fad, nor from the writings of a contemporary futurist. It is, rather, a strategy as old as the human spiritual journey itself, rooted deep in our collective unconscious. It is a strategy borrowed from the past and given contemporary relevance. It is a strategy applicable for both our superficial daily challenges and our deep spiritual pilgrimage, for us as individuals as well as for our collective spiritual transformation.

The strategy for becoming user-friendly with change is none other than the archetypal heroic journey. The heroic journey is so fundamental a process of empowerment, so common throughout human experience, and manifested in so many different cultures, that Joseph Campbell entitled his classic book about it, *The Hero With A Thousand Faces*. It is a very specific pattern found throughout human cultures with a multitude of expressions. It is the same song of spiritual empowerment sung in all the world's different languages. It is the same picture painted in all the different colors of the rainbow. It is so fundamental to the human experience that Campbell borrowed James Joyce's term and called it humanity's "monomyth." It is the master myth of human spiritual empowerment. It also provides us with a very practical strategy for handling day-to-day changes in our lives. It is a remarkably effective strategy for guiding us through either the most grandiose of life changes or the most mundane of everyday changes.

The heroic adventure, the monomyth, has just three stages: first, departure or separation from the world as it is; second, initiation into new found power and; third, a return to the world to serve, in light of that empowerment. Separation, empowerment, and return—a three stage journey gleaned from humanity's past experience which provides our Epoch III strategy for utilizing change as a spiritual catalyst. It is a resource gleaned from deep in humanity's psyche that can facilitate our future health and well-being.

Since it is a strategy as old as human culture we have plenty of role models, many people who have already experienced this empowering process. It is the process used in many native cultures for "coming of age" transitions. "Rites of passage" varied from culture to culture but they have usually involved the same basic three stages of separation, empowerment, and return. In many native cultures this process was used as the means by which a person was given their name, an indication of their power animal, or their particular contribution to the community.

The heroic journey also describes the life process for the central figures in some of the world's major religions. Take the Buddha, for instance. In the sixth century B.C. prince Gautama Sakyamuni, at age twenty-nine, renounced his life of luxury, slipped out of his father's palace at night, and rode his horse into the wilderness. He sheared off his royal locks, put on the garments of a monk, and became a beggar. He spent seven years in the wilderness encountering various powers—temptations, miracles, and initiations. On the last night, sitting under the Bo tree, he acquired "knowledge of his previous existences. . . the divine eye of omniscient vision, and. . . understanding of the chain of causation. He experienced perfect enlightenment at the break of day."[7]

Gautama returned to the world as the Buddha, the enlightened one, and for the next forty years served a ministry of sharing his knowledge of the Way throughout India. Separation, initiation, and return—the Buddha's life journey.

Six centuries later Jesus of Nazareth lived out his version of the monomyth. It has remarkable similarity to that of the Buddha's, only each stage for Jesus was substantially shortened.

Jesus, also at about age 29, entered the wilderness following his baptism in the river Jordan by John the Baptist. In contrast to the Buddha's seven years Jesus spent forty days in the wilderness, but like the Buddha, Jesus' experience in the wilderness was that of facing temptation and discovering his innate power. And in contrast to the Buddha's return to a forty year ministry, Jesus returned for a ministry of only about three years before he was crucified. Separation, empowerment, and return to serve—the monomyth again lived out in a major spiritual journey.

The point here is that this heroic adventure of three stages is an effective strategy for everyone of us—for the nitty-gritty experiences of change that we face in our daily life, or for our entire life journey. It is a radical democratization of the most profound process of spiritual transformation. You and I can utilize the same process that characterized the lives of Buddha and Christ and use it as a strategy for our own life, transforming unwanted or scary change into a spiritual and productive journey.

Let's take a more specific look at how each stage works and then examine some examples of how we can plan heroic journeys through changes. We will also explore how we can respond heroically to changes which are thrust upon us involuntarily.

Separation

The first stage of the heroic journey is becoming separated from the past or from the status quo. The transformation from victim to victor takes place when we interpret the separation not as something to be condemned but as an opportunity for an empowering adventure. We can choose to make the act of separation into an act of growth, whether it was self-selected or destiny calling us forth.

The first challenge one faces, and the triumph necessary to even begin the process, is simply the willingness to separate. Campbell speaks of this challenge, again in mythological terms, as the necessity to confront and slay the "monster of the status quo: Holdfast, the keeper of the past." Knowing about and learning from the past are beneficial aspects in one's life, but the past becomes monstrous if we hold onto it, if we try to rigidify life and not let the future be born. Transitions are pregnant moments in one's life, and the question is whether we will deal with them in ways that give birth to a new life or leave our future possibilities stillborn.

If we reluctantly enter an experience of separation with eyes glazed over because of fear or resistance, we will be blind to the possibilities of empowerment. In contrast, however, if we look at transitions with sacred eyes we can sing with amazing grace, "I once was blind, but now I see."

A revealing personal test is to candidly examine one's basis for self-identity. If our self worth and identity are rooted rigidly in something or someone in the past or present, the monster of Holdfast will keep us from moving into the creative and empowering future. This is why change is experienced as threatening—it threatens our very sense of who we are. When we are captive of the monster Holdfast it is no wonder we resist change.

Various religions have waxed eloquent about the virtues of detachment and the sin of idolatry. We can be idolatrous by worshiping the past—whether the object of our worship be a person, a person's experience, an institutional history, or our own past self image.

Dr. Scott Peck starts out his book that has so remarkably fed a spiritual hunger in the general public, *The Road Less Traveled*, by stating bluntly, "Life is difficult." He goes on to discuss mid-life crises and says that to move through the major transitions of life in a healthy manner:

> We must give up cherished notions and old ways of doing and looking at things. Many people are either unwilling or unable to suffer the pain of giving up the outgrown which needs to be forsaken. Consequently they cling, often forever, to their old patterns of thinking and behaving, thus failing to negotiate any crisis, to truly grow up, and to experience the joyful sense of rebirth that accompanies the successful transition into greater maturity.[8]

Peck's words have a double meaning for our discussion. What he says is true for the individual, in terms of growing up, and it is true for the larger collective maturation of humanity that provides the central theme of this book. We are living individual adventures in and through change in the midst of a collective transformation. We can choose to participate in making both our own story and humanity's story the heroic journey out of the past and into a more empowered future.

Encounter with power

Having taken the first step in the hero/heroine journey—separation—the door opens wide for new perception, a change of consciousness, and the acquisition of new power. Having separated from ordinary reality, if we are looking with sacred eyes, we can see the extraordinary power available to us.

The separation from the status quo and the encounter with new powerful possibilities is not always a pleasant process. It can be downright scary, which is why courage is a necessary element. That, however, should come as no surprise—after all, it is called an heroic adventure. But as we discussed in the last chapter, we have access to a profoundly powerful source of courage at the core of our being. We need only remember who we are, and the courage is available.

There are many stories told throughout every culture of this courageous leap into the future and the encounter with and acquisition of new power. Jacob, in the Old Testament, is one such story: another role model out of the past who can give us hints as to how we can face our own future.

The particular experience I am referring to started with Jacob sleeping in the wilderness by a stream. Whether it was a dream or a waking mystical experience we are not sure, but Jacob was jolted out of his ordinary experience and into an extraordinary encounter with power.

Jacob was jumped upon by a divine spirit and they had a wrestling match. It wasn't a pretty or pleasant experience. It was down and dirty. It was a long ordeal, lasting the entire night.

Jacob demonstrated courage in the face of this powerful spiritual confrontation. He did not whimper in fright, call out for mercy, nor try to run from the encounter. He recognized it as an important opportunity in his spiritual journey and was determined to come away from it more whole and more informed. He refused to give up the struggle until he had found out the meaning of the struggle—"I will not let you go unless you bless me," Jacob declared. The divine spirit responded by telling Jacob, "Your name shall no longer be Jacob, but Israel."[9]

A person's name, in Jacob's time, was not simply a whim or fancy of one's parents. It was a very personal identification, indicating who you really were as a person. Consequently, the name change suggested by the divine spirit was a very significant event. It was literally a description of a change in identity. It revealed Jacob's inner essence, namely, "Israel" which literally means "to be a wrestler with God."

To be a wrestler with God meant that Jacob's role, his power, was to be as one who takes the spiritual journey seriously. He was meant to grapple with the really important issues of life. Jacob said he would not let go until the divine spirit blessed him. And, indeed, he was blessed with a new identity, a new name, and a "calling." Jacob followed that blessing into a life of spiritual leadership.

It is significant that Jacob's heroic process took place in the wilderness, just as it is significant that the wilderness played such a major role in the spiritual journeys of the Buddha and the Christ. It was in separating ourselves from the wilderness that we collectively entered our adolescence and it is in the wilderness that much of our lost power resides. It is in the wilderness that life is untamed, uncontrolled, and unpredictable. We civilized people have tamed, controlled, and predicted a lot of our power—with our disempowerment as the result.

Notice, for instance, that in Jesus' experience it was not the Devil that led him into the wilderness, but the Holy Spirit. It was the Spirit of the Holy, the Spirit of Health, and the Spirit of Wholeness that led him into a confrontation with his dark, repressed, and wild nature.

So it is with any change in our lives, large or small. In the separation from ordinary reality we can encounter the powers of revelation, showing us something new about ourselves. In the more dramatic instances we are given a new identity and a new agenda for the next phase of our lives—in doing so we become, in a sense, a Buddha, a Christ, or an Israel.

Whether pleasant or painful, delightful or scary, the encounter with power can be an incredible blessing. As we discussed earlier, to follow one's blessings is an essential element of Epoch III spirituality. And that brings us to the third stage of the heroic journey.

Return to Serve

Contrary to some of the adolescent versions of spirituality manifested in Epoch II, mature spirituality always balances the inner search with outer service. So, also, with the heroic monomyth. The journey does not conclude with revelation or empowerment but with a return to the world to serve. There may be a deeply personal and solitary process of separation and of encounter with power, but the journey is spiritually mature only as the power is then shared with others for the purpose of greater health and wholeness for humanity and the planet.

In appropriate Epoch III manner there is a recycling dimension to the heroic journey. We seldom experience only one change in life. So after returning to serve, another separation invariably comes along and we are off on the classic adventure again. Separation, empowerment, and return—again and again. With each adventure we become more empowered—more healthy, holy, and whole. And with each adventure we become more user-friendly with changes in our lives and are able to contribute more to the world.

So, from across the ages and from the depths of the collective human unconscious, manifested in numerous cultures and religions, we are given an incredible gift—a rather clear and simple, though not simplistic, strategy for spiritual growth and for handling change in an effective and productive manner. It can be a *macro* strategy to guide our entire life journey, and/or it can be a *micro* strategy for growth and development within the little changes of everyday life. Living the monomyth can integrate the most grandiose experiences of our lives with the mundane changes we experience almost daily. It can give meaning and purpose to our experience of change. In short, it can sanctify our daily lives.

We turn now to some brief examples of how the monomyth can be an effective strategy in our planned intentional changes, before turning to the unplanned and unintentional experiences of change.

III. Planned Heroic Adventures

[We must] always remain acutely conscious that [our] condition is that of a traveller. . . homo viator. . . It is precisely the soul that is the traveller; it is of the soul and of the soul alone that we can say with supreme truth that "being" necessarily means "being on the way."
—PHILOSOPHER GABRIEL MARCEL

Meditation

Meditation can be a brief yet powerful experience of the monomyth. In just fifteen or twenty minutes one can separate from the superficial world of rapid, sometimes frantic brain activity and nitty-gritty daily chores, gain a new level of empowerment, and return to a life of greater service.

Each experience, taken by itself, may seem to make only a small gain in empowerment and service but the accumulation of such experiences can have a powerful life-enhancing effect. On the other hand, don't count out the possibility of a dramatic breakthrough coming from any one such experience—profound changes can occur with a suddenness that boggles our linear time-oriented mind.

There are many "methods" regarding the meditative experience. My purpose here is not to survey all the various forms of meditation—there have been many of us who have written entire books on the subject—but simply to recommend it as a marvelous intentional version of the heroic journey.

The empowerment may come from the Eastern preference of experiencing the "void," or the more Western propensity of paying attention to the images or insights that emerge from deep consciousness. Whatever. The point is that incredible power is available from our depths when we intentionally separate from our ordinary superficial daily routines. Meditation is one of the most accessible, brief, and potentially powerful forms of the heroic journey.

One aspect that deserves an extra comment, however, is the value derived from learning to control attention. The ability to focus attention, to concentrate, is one of the several benefits of a meditative discipline, and a skill extremely valuable in many other aspects of one's life. Developing the ability to laser the light of your consciousness can play a powerful role in your life—superficial daily activity or major enlightenment, business or professional skills, sports, music, or education.

William James, a Harvard psychologist of almost a century ago, pointed out how this skill would enhance education in general: "The faculty of voluntarily bringing back a wandering attention over and over again is the very root of judgement, character and will. . . . An education which would improve this faculty would be education par excellence."[10]

As Epoch II fades and Epoch III begins to emerge it is understandable that we would have an increase in dissatisfaction with the old models of education and a increasing desire for reform similar to what occurs in many fields at such a soul-transition time. The problem is that we often have Epoch II minds trying to suggest reform, rather than putting Epoch III imaginations to work on the substantive changes needed in the educational enterprise.

The above quote from William James is a case in point. He talks with an Epoch III quality, suggesting that education would serve us better if basic skills like concentration were taught rather than just learning facts that soon change or are out of date. Concentration is one of those skills which have many spin-off benefits, which provide tools for life-long learning, and which can help us become user-friendly with a world of rapid change.

I could go on and on about Epoch III education—it is such an important realm regarding our future health and well-being—but educational reform is not the main subject in this chapter. Both the glory and the agony of a holistic paradigm is that any one subject is in some way interrelated with every other subject. Thus, the temptation for tangential discussions. But, for now, back to the survey of intentional means of becoming user-friendly with change via the heroic adventure.

Retreats

A more mainstream way of experiencing a relatively brief journey of empowerment is what is commonly called a "retreat." Whether it be a day, a weekend, or a longer period of time, a retreat is an opportunity for the heroic adventure—departure, empowerment, and return.

Simply going away or taking some time off from one's regular schedule obviously does not automatically make it a heroic adventure. It takes some intentionality to transform a leave-taking from that of only leaving to that of a readiness for new insight and empowerment. It can be just a break in the action, or it can be a breakthrough to a new level of living. It can be mind-boggling, spirit-stretching, life-changing, and world-shaking to stop and smell the roses.

It is interesting how often we choose nature as the place for our experience of the monomyth. There is apparently something deep within us wanting to recover what we lost when we separated from nature. We long for the power available in our collective "inner child."

As we transit from Epoch II into Epoch III, as we come of age into the fullness of adult maturity, our desire to rediscover our connection with nature is increasing. In unprecedented numbers those who can afford to do so are moving to the country, having a "retreat" second home in the country, or are availing themselves of special times in nature—camping, back-packing, hiking in the mountains, and/or wilderness trips of great variety.

Shamanic Journeys and Vision Quests: Ancient Roots and Contemporary Experiences

Among those on the leading edge of cultural transformation there has been an explosion of interest in the ancient models of the heroic adventure—namely "shamanic journeys" and "vision quests."

There are at least seven remarkable features about shamanism and the various forms of vision quests that are relevant to our discussion. One is that, as a process for spiritual enlightenment, they are extremely old and wide-spread. Shamanism, in its various forms, has been an integral part of the spiritual quest for native peoples for thousands of years with some anthropologists tracing it back at least 20,000 years. Shamanic practices are found in native cultures all around the globe.

The second remarkable feature is how they all follow the classic heroic adventure's three stages. Whether initiated through drumming, chanting, breathing, sacred drug use, or the crisis of an illness, the shaman separates from normal consciousness and enters an altered state of consciousness. The trip to the "under-world" is for gaining new insights and/or encountering new power. And, of course, the return to serve is the third stage.

The third feature relevant to our discussion, particularly as an expression of Epoch III spirituality, is the democratization of spiritual power. Although some of the ancient roots may manifest the Epoch II elitism, clearly the current widespread interest in shamanic practice is that it is available to everyone. Thousands of housewives, business executives, and professional therapists are taking weekend workshops from anthropologist Michael Harner, and he reports that some 90 percent are able to experience genuine shamanic journeys. People moving into Epoch III spirituality are turning their backs on institutional and theological imperialism and experiencing spiritual empowerment themselves.

The forth special feature has to do with the unique individual quality involved in a shamanic journey or vision quest. In the twelfth and thirteenth-century versions of the heroic journey—the quest for the Holy Grail—the knight-hero went in direct opposition to the medieval church which wanted conformity in the spiritual life of its followers and which promised vicarious salvation through the Holy Mass. Joseph Campbell translates an Old French text with what he suggests is the central element of the Grail quests: "They agreed that all would go on this quest, but they thought it would be a disgrace. . . to go forth in a group. So each entered the forest at a point that he, himself, had chosen, where it was the darkest and there was no path."[11]

The fifth remarkable part of these stories is how often they involve the wilderness, the forest, and/or animal powers. For instance, among Native Americans the vision quest was often the ritual facilitating one's passage into adulthood and frequently the event for discovering their personal name. Names were gleaned from particular personal qualities, religious experiences, or power symbols discovered in the vision quest. Native American writer Jamake Highwater reports that in a typical vision quest an animal power will appear: "teaching a song or revealing secret and powerful images that [the initiate] was instructed to paint on the body, clothing, shield, and tipi as a manifestation of personal power."[12]

The sixth element, remarkable precisely because of the individuality of the journey, is how often the common theme of unity with nature occurs. Again, Harner reflects on the thousands of people who have experienced shamanic journeys in his workshops:

> The experiences that come from shamanism tend to foster a

great respect for the universe, based on a feeling of oneness with all forms of life. By getting into harmony one has much more power available to help others, because harmony with the universe is where the true power comes from. Then one is much more likely to lead a life that emphasizes love rather than hatred, and which promotes understanding and optimism.[13]

The seventh remarkable feature of these ancient roots and contemporary experiences is the pragmatic synthesis of the esoteric and exoteric—the essential link between inner experience and outer service. As I have emphasized throughout our discussion, this balance of the cosmic and the personal, the esoteric and the exoteric, the inner and the outer, head-tripping and heart-giving are all essential elements in the Epoch III maturity of spirituality. The heroic journey is never complete without the return to service. A strategy for dealing with change is never fulfilled, nor fulfilling, without this link between discovery of inner power and the linking of your power with the world outside.

Major Life Reconstruction

Whether it is facilitated by any of the smaller or shorter experiences, as those listed above, or done through one's own unique process, a particularly courageous version of the intentional heroic adventure is that of a major life change. It is usually not a simple nor easy decision to make when considering family, professional, and/ or financial consequences, but sometimes it is simply a spiritual necessity to redirect one's life.

Sometimes it is a sudden realization—such as when an executive invests decades in climbing the corporate ladder only to discover that, for him or her, the ladder is against the wrong wall. Sometimes it is simply the gradual development of a feeling that you have exhausted all the creative possibilities out of your current direction in life and your soul is calling for a change. Perhaps you have tried a particular style of living and/or relating and it just doesn't work anymore. With sacred eyes we see our way into a new and different future.

If we are living a life that responds to soul-level energies we may be "called" by the spirit of health, the spirit of wholeness, and the spirit of the holy to separate from the past, go into our wilderness, discover new power, and reconstruct our life. Such a radical change may in the eyes of friends or family look like foolishness. Some may call it irresponsible, naive, or "flipping out." But that is precisely why it takes courage. Your version of the heroic adventure will not always be understood or appreciated.

The issue, of course, is this—if your soul's purpose calls for a radical transformation, can you afford *not* to heed the call? Can you refuse the adventure without risking greater consequences? I wonder how much of our emotional and spiritual dis-ease and physical disease is the result of blocking such soul-level energies? In the same vein, I wonder how many of us would experience seemingly miraculous growth spurts in meaning and purpose, or in physical healing, if and when we would resonate with that flow.

IV. Unplanned Heroic Adventures

Every journey has a secret destination of which the traveler is unaware.

—Martin Buber

We have looked at some of the ways we can intentionally take responsibility for our spiritual journey while learning the skills of the monomyth. There are many times, however, when we do not so much choose separation from our ordinary reality as it is thrust upon us. So often the heroic journey is not so much a selection as it is a reaction. But this is where the skills of response-ability come into play. How will we choose to respond to changes thrust upon us— with fear and resistance or with a courageous process of claiming new empowerment?

Let's take a brief look at some of the ways in which, although not choosing the separation, we can choose not to ignore it, resist it, or abort it. Instead, we can choose to follow the separation into a new world of power and service.

Dreams

We have several dreams every night. We have been in a culture, however, which has not valued their messages and their opportunities. Most of us, therefore, simply ignore them. If we do remember our dreams, our primary tendency in Epoch II has been to look at them literally, thus missing the rich symbolic meaning that can make our dreams important steps in our spiritual journey.

Every night we separate from ordinary day-time consciousness, from dealing with the external activities of our lives, to let the body rest. The unconscious, however, needs no rest and uses the night as an opportunity to provide us with a journey into profound subterranean powers.

Particularly creative people have long known that extraordinary solutions to life's problems are available in our dreams. Norman Lear finds the unconscious to be "a terrific partner" in his creative endeavors. "It slips you pieces of paper with the answers on them and ideas like letters dropping into the mailbox. One must keep the lines open to the unconscious and be there when the phone rings." [14]

The poet Hugh Prather put it in dialogue form:

> Me: There is something wrong with my life and I don't
> understand what it is.
> Dream: Look, I'll draw you a picture.[15]

I have never known anyone more profoundly in touch with her
dreams than my wife, Diana. She not only remembers them with
remarkable ease but brings an innate talent to understanding the
symbolic relevance to her life. I have seen her use her dreams many
times as the source of small, and in some cases, large heroic
journeys.

Diana was going through a real tough time in her life, experiencing what she described as "a thousand deaths." Many of her
relationships were changing, some ending, and it was a very
painful time. Her professional career as a teacher, psychotherapist,
and business-woman was undergoing dramatic changes. It was
frightening, for elements in her life that she had counted on were
changing, if not dying. She wasn't sure what was to follow. The
dying was obvious, but what was being born was not so obvious.

Sure enough, the resourcefulness of her depths came to the
rescue—she had a powerful dream that moved her through her
agony. She relates how

> I was with a woman who appeared to be my teacher. I
> listened carefully as she explained the value of releasing old
> energy patterns. She said there was really nothing wrong with
> the energy I was carrying around except for the fact that it was
> old, stale, and flat. The energy flowing through my activity had
> lost its sparkle and the vitality it once had.
>
> In a ritualistic manner, my teacher began to remove the old
> patterns from my life—the old images, the old objects, and the
> old feelings—while simultaneously replacing them with exact,
> but renewed replicas. I did not look any different and exter-
> nally my life did not appear to be changed. But at the energetic
> level everything was transformed. The changes were subtle but
> I began to experience a deeper and clearer connection to all that
> surrounded me. I felt more loving and more present with my
> life, personally and professionally, and a sense of appreciation
> and joy grew within me.
>
> Endless aspects of my life were brought to my awareness
> and subtly transformed—the energy in our house, our furnish-
> ings, the art, the spaciousness of each room, the light and the
> color—it all came to life in a new way. Food was placed before
> me, then replaced with food more representative of the essen-
> tial life energy.

The view from our living room of the mountains became sacred. The loving energy connecting me and Spirit [our dog] became crystal clear. My marriage with you, Bob, and all its healing qualities—the beauty, the power, and the love—clarified to remind me of how richly blessed I am. I stood with my teacher feeling renewed and truly alive.

When one takes a heroic journey with one's dreams it is amazing with what power and depth it enables change. Diana started the new day with a calm confidence that out of her depths her life was being positively transformed. The dying she felt so vividly the day before was replaced with the feeling of being born anew.

Diana's dream reminded me of a great line by the comedian Stephen Wright, when he said in his characteristically deadpan manner and monotone voice: "Somebody slipped into my house last night, stole all my furniture, and replaced everything with exact replicas." To the outside observer, Diana looked pretty much the same as the day before. On the inside, however, she was transformed. Despair was replaced with hope, depression replaced with a vibrant and hopeful faith in a renewed future.

It is a real treat to watch Diana work with another person in helping that person find the transforming power in their own dreams, and the process of the journey that leads them into their depths and then out into the world to serve. Most of her work is in the privacy of individual therapy but once in a while I see her "ministry" at work in a group setting.

One such experience was in a workshop we were conducting for a group of clergy. One of the participants was Gene, a United Methodist minister, who had stated that this was a particularly tough time for him. It was a time of struggle for meaning, a time of frustration with his life and career. One morning during the workshop Gene shared a dream that he had the night before, the meaning of which he could not understand.

In his dream Gene was on a Kansas farm like the one on which he grew up. For most of the dream, he said, he was plowing the fields and was preoccupied with plowing straight furrows with an old-fashioned plow being pulled by a horse. But then he became aware of the fact that the horse was invisible. Somehow he knew the plow was being pulled by a horse, but he could not see the horse.

The group brainstormed the dream but Gene was not satisfied with any of the suggested interpretations. None of our guesses felt on target for Gene, regarding the meaning of his dream. We appeared to be at a dead end.

Having waited patiently for us to deal intellectually with the dream, and seeing us come up empty, Diana took over. She led Gene into a meditation—deep into the state of consciousness from which his dream had emerged. She suggested that he imagine entering a movie theater where he would see his dream played out again, this time on the movie screen. She suggested that at the end of the dream/movie the title would appear on the screen which would give him a clue regarding the meaning of his dream.

In other words, Diana was suggesting that the unconscious which had created the dream/movie would know the meaning of it all. We needed only to trust those depths and be open to hints from the unconscious regarding the meaning and purpose of the dream.

Gene was deep into it and quiet for a long period of time as he watched his dream being played out on the movie screen of his imagination. At the end of his dream/movie the title appeared and Gene burst into laughter. "This is really incredible," laughed Gene, "the unconscious sure does have a sense of humor." Naturally, we were intensely curious. "What," we asked almost in unison, "What was the title?" Still chuckling Gene told the group that the title of his dream was, "The horseless headsman."

With an enthusiasm that only comes when one is touched very deeply with a new and profound insight Gene continued. The dream, he admitted, was saying something he knew down deep, but had not yet consciously admitted—he had been head-tripping his entire life and it was no longer adequate or fulfilling. He was so accustomed to intellectualizing, philosophizing, and theologizing everything in his life, he was out of touch with his emotions. The horse, Gene realized, symbolized the animal power—the instincts and the feeling level of his life, which was the essential power "pulling the plow." Yet, he was so much of a "headsman" he was out of touch with that body-level power. He was blind to the presence of the horse. "I guess my dream is indicating," Gene concluded, "that I need to get more in balance, integrating my head and my body, my intellect and my emotions, my rationality and my instincts. It feels like an incredibly important insight for my health and well-being."

Whether it is for proposed changes in the interest of health, or giving us clues regarding how to deal with change being thrust upon us, our dreams are regularly occurring treasure-houses of information, coming from deep down in our unconscious. The trouble is, as Joseph Campbell put it, most of us leave our miracles down there.

Our Epoch II culture has ignored, if not denigrated, this resource for health and wholeness. In Epoch III we will begin to appreciate what an incredible source of creativity we have emerging nightly from our inner depths. We don't choose to have dreams, we all have them. But we can choose to pay attention and make them into empowering journeys.

Crises

The major crises that come crashing into our lives certainly are not chosen. The crisis of a major illness or accident, the unwelcomed stress of having a child with a birth or genetic defect, the blow to self-esteem of divorce or a business failure, or the despair involved in the death of a spouse. Various and sundry crises are unwelcomed companions thrust into our life's journey.

We can, however, choose how we respond to such crises. We are not helpless victims to feelings of despair and hopelessness. Eventually—perhaps not immediately, but eventually—we can reconnect with the inner power to choose our victor response.

A friend put it this way: "It felt like I got pushed off a precipice. The fear of helplessly falling and of the inevitable crash was incredibly intense. Part way down, however, I decided it was about time to learn how to fly." Indeed. The heroic adventure is the strategy for flying out of trouble.

If life has thrown you off your previous "ground," the hero or heroine views it as the first step in an empowering journey, even if they did not choose to take it in the first place. When pushed or shoved the heroic response is to fly into new power and land on new "ground" to serve in a new or better way.

The Chinese pictogram for "crisis" is made up not of one but of two signs: one meaning "danger," and the other meaning "opportunity." If we respond to the changes involved in a crisis with a preoccupation of danger, change will continue to be the enemy. If, however, we respond with sacred eyes looking for opportunities involved in the change—even a dangerous opportunity—then we are in the company of heroes and heroines.

In almost every community we can find those who went through danger and into opportunity. Just about everyone reading these words is one, or knows someone, who is serving others in light of or perhaps because of a crisis they went through. Most of the self-help health organizations, as well as many issue-oriented citizen groups, have been formed because someone experienced a terrible separation, an encounter with danger or terror, and found the power in their own healing to serve others.

The heroes and the heroines are those who turn a crisis they did not choose into a spiritual journey. That is response-ability. That is sanctifying a wounding experience and making it a sacred wound. That is living the classic monomyth.

We could survey many other forms of unintended and unchosen crises to which we can choose the heroic adventure as our response— mystical experiences, spiritual emergence, out-of-body experiences, and near-death experiences, just to mention a few. It is how we choose to respond that can empower change, even unwelcomed change, rather than have it ruin our lives or leave us in fear.

If we enlarge this subject, from a total focus on individual crises to the level of our collective crises, we are back into the subject of Chapter Six, our dark night of the soul. The same challenge of danger and/or opportunity exists at the collective level as it does at the individual level. Our world is in a crisis—we have been for three decades—and we, as participants, can make it a heroic adventure. Some are preoccupied with the danger and are literalizing the symbols of death and destruction emerging from the unconscious. Heroes and heroines, however, can make this extraordinary time in history a time of empowerment and greater service. It is the matter of having historical integrity in and with our time. And it is on such people that the world rests its hope for a brighter future.

Aging

It may seem a bit strange to identify aging as an opportunity for the heroic journey. But think about it. If we want to be alive we can't choose *not* to age. We can, however, choose how we respond to the aging process. Aging certainly confronts us with challenges regarding how we choose to deal with changes—resentment or welcome, resistance or going with the flow, danger or opportunity, falling or flying.

Particularly in America we have idolized youth and have despised getting old. We are a culture overflowing with ageism. People have made fortunes off our fear of looking older—we plaster this or that on our faces, do this or that to our hair, vacuum fat cells out of our bodies, implant this, tuck that, and search endlessly for the fountain of youth.

Perhaps no major area of our lives is more applicable to Jean Houston's words about mythologizing rather than pathologizing. It is reflective of a materialistic culture that puts an almost total focus on the deterioration of the body in the aging process, rather than on the ascension of the mind and spirit. An entropic mindset focuses on the deterioration of the physical, whereas an evolutionary perspective is aware of the growth and development potential in the mental and spiritual aspects of life.

Carl Jung spoke about the normal aging process, wherein during the first half of life our attention tends to be on physical development and making one's place in the world in terms of profession, finances, and family. In the second half of life, the healthy person turns more to the inner life of spiritual and emotional maturity, establishing meaning and purpose in one's life, and the legacy one will leave.

Joseph Campbell, in the now famous PBS series on *The Power of Myth*, was asked by Bill Moyers about how myths assisted him in his own aging process. Anyone who watched Campbell in his seventies and eighties knew that we were witnessing a master at work regarding mythologizing rather than pathologizing aging.

> The tradition in India, for instance, is of actually changing your whole way of dress, even changing your name, as you pass from one stage to another. When I retired from teaching, I knew that I had to create a new way of life, and I changed my manner of thinking about my life, just in terms of that notion— moving out of the sphere of achievement into the sphere of enjoyment and appreciation and relaxing to the wonder of it all.
>
> The problem in middle life, when the body has reached its climax of power and begins to decline, is to identify yourself not with the body, which is falling away, but with the consciousness of which it is a vehicle. This is something I learned from myths. What am I? Am I the bulb that carries the light, or am I the light of which the bulb is a vehicle?[16]

As we get older even the healthiest of bodies diminish. There are some things we can't do physically at fifty-five that we could do at twenty-five. And the body generally is not able to do at eighty-five what it could do at fifty-five.

If we are influenced by the late adolescent materialism and the preoccupation with the physical aspect of life, then entropy is our "school of thought" and change is viewed as negative. If, in contrast, we move into the spiritual maturation of Epoch III when the *meta*physical aspects of life come into sharper focus, transformation and evolution shape the "curriculum" of our school of thought and we see change as an opportunity. With materialistic eyes we see only the beauty or deterioration of the body. With sacred eyes we can begin to see the beauty of soul growth and development.

The mind and spirit can be on an evolutionary ascent all the way through life and into and through death, if we choose to remain alive and growing in these regards. Thus, the heroic adventure is the strategy by which to shift from a truncated physical perspective into the spiritual possibilities, and a way of enabling us to become user-friendly with change.

Take the metaphysical power of love, for instance. Nothing that happens to the body is significant compared to growing in the understanding and application of love. Whereas the physical aspects of love are wonderful—not a bad perk for this journey in and through materialized spirit—it is simply shallow and unfulfilling if not combined with the maturation of the metaphysical aspects of love. The latter is what we learn more of with each heroic adventure.

Every time we realize that a "can" of the past has turned into a "can't" of the present, it is a moment of separation—the first step in the heroic journey. We have all those new encounters with new initiations, new trials, and new encounters with power—the special power of a new age. In this sense, every healthy aging person is a "new ager," for they find in every new age they enter—whether they measure that in days, weeks, months, years, or decades—new power and new opportunities.

For every one of us aging is a marvelous opportunity to choose to live the ancient monomyth rather than begrudging every new day, to choose to be a hero or heroine rather than a coward in facing one of the inevitabilities of life, and to welcome change as an opportunity for discovery and empowerment. For every door that aging seems to close there is a door opening up to an adventure into new possibilities. We will see those doors opening up if we cultivate sacred eyes, the kind of in-sight no cataract can cloud.

Give it a try. Cultivate sacred eyes. Develop the heroic art of living an improvisation. For if you do, you will gain new in-sight for improvising your way through heroic adventures. With the succession of added years, and with the increased skill in and familiarity with the heroic adventure, we old whippersnappers will show those young codgers a thing or two about living until it is time to die. We will perfect the heavenly art of dying young—as late in life as possible.

V. BEYOND STRATEGY

Attempting the mastery of fear is useless. In fact, it asserts the power of fear by the very assumption that it need be mastered. The true resolution rests entirely on mastery through love.
—A COURSE IN MIRACLES

Although a strategy for becoming user friendly with change is essential as the pace of change escalates, there is something even more important: grounding ourselves in love. The heroic journey is certainly the strategy by which we can glean growth and empowerment from the changes we experience, but ultimately, the only way to deal with the fear of change is knowing—I mean really knowing, not just believing in—the ontological love that is at the core of our being.

No matter how much we perfect a strategy for dealing with change, a strategy is still at the "doing" level. The ultimate in dealing with our inner fear of change is, however, at the "being" level. Being always undergirds the doing. We may have highly developed skills in the strategies of doing, but if we don't have peace at the deep levels of our inner being we will forever be fearful of change. On the other hand, if we are at home with our inner depths we will be comfortable with life, changes or not. We might not learn as much from changes, as we would with the heroic strategy, but we would not be fearful of change. And so that which lies beyond strategy is the "being-ness" of love.

Consistent with our earlier discussions regarding love, we are not talking here about something we have to do to gain love, or do to merit love. Since love is ontological, love is the essential power, the within-ness, of the universe, and therefore, at the core of every physical and spiritual cell of our being. It's there. We don't have to earn it. We can't make it happen. It's just there.

Consequently, the appropriation of love is simply accepting the grace of its presence. It may seem quite contrary to our make-it-happen, nothing-is-of-value-unless-we-work-for-it kind of world, but that is precisely the nature of spiritual love. We are loved by that which is most essential in the universe, and if we know that, accept that, and live that, we have no fear of changes.

Our bodies provide a marvelous metaphor for this spiritual reality. Our physical body is constantly undergoing changes, yet it doesn't forget who it is. Similarly, our spiritual depths can be secure in knowing that we exist within ontological love, and not forgetting that regardless of changes in our external lives.

Consider that in more detail. The endocrinologist Dr. Deepak Chopra gives us some specific data regarding how thoroughly our bodies change. Every second, two and a half million red blood cells die and a similar number are born. The lining of our stomach is renewed every week. Our skin is replaced every month and our liver every six weeks. That seemingly hard, permanent skeleton of yours is actually totally replaced every three months. Your brain cells are replaced every year. In fact, Chopra says that 98 percent of your entire body is different than it was just a year ago.

Nevertheless, your sense of "you" is not entirely different than it was a year ago. Somehow, without working hard at the task, all the new material of your body comes and goes without losing your sense of "you," without losing your memories of the past, and without fear. And that's the point; your natural physiological changes take place without fear of the future, without fear of change. The "knowing" somehow transcends the physical changes. Who you are is somehow more than and different from the material components of your body. The material changes, but a sense of "you" remains.

Likewise, who you are at a spiritual level—an at-one-ment with the ontological love of the universe—transcends any changes that may take place in your life. There is nothing to fear, if you are at home in that love.

Ontological love heals the fractures created by fear—the gap between the known and the unknown, between past, present, and future, and between the now and the not-quite-yet.

The deep values emerging in our transition into Epoch III thus become manifest in our depths. We are loved precisely because this is a holistic universe, for love is the allurement, the gravity, which pulls it all together. We are empowered by this love. And by becoming so empowered, we have that which transcends all strategy in terms of dealing with change.

CHAPTER 11

RE-MEMBERING HUMAN-NATURE

For my part, I would take it to be little short of a counsel of despair if I thought the fate of the living planet depended wholly on the moral fervor of some small number of our species, overworked groups of ecological activists, each focused on a separate environmental horror with nothing more to draw upon in addressing the world around them except ethical denunciation, panic, or even enlightened self-interest. Is there an alternative to scare tactics and guilt trips that will lend ecological necessity both intelligence and passion? There is. It is the concern that arises from shared identity: two lives that become one. Where that identity is experienced deeply, we call it love. More cooly and distantly felt, it is called compassion. This is the link we must find between ourselves and the planet that gives us life.

—HISTORY PROFESSOR THEODORE ROSZAK

A Long Forgetting—and Now A Remembering

IT TOOK A 10,000 YEAR JOURNEY—a journey characterized by amnesia, fear, and hostility—before we began remembering the nature of human nature. It was, however, a necessary trip.

Before humanity could take its mature role in relationship to nature, and before we could become fully human, we had to develop a separate self-identity. We started our adolescence by distinguishing ourselves from nature, left our childhood's feminine value system in favor of a masculine value system, and switched our worship from Mother Earth to Father God. Such was the process of developing the human ego and sense of identity.

Like all such adolescent journeys we were filled with fear and trepidation and quite insecure throughout the entire process. We were constantly afraid that, without persistence and diligence, we might drift back into the wild nature from which we were trying so hard to ascend. We developed "civilized" notions that sex and other such nasty behavior had to do with base animal instincts and certainly did not represent the highest and best of being human. At one point we had a Victorian preoccupation with cleanliness as a primary way of distinguishing ourselves from the beasts and, in fact, "bestiality" was considered to be among the worst of crimes, actually punishable by death from the late sixteenth century up through the middle of the nineteenth century.

The fear of werewolves, the violence against anyone called a witch, and the labeling of our enemies as "savages" were all manifestations of an adolescent ego trying desperately to separate itself from its natural roots. I suspect that the zest and vigor with which Christian fundamentalists opt for "creationism" rather than evolution is similarly motivated.

To begin our adolescence we left the wilderness, denied our natural and innate connection to wildness and tried to make human life tame, as opposed to wild.[1] It may seem like a large jump in logic—remember that we are having to paint a very large picture in order to cover the canvas of the entire human journey—but I strongly suspect that our beginning adolescent need to leave the wild and become preoccupied with the tame is at the root of the modern human's excessive need to exert control. And it is this need to control, as opposed to "going with the flow," that contributes to the prevalence of coronary heart disease today. It is a large jump, but today's health challenges have deep roots and we just don't have the space in this book to trace every step of that journey.

Now, however, we have arrived at the point in history when a soul-level transformation is taking place, telling us that we can now transcend those adolescent fears. We have moved through our adolescence and need not live in fear of losing control over our humanity. It is a deep change that is now taking place in the human psyche. The transformation from adolescence into adulthood represents, among the other things we have been discussing, a maturation of our relationship with our long lost brothers and sisters throughout nature and a reunion with our Mother Earth. From our soul emerges the organic maturational energies. We are now re-membering that which we dis-membered some ten thousand years ago.

All that we have witnessed in the ecological and environmental movements over the past two or three decades is testimony to the emergence of this deep value of Epoch III. Many books dealing with this subject are how-to books—how to become environmentally responsible, how to be an animal rights activist, etc. They are needed and play an important role. This book, however, will not attempt to cover that same ground. This book is not so much about what to do as about how to think.

You will not, therefore, find here a list of things to do, although I certainly do not diminish the need of doing. Rather, what this book is about is the deep value changes taking place and the kind of thinking that emanates from those deep values. The way of thinking precedes and directs the way of doing.

Perhaps it should be said again—we are not talking about going back. We are not going to devolve back before our collective adolescence. The adolescent ego development and separation was an essential stage in our growth. Now is the time, however, to take the next evolutionary step forward and gain a new, more mature, more synergistic reunion with nature. In so doing, we will come to an even greater understanding of human nature.

Science Jogs Our Memory

It may be popular among some environmentalists to decry the role of science, for science has provided a great many of the means by which we have assaulted the earth and the environment. But it is not science per se that should be blamed. It has merely provided us with the tools to carry out our values. It is with an examination of our values that we should start. When we had a deep primary value of being above and outside of nature, and a theology which gave us the permission, indeed the calling, to have dominion over nature, then science helped provide us the means with which to do just that.

But the fact is, science has also played a major role in bringing the new deep values of Epoch III to the surface. Science has been able to do that precisely because it has been the object of our worship in late Epoch II. We pay attention to anything that we think is scientific.

And what has science done but give the lie to our favorite adolescent need. We have tried so hard to separate humanity, as far as possible, from all the wild natural world—namely, all that which is not human or domesticated by humans. But modern science has shown us that we are incredibly, and inextricably, mixed up with all of nature.

As we discussed before, there is a constant flow between life and non-life, between that which is organic and that which in inorganic, between humans and the rest of nature. Every atom in our bodies has been elsewhere and will be again. Literally, with every breath we exchange matter with the rest of humanity and the rest of nature. The notion that we are solid, separate, distinguishable hunks of matter, always human, is quite simply an illusion.

The human genome project, launched in 1990, is a marvelous case in point. It has the ambitious goal of understanding the genetic makeup of humans "by sequencing the three billion pairs of chemical bases that make up the spiraling DNA strands inside the nucleus of each of our cells."[2] It is estimated to take fifteen years and about three billion dollars to complete the project. But even before doing that, scientists know that our genetic makeup is about 99.9 percent identical to any other human on this planet. And—this is where our adolescent ego starts into spasm—our genetic makeup is about 99 percent the same as a chimpanzee's. Hundreds, perhaps even thousands, of our genes are the same as found in all other life forms on this planet.

Not only are we very closely related to all other life forms, but we are having a constant exchange of the very material of our bodies with the "outside" world. What is fascinating is that the stuff of our bodies is in consistent and total turnover, yet we retain a sense of self. That may be one of the important contributions of our adolescent ego development.

Humanity has been given a special role to play, as has every other participant in this dance of life, and we needed an ego for that purpose. We'll get to that purpose in a moment, but we are not through with the important contributions science has been making in surfacing the new Epoch III value of re-membering humanity and nature. Two very important contributions came from one of the crowning achievements of Epoch II technology, the space program.

First of all, it provided the leading metaphorical image of a whole, integrated and living planet—the Gaia Hypothesis. The pinnacle of mechanistic science ended up providing the organic planetary image of Epoch III.

In the 1960s James Lovelock was designing instruments for the space program with which to discern whether or not there was life on Mars. In the process he discovered that the Earth Herself gives all the indications of being a living entity—self-organizing and self-renewing. This provided the scientific basis for a resurgence of interest in Mother Earth.

Secondly, the space program provided the opportunity for human beings to see this home planet from the outside. The view had profound effects, for it changed our mind about ourselves and our planet.

Anthropologist Lyall Watson points out that you have to be outside something before you can really understand it. Fish, for example, are not the ones to tell us how water fits into the overall context of the planet, and we can't perceive the forest until we move beyond seeing only one tree. It was the space program which finally helped us move from theory to understanding regarding the life-fullness of our Mother, the Earth.

Consider, for instance, what some of the astronauts and cosmonauts said when they saw, first hand, the view of the Earth from outer space. Rather than just a brief quote or two, I would like to share several of them with you, asking you to let their words wash over your mind and spirit. They were our first eyes to witness that sight—a sight which transformed scientific eyes into sacred eyes.[3]

> We went to the moon as technicians; we returned as humanitarians. . . . There was suddenly a very deep gut feeling that something was different. . . I experienced the universe as intelligent, loving, harmonious. . . . Only when man sees his fundamental unity with the processes of nature and the functioning of the universe—as I so vividly saw it from the Apollo spacecraft—will the old ways of thinking and behaving disappear. Only when man moves from his ego-centered self-image to a new image of universal man will the perennial problems that plague us be susceptible to resolution. Humanity must rise from man to mankind, from the personal to the transpersonal, from self-consciousness to cosmic consciousness. *(Edgar Mitchell, USA)*

> Before I flew I was already aware of how small and vulnerable our planet is; but only when I saw it from space, in all its ineffable beauty and fragility, did I realize that humankind's most urgent task is to cherish and preserve it for future generations. *(Sigmund John, German Democratic Republic)*

> One morning I woke up and decided to look out the window to see where we were. We were flying over America and suddenly I saw snow, the first snow we ever saw from orbit. Light and powdery, it blended with the contours of the land, with the veins of the rivers. I thought—autumn, snow—people are getting ready for winter. A few minutes later, we were flying over the Atlantic, then Europe, and then Russia. I have

never visited America, but I imagined that the arrival of autumn and winter is the same there as in other places, and the process of getting ready for them is the same. And then it struck me that we are all children of our Earth. It does not matter what country you look at. We are all Earth's children, and we should treat her as our Mother. *(Aleksandr Aleksandrov, USSR)*

During a space flight, the psyche of each astronaut is reshaped. Having seen the sun, the stars, and our planet, you become more full of life, softer. You begin to look at all living things with greater trepidation and you begin to be more kind and patient with the people around you. *(Boris Volynov, USSR)*

A Chinese tale tells of some men sent to harm a young girl who, upon seeing her beauty, became her protectors rather than her violators. That's how I felt seeing the Earth for the first time. I could not help but love and cherish her. *(Taylor Wang, China/USA)*

From space I saw Earth—indescribably beautiful with the scars of national boundaries gone. *(Muhammad Ahmad Faris, Syria)*

The first day or so we all pointed to our countries. The third or fourth day we were pointing to our continents. By the fifth day we were aware of only one Earth. *(Sultan Bin Salman al-Saud, The Kingdom of Saudi Arabia)*

The Earth reminded us of a Christmas tree ornament hanging in the blackness of space. . . . That beautiful, warm, living object looked so fragile, so delicate, that if you touched it with a finger it would crumble and fall apart. Seeing this has to change a man, has to make a man appreciate the creation of God and the love of God. *(James Irwin, USA)*

Now I know why I'm (on the moon). Not for a closer look at the moon, but to look back at our home, the Earth. *(Alfred Worden, USA)*

For me. . . orbiting our beautiful home planet, fascinated by the 17,000 miles of spectacle passing below each hour, the overwhelming experience was that of a new relationship. . . the unavoidable and awesome personal relationship, suddenly realized, with all life on this amazing planet. *(Russell Schweickart, USA)*

I don't know about the impact of those statements upon you, but they give me the feeling that something very important happened when representatives of humanity finally saw our "home" from the outside. It was a turning point in history, a re-birth of awe and wonder, a transformational catalyst.

The word wonder, of course, has two very useful meanings. One refers to being awe-struck, and that certainly was one major emotion shared by those who viewed our planet from the outside. The other meaning of the word refers to questioning, and these comments by astronauts certainly raise some questions in my mind.

I can't help but wonder if our best defense against wars might not be to take at least some of the money we put into armaments to send the leaders of the combatant nations up into outer space to negotiate while looking back at Earth. I wonder if we wouldn't save a lot of money in the long run by sending executives of polluting companies up there for a consciousness-raising, mind-blowing and spirit-stretching experience. I can't help but wonder what myriad of problems, problems that seem so intractable to our small Epoch II perspective, would be solved it we invested in sending more people into outer space. I wonder.

The experience of being up there transformed Epoch II scientific eyes into Epoch III sacred eyes. It would take a major shift in our priorities to do what I suggested above. I wonder if we have the will, and the political leadership to do it? Could the United States turn from being the world's leading arms dealer to becoming the world's leader in transforming in-sight and eye-sight? I wonder.

At the least, we have in the space program a marvelous symbol of the transition from the Epoch II reductionism that separated science from spirituality, and one that considered the world and human beings as machines, to the Epoch III holistic synthesis of the best of science and the best of spirituality, both sharing the perception of a living, organic world. We have scientists who were trained in Epoch II mentality coming back from outer space with their view of life transformed. We have the technology of Epoch II acting as an important catalyst for the emergence of Epoch III. The old science, in one of its most masterful accomplishments, jogged our memory. It has helped us, after thousands of years of amnesia, to remember who we really are.

Remembering Our Native American Roots

For the European-Americans living in North America there is a very specific example of our journey from adolescence into adult maturity—our relationship with the Native Americans. When we came to this land we considered the people living here to be "savages," which gave us the rationale to treat them as we treated the rest of nature—like trash. And it is no coincidence that, as we move toward Epoch III, there is a renewed interest in and respect for Native Americans themselves, their traditions, and particularly their spirituality—an earth centered spirituality.

Consider the legend of the White Buffalo Woman as told by the Ogalala Sioux medicine man, Black Elk.

> A very long time ago, they say, two scouts were out looking for bison when they came to the top of a high hill and looked north. They saw something coming a long way off, and when it came closer they cried out, "It is a woman," and it was. Then one of the scouts, being foolish, had bad thoughts and spoke them; but the other said: "That is a sacred woman; throw all bad thoughts away." When she came still closer, they saw that she wore a fine white buckskin dress, that her hair was very long and that she was young and very beautiful. And she knew their thoughts and said in a voice that was like singing: "You do not know me, but if you want to do as you think, you may come." And the foolish one went; but just as he stood before her, there was a white cloud that came and covered them. And the beautiful young woman came out of the cloud, and when it blew away the foolish man was a skeleton covered with worms. Then the woman spoke to the one who was not foolish: "You shall go home and tell your people that I am coming and that a big tepee shall be built for me in the center of the nation." And the man, who was very much afraid, went quickly and told the people, who did at once as they were told; and there around the big tepee they waited for the sacred woman. And after a while she came, very beautiful and singing, and as she went into the tepee this is what she sang:
>
>> With visible breath I am walking,
>> A voice I am sending as I walk.
>> In a sacred manner I am walking.
>> With visible tracks I am walking.
>> In a sacred manner I walk.
>
> And as she sang, there came from her mouth a white cloud that was good to smell. Then she gave something to the chief, and it was a pipe with a bison calf carved on one side to mean

the earth that bears and feeds us, and with twelve eagle feathers hanging from the stem to mean the sky and the twelve moons, and these were tied with a grass that never breaks. "Behold," she said. "With this you shall multiply and be a good nation. Nothing but good shall come from it. Only the hands of the good shall take care of it and the bad shall not even see it." Then she sang again and went out of the tepee; and as the people watched her going, suddenly it was a white bison galloping away and snorting, and soon it was gone.[4]

"This they tell," Black Elk went on to say, "and whether it happened so or not I do not know; but if you think about it, you can see that it is true." The kind of vision Black Elk is talking about comes from sacred eyes. "I had a vision," he said, "because I was seeing in the sacred manner of the world."[5]

Such sacred vision is, as Black Elk knew, "of the world." It sees, first of all, that the message from the legend of the White Buffalo Woman is that nature represents feminine power. Back when we separated ourselves from nature, in order to begin our adolescence, we separated ourselves from our innate feminine power—thus, our adolescence was one of masculine values. This Native American legend reminds us that when we re-member our feminine power, we will gain a greater organic wholeness.

Secondly, the White Buffalo Woman sings of visible movement—in other words, material, physical evolution. A natural earth in movement, always involved in changes, is an organic reality Native Americans have known and which our psyche is just now catching onto.

Thirdly, it is a legend that states again that the earth and the animals form a unity with humanity, if we but have the sacred vision to see it.

But most of all, this legend gives us a message desperately needed at this particular stage in history—that we have the free will to choose what we will do with the feminine earth, but we do not have the freedom to choose the consequences to our actions.

The White Buffalo Woman told the scouts that they could do as they wished. The foolish one went to her with bad thoughts and suffered the consequences of death. In like manner Mother Earth is soft and permissive, in that sense, allowing us to express our developing ego and to utilize our technology according to how we think. But make no mistake about it, we cannot escape the consequences of our thoughts and actions.

Because of the thinking of most Europeans who came to America, this country was colonized but not "discovered." People had already been here for 20,000 years, people who had a rich heritage and an earth-based spirituality. The European colonizers, by and large, did not discover those riches at all. Instead, they saw a land free for the taking, inhabited only by "savages," and a religion to destroy and suppress in favor of the Christianity they brought with them. We are just beginning to realize the consequences of such narrow, parochial and arrogant thoughts to our collective soul.

What happens to our soul when we think a land is to be "conquered" rather than lived with in mutual harmony? What happens to our soul when we think of nature as an "it" rather than a "thou"?

What happens to our soul when we honor as a hero a man who thought as did General William Tecumseh Sherman? Sherman, whose middle name was ironically that of a Native American prophet murdered by the whites, turned his mind and guns on the Indians following the Civil War:

"The more we can kill this year, the less will have to be killed the next war," wrote General Sherman, "for the more I see of these Indians the more convinced I am that all have to be killed or maintained as a species of pauper. Their attempts at civilization are simply ridiculous."[6]

In contrast, read the words attributed to Chief Seattle of the Suquamish tribes around Puget Sound. This is, ostensibly, the response Chief Seattle gave to the United States Government's desire to purchase tribal lands. Although its authenticity is now under question, it certainly is a true representation of Native American spirituality regarding the earth—the kind of "savage" thinking Sherman thought should be killed.

> How can you buy or sell the sky, the warmth of the land? The idea is strange to us. If we do not own the freshness of the air and the sparkle of the water, how can you buy them? Every part of this earth is sacred to my people—every shining pine needle, every sandy shore, every mist in the dark woods, every clearing and humming insect is holy in the memory and experience of my people. . . .
>
> This shining water that moves in the streams and rivers is not just water, but the blood of our ancestors. If we sell you our land you must remember that it is sacred, and you must teach your children that it is sacred, and that each ghostly reflection in the clear water of the lakes tells of events and memories in the life of my people. . . .
>
> We know that the whiteman does not understand our ways—

one portion of land is the same to him as the next, for he is a stranger who comes in the night and takes what he needs. The earth is not his brother but his enemy, and when he has conquered it he moves on. . . .

The sight of your cities pains the eyes of the redman, but perhaps it is because the redman is a savage and does not understand. There is no quiet place in the whiteman's cities— no place to hear the unfurling of leaves in spring or the rustle of insects' wings. . . . The clatter only seems to insult the ears. And what is there to life if a man cannot hear the lonely cry of the whippoorwill, or the arguments of the frogs round the pond at night? . . .

But if we sell you our land, you must remember that the air is precious to us, that the air shares its spirit with all the life it supports. The wind that gave our grandfather his first breath also receives his last sigh. The wind must also give our children the spirit of life. And if we sell you our land, you must keep it apart and sacred as a place where even the whiteman can go to taste the wind that is sweetened by the meadow's flowers. . . .

So we will consider your offer to buy our land. If we decide to accept, I will make one condition; the whiteman must treat the beasts of his land as his brothers. I am a savage and I do not understand any other way. I have seen a thousand rotting buffaloes on the prairie, left by the whiteman who shot them from a passing train. I am a savage and I do not understand how the smoking iron horse can be more important than the buffalo that we kill only to stay alive. What is man without the beasts? If all the beasts were gone, man would die of a great loneliness of spirit, for whatever happens to the beasts soon happens to man. All things are connected. . . . Teach your children what we have taught our children—that the earth is our mother. Whatever befalls the earth befalls the sons of the earth; if men spit upon the ground, they spit upon themselves. This we know—the earth does not belong to man, man belongs to the earth. This we know. All things are connected, like the blood which unites one family. All things are connected. Whatever befalls the earth befalls the sons of the earth. Man did not weave the web of life, he is merely a strand in it. Whatever he does to the web he does to himself. . . .

One thing we know, which the whiteman may one day discover—our God is the same God. You may think now that you own Him as you wish to own our land, but you cannot. He is the God of man, and His compassion is equal for the redman and the white. This earth is precious to Him, and to harm the earth is to heap contempt on its Creator. The whites too shall pass, perhaps sooner than other tribes. Continue to contaminate your bed and you will one night suffocate in your own waste. But in your perishing you will shine brightly, fired by the strength of the God who brought you to this land and for some special purpose gave you dominion over this land and over the redman. That destiny is a mystery to us, for we do not understand when the buffalo are all slaughtered, the wild horses are tamed, the secret corners of the forest heavy with the scent of many men, and the view of the ripe hills blotted by talking wires. Where is the thicket? Gone. Where is the eagle? Gone. And what is it to say good-bye to the swift pony and the hunt? The end of living and the beginning of survival. . . .

When the last redman has vanished from this earth and his memory is only the shadow of a cloud moving across the prairies, these shores and forests will still hold the spirits of my people. For they love this earth, as the newborn loves its mother's heartbeat. So if we sell you our land, love it as we have loved it; care for it as we have cared for it; hold in your mind the memory of the land as it is when you take it; and with all your strength, with all your heart, preserve it for your children and love it, as God loves us all.[7]

So what are the consequences for us, at a soul level, when we call people like General Sherman civilized and consider the Native Americans with this kind of reverence for the earth to be something less than human?

We have grown up to the point of having the freedom to think and to act in whatever ways we want. Mother Earth and Father Sky—or whatever we want to call the divine Spirit of the universe— do not *make* us believe in a particular way. Spirit, in this sense, is quite permissive. But we *will* experience the consequences of our thoughts and actions; you can count on it.

What are the consequences of thinking we can treat the Earth as simply a material resource to be plundered and pillaged? What are the consequences of racial, sexual and cultural arrogance and violence?

Instead of thinking of Native Americans as savages or their spirituality as primitive—both of which we thought were inferior to "civilized" Europeans and the Christianity they brought with them— we are assisted in our maturation into Epoch III by their ancient understanding of the human-nature relationship.

Remembering Human Nature

So who are we, really? If we re-member that which has been dis-membered, can we recall who we are to be in our future maturity? If maturation means to be fulfilling our destiny, what is that destiny? If we're not to have dominion over nature, what is our appropriate relationship with the earth?

The suggestion here is that soul-level deep value changes are bringing into our awareness an innate, organic connection with nature and a cooperative, synergistic relationship. That message is bubbling to the surface all across the culture's landscape as we begin to grow up out of our adolescent ego agenda and into a more mature spirituality. All sorts of "secular" institutions, organiza-tions, and businesses are affirming and articulating this new "geo-theology" and are rushing to out-green the competition, even if being religious is the farthest thing from their minds.

More specifically, emerging from the current soul-level, epoch-sized transformation is a new self-image for humanity—the plan-etary psyche in relationship to the rest of the planetary soma. We are becoming, as Peter Russell put it, the "global brain."

In Her own growth and development, Mother Gaia developed Her lithosphere (stone), Her hydrosphere (water), Her atmosphere (air), Her biosphere (life), and finally Her noosphere (mind). We participated in Her entire journey of maturation, the sacred evolu-tionary journey toward health and wholeness, and are just now becoming ready for our unique contribution. We are Gaia's matur-ing mind, Her noosphere. We are matter become conscious, Gaia's central nervous system. We are the developing neo-cortex of the planetary body.

Being the planetary mind is our special role, our special capacity, and our special responsibility. There is little remarkable about us physically except for our brain power. There are many other forms of life that are stronger and/or faster. Many forms of life live longer than we. Some can even grow replacement parts, change colors, etc. Our contribution to the planet is in the role of psyche—mind and soul. We developed our mental capacities to an extraordinary degree throughout our adolescence and now, with the added agenda of spiritual maturation, we are discovering our full capacity to contribute to a healthy planetary whole.

The metaphors we use to think about, understand, or describe our world and ourselves are incredibly influential—they influence what we see in the present, what we consider to be appropriate action, and what we think is possible or impossible in the future. We have had three hundred years of thinking in mechanistic metaphors. The universe, we thought, was dis-spirited and ran like a well-made clock—no need any more for the clock maker. Human beings, this Epoch II thinking went, are also like machines—hearts like pumps, brains like computers—and needing only a highly skilled mechanic to diagnosis the problem and fix or replace any part that wears out.

But we now enter the age of organic metaphors, spirit-filled life, and humanity as the planetary mind. Immediately, this way of thinking opens up new possibilities.

One new possibility—new only in the sense that it has not been a part of our adolescent mentality, but old in the sense that it was dominant throughout our childhood and has been retained in native cultures—is the sense of humility that comes from realizing our interconnection with all of nature. We are ecologically related to everything else, not a separate part which can survive, let alone thrive, in isolation. The mind simply cannot live without the body. Only in some Epoch II science fiction do we see, or presumably would even want, a disembodied head kept alive with advanced technology. In "real life" we simply can't go it alone. Arrogance and presumed isolation are simply wrong and of course, also suicidal. The head needs the lungs, the heart and the liver, just to name a few other parts, if it is to remain alive and healthy.

Then there is the connection with the biological wilderness. We don't control the many natural biological functions that keep us alive. In our Epoch II need for cleanliness and making the wild tame, we disdained the body's natural functions and urges, called them "animal needs," and denied anything emotional. We overvalued rationality as we became disembodied, de-sexed, unemotional, and devoid of spirituality, as we "rose above" nature.

That Epoch II arrogance combined with the adolescent propensity for hierarchy so that we interpreted our superior brain power to be evidence that we were above all of nature in importance. We considered ourselves to be the pinnacle of evolution, higher than, better than and more important than the rest of nature.

The emergent deep value Epoch III—deep ecology—has us remembering who we really are, the planetary mind. But the special purpose is *function*, not hierarchical arrogance. Each and every part of nature has a special function and does not need to think in "better than" hierarchical arrangements.

The head is at the top of the body, not to be "higher than," but because a special function of the psyche is vision—being near the top the eyes can see farther. By being able to see the entire sweep of history and evolution, being able to look deeply into the night sky and deeply into the earth—all of which means deeply in time—we can gain perspective on life's overall meaning and purpose and help usher in a healthier future. We have powerful responsibilities precisely because we have powerful abilities to contribute to planetary health and well-being. From Epoch II self-centered and tunnel-visioned ego development, we are moving on up to the maturity of caring for the larger, natural family.

Imagination is one of the most important capacities of the mind, and as the planetary mind we have the special responsibility to use our imagination to envision a more mature humanity as well as a healthier planetary body. Imagination gives us the vision to work toward those ends.

To bring the point closer in, let's consider a thought-experiment. Imagine that we are collectively experiencing what some individuals have gone through personally—namely, what is called a "Near Death Experience" (NDE). There probably have always been people experiencing clinical death prior to being revived. What is unusual in recent years, however, is the interest in researching this phenomenon and the fascinating information that has emerged from such research. Consequently, we have learned a great deal about the NDE, the numbers of people having such experiences, and the impact such an experience has on a person.

Dr. Kenneth Ring is professor of psychology at the University of Connecticut and the president of the International Association for Near-Death Studies. "In the United States alone," reports Dr. Ring, "literally millions of people are now known to have had near death experiences."[8] In other research it is reported that as many as 15% of the population have had an NDE.

The pattern is usually quite similar, regardless of whether the NDE occurs because of an auto accident, a near drowning, attempted murder, or any kind of medical emergency. The person first has an "out of body experience," in which they find themselves above and outside their body looking down and observing the entire scene— rescue activity, attempts to revive them, etc. There is no pain, discomfort, or fear. Then they experience a movement through a dark tunnel, again with no fear, and a sense of vast speed and an expected destination. At the end of the tunnel is a pinpoint of light which grows larger and brighter. It is a brilliant golden white light, but it does not hurt to look at it. As they near the light they are overwhelmed with and totally penetrated by a powerfully good feeling of what is usually described as "pure love." At this point all time seems to stop, eternity seems to be experienced, and they feel at home in the light.

Involved in this light is the sense of divine presence—regardless of previous religious persuasion or even having considered oneself an atheist. This presence lets them know that they face a decision—stay or go back.

At this point the person usually observes, without judgment, an overview of their life including its essential meaning. It is within this moment that they see clearly that they are not finished and must go back. This decision frequently focuses upon the notion that their children still need them. The transcendent experience comes to an end and the person finds themselves back in their body, experiencing all the pain of the physical trauma.

People having experienced an NDE know it was not a hallucination, a dream, or a fantasy. They feel certain that it was not "just their imagination," although family, friends, or medical and psychological professionals give them little affirmation and understanding. It feels like the most real thing that has ever happened to them, yet words seem inadequate to explain what they experienced. Most importantly, it is quite simply the most profound experience of their lives and it leaves them vastly changed. They are transformed.

What is truly amazing about the research on NDE's is how common the results are, in spite of how different the people were before they had their near death experience. Regardless of demographics—gender, age, race, social class, education, nationality, or religious persuasion—the aftereffects are similar. Particularly important for our discussion here is how the aftereffects could lead to a healthier future for humanity and the planet. The changes experienced by all these very different kinds of people are not only remarkably similar, but the "pattern of changes," reports Dr. Ring, "tends to be so highly positive and specific in its effects that it is possible to interpret it as indicative of a *generalized awakening of higher human potential.*"[9]

According to the extensive and scientifically careful research there are three broad categories of transformational change experienced by almost everyone who has gone through an NDE:

A.CHANGES IN SELF-CONCEPT AND PERSONAL VALUES:

People going through the NDE come out with a greatly enhanced sense of self-worth. It appears not to be a matter of ego inflation but rather a greater acceptance of themselves because of the "tremendous sense of affirmation they receive 'from the light.'" They have a heightened appreciation of life and an increased concern for others. They manifest greater compassion, tolerance and patience with other people and an increased desire and ability to express love.

B.CHANGES IN RELIGIOUS OR SPIRITUAL ORIENTATION.

Although they may not be more outwardly religious, such persons feel a profound change in their spiritual perspective, one they describe as "universalistic." They are more people oriented and less materialistic. They are less concerned about the worldly notion of "success" and have less of a need to make an impression on those around them. NDE survivors have a profound sense of the unity of all people and of all spiritual paths. Narrow or exclusive religious practices and beliefs are felt to be too small and inadequate. There is usually an enlarged belief in life after death and more openness to the idea of reincarnation.

C.CHANGES IN PSYCHIC AWARENESS.

The NDE appears to "trigger an increase in psychic sensitivity and development—that following their experience they become aware of many more psychic phenomena than had previously been the case."[10] They personally have an increase in telepathic, clairvoyant, precognitive, synchronistic and out-of-body experiences. The essential element in all this is that an NDE transforms a person's experience of life from the Epoch II reductionistic paradigm into the Epoch III holistic paradigm. Only when we thought aspects of life could be isolated and insulated from one another did we think psychic phenomenon was impossible. Within a holistic universe, wherein everything is interrelated and interconnected, it makes sense that we would know things and communicate with people in ways not even understood during Epoch II.

The point here is that people experiencing an NDE have been involuntarily thrust into the new spiritual paradigm. Perhaps this is the species breakthrough to what Lewis Mumford called the "higher trajectory" for humanity that is coming as we leave Epoch II and enter Epoch III. For those who actually experience an NDE, their lives are changed. For the rest of us, this is where the special capacity of the neo-cortex, imagination, comes into play.

Anyone with just the slightest bit of imagination knows that collective humanity *is* in an NDE. We are, and have been for a number of years, within moments of killing humanity in a nuclear holocaust. Our imaginations have been sensitized increasingly in recent years to how we are ecologically creating an NDE. Heightened imaginations are now an important ingredient in bringing about our sense of participation within a larger human family, with *all* life on this planet, with Gaia Herself, and with our responsibility within the entire matrix.

Imagination may be the quality of Gaia's neo-cortex that plays the central role of enabling us to mature into Epoch III rather than committing an adolescent suicide, the difference between a future of despair and a future of hope. If we intentionally use this leading-edge quality of evolution we can participate in conscious evolution. We can co-create a mature planetary mind.

Imagine an entire universe participating in meaning and purpose, heaven-bent on creating and fulfilling a whole, healthy and holy life. Imagine the many wonderful and complex ways in which the universe and Gaia conspired to enable us to arrive at this point in evolution. Imagine Gaia giving birth and growing a humanity which has come to its special role in the whole of life. Imagine humanity growing through the physical development of childhood, then the ego and mental development of adolescence. And imagine us now ready to get our body/mind/spirit act together with a maturational and spiritual growth-spurt into full adult participation and responsibility.

Imagine yourself as one neuron in the planetary mind, sending images of health and wholeness across the synapses to all the other neurons. Imagine enlarging your definition of self to include all of life. Imagine your are in an NDE and acquiring all those advanced qualities of spiritual maturation. And imagine each of us, with sacred eyes, seeing into our spiritual and physical DNA so clearly that we re-member human nature.

CHAPTER 12

ON HAVING HISTORICAL INTEGRITY WITH AN EMERGING EPOCH III

IT IS TIME, AGAIN, TO GET PERSONAL. As we did in Chapter Seven following our discussion of Epoch II, we again shift from considering humanity's collective journey to looking deeply at our own individual journey. Again we shift from Biography to autobiography to consider how the "text" of our individual lives fits into the "context" of humanity's evolutionary journey. Again we are challenged to consider the matter of historical integrity—how our lives have integrity within the time of our lives. And, again, as I did in Chapter Seven, I will candidly share some of my own struggle with historical integrity as a way of encouraging you, the reader, to do the same.

Since we are living in such an epoch-sized transformational time, the matter of historical integrity, the matter of how our own stories fit into the larger context, is a matter of special and unique spiritual importance. We may have had all the ingredients before—evolutionary change, humanity's story, our individual stories, etc.—but there has never been a time just like this before, with its level of import and crisis.

The philosopher Sam Keen provides us with the words and images by which we can begin to consider our historical integrity with the emerging Epoch III.

> The identity of traditional man was based upon his ability to find his way in the forest, to light the fire, to say the prayer, and to tell a story that placed his life within an ultimate context. . . .[but]. . . Modern man has lost his way in the forest, he cannot

light the fire or say the prayer, and he is dangerously close to losing his ability to see his life as part of any story."[1]

In his customary way Keen has cut right to the essentials—the role of wilderness, the fire that enlightens and transforms, the desire to connect consciously with Spirit, and a personal story that integrates us within the larger context. Furthermore, Keen suggests that humanity in the modern era has lost touch with those essentials.

We have become lost, in part, because of the long-term impact of separating ourselves from the wilderness. What started ten thousand years ago as a natural process of adolescent ego development has now run its course. In developing our ego we lost our sense of connectedness with nature. We came to think of ourselves as essentially different from, and above and outside of nature. In the process we lost touch with our innate feminine power, began a head-trip which separated everything including head from heart and body. We projected power externally and developed what has now reached almost pathological proportions, a need to control through belief systems and violence. In our childhood we were at home in the wilderness and in our own wildness. In our adolescence we tried to tame everything and gain control over the lost power in our lives.

Fire and prayer are related. In late Epoch II our relationship with the holy has predominately taken one of two directions. Some of us have stuck rigidly and defensively with out-dated religious motifs worshiping the gods of stasis at the altars of static belief systems. Others of us, in our desire to be progressive and modern, have come to think of the holy as being irrelevant and have considered talk of such things as enlightenment or transformation to be the immature babblings of childish New Age woo-woo minds hanging out together in left field. In either case, the fires have been extinguished and we have lost touch with a living and dynamic Spirit.

In Keen's quote, and in our own lives, we eventually come to the matter of stories. It is not an accident of timing that as we experience our collective "dark night of the soul" we discover a renewed interest in story—individual stories, the "new story of science," and the largest story of the universal context within which we find ourselves. We know intuitively that part of our transformation at this crucial transition in history has to do with finding how our personal story fits within the new Cosmic Story.

This is not a new phenomenon, per se, for we have always had stories. As far back as we can discover, telling stories seems to be a strong human trait. It is just that we are now more aware of how the large religious and cosmic stories change with time and how they influence and interact with our own stories. In Epoch I we had our Childhood Story—a feminine story, a story about being one with nature, a story of a nourishing Mother Earth and a story in which we worshiped the Goddess. In Epoch II we had our Adolescent Story—a masculine story, a story of separation from nature and a story of fascination with external power, manifested first of all in a Father God and in male prophets, priests and saviors, then in technology and in the scientific priesthood.

In the late twentieth century we have a radically changing universal story—a story about humanity coming of age into a collective Adult Story. It is a story of synergy between science and spirituality, intellect and intuition, objectivity and subjectivity, human and planet. It is a story of wholeness, of empowerment, of becoming familiar with change and of re-membering our human-nature. And precisely because it is a time of change in the large story there is a renewed interest in talking about our individual stories and placing them in context. It is the spiritual impulse within us that wants a meaningful and purposeful context for our lives.

The late adolescence of collective humanity—the modern era—has been a particularly tough time on our self-identity and self-esteem. That should not surprise us, for any transition from adolescence into adulthood tends to be that way.

At one time we thought we were living on a planet at the center of the universe, which put *us* at the center of the universe—then we were told that story was wrong. We then hooked our developing ego to the belief that we were created by God as is and, therefore, had no relationship to "lower animal forms"—then we were told that story, too, was wrong. Then we got head-strong, accepted rationalistic and materialistic science as our god and denied that Spirit was any longer an accepted part of the modern intelligent life. We were wrong about that, too, and our mistake led to an enormous illusion. As our dis-spirited mind discovered an expanding universe, we deluded ourselves into a shrinking self-image. The universe was huge and incomprehensible and humanity was insignificant. The result of this recent story has been spiritual malaise and the paradox of a large ego and low self-esteem. We lost any sense of a meaningful story within story, of autobiography within Biography.

This is precisely why, in a book dealing with the large story of cosmic evolution and humanity's long journey of maturation, we place so much importance on the personal story—in Chapter Seven and here again in Chapter Twelve.

I have been told by "experts" that this book tries to do too much, that it is too comprehensive in its scope and too ambitious in its vision. I have been told that this book will not fit neatly within the conventional categories of publishing and book-selling and that it, consequently, will not sell. Bookstore owners will not know what shelf to put it on they tell me.

All of that notwithstanding, I believe our times demand a large sweeping perspective that integrates our lives with the time of our times, our stories within the largest story. The dark night of the soul that we are experiencing in the latter few decades of the twentieth century is in part, if not primarily, because we have lost touch with Spirit, and what is spirituality if not finding a meaningful and purposeful context for our lives. What we desperately need right now, at this dramatic transformational time in history, is the most ultimate and largest context we can imagine, a story which inspires the highest and best within us, and a story which can nourish and nurture the smallest of daily activities. The emergent Epoch III spiritual maturity demands that we transcend the convenient divisions of our adolescence between science and spirituality, between scholarship and autobiography, between the rational and mystical experiences of life, and between story and story. We can no longer stay within the narrow categories of Epoch II.

We may have been accustomed to reading health books separately from spiritual books and cosmology or astronomy separate from biographies. But the ancient etymological wisdom that connected health, wholeness, and the holy is a wisdom to be rediscovered in our time. It is a time for synthesis. It is a time for synergy between ourselves and our universe. It is a time to find new meaning and purpose in the way our individual lives fit within the largest story which science and spirituality are capable of providing. It is a time to think big—with integrity.

So, again, we ask—Why me?—Why now?—Why here? Can we delve deeply enough into our soul to rediscover our wilderness, to reconnect with Spirit, to experience again the fire of enlightenment and transformation, and to find our own story within the collective story? How do our particular gifts and our particular blessings provide particular opportunities in this particular time and place? How can our individual uniqueness assist humanity in moving toward health and wholeness? How can our particular version of Spirit contribute to the collective experience of Spirit? How does the part participate in, receive from and contribute to the whole?

I. Out of My Wilderness, My Fires, and My Prayers—My Story

The Blessing From Hell: Severe Chronic Pain

In Chapter Seven I shared the first part of this story. I told how the glorious feelings of athletic enjoyment turned into the agony of severe pain, how my blessing of body-mind-spirit coordination turned into a curse of crippling, how my heaven was transformed into a hell. I told how the medical authorities all concluded I would just have to accept my predicted fate—for the rest of my life, they said, I would be in severe pain, taking strong drugs, and confined to a wheelchair.

I also commented on what I consider to be the most fundamental condition upon which a healing is based—a determined victor rather than a helpless victim attitude. I won't rehash all of that but simply reiterate that none of the following would have been possible had it not been for that starting point. Before any "techniques" of mind-body healing could be helpful I had to make that all-important shift in attitude. I became absolutely determined to live into a better future than that which was predicted. I was *not* going to be a victim for the rest of my life, in spite of all the expert prognostication to the contrary.

With that as the preliminary and crucial first step I promised earlier to share the rest of the story. Basically, the rest of the story falls within three categories—discovering the role stress plays in the experience of pain, a cluster of mind-body-spirit strategies in synergy in order to experience the "more than" of healing, and finding the best healing energy of all—the deep and abiding love of and with, to and from, Diana.

First of all, stress. The role of stress in the chronic pain experience cannot be over-emphasized—in its creation, its intensity, its duration, and in pain's elimination or solution. I discovered it first experientially and then went on to make the study of stress in health and illness a major part of my doctoral work. It is not my purpose here to lay out a long and detailed scientific analysis of all the research on stress and pain—this chapter is for personal sharing not surveying the professional literature. Nevertheless, between my doctoral research and my personal experience and experimentation I have become convinced that the experience of life as inescapably stressful, or in contrast, the skills of modifying and managing life's stresses play enormous roles in our experience of health or illness.

For me, the first and the toughest challenge of stress management had to do with my first marriage. I have always been reluctant to talk about this for fear of being unfair to my first wife, who obviously cannot present her perspective or her experience in these same pages. There is never just one story in a relationship, although I can only speak for my story.

My reluctance has been such that I even wrote an earlier book about my healing, never mentioning this as a causal factor. I have come to understand, however, that I cannot be truthful and forthcoming without dealing with the fact that a stressful marriage was a very influential component in my experience of severe chronic pain.

Perhaps the fair way to put it is to say that Lee and I had some fundamental differences in some very crucial areas of a marriage relationship—namely, the role and experience of intimacy, nurturance, and essential affirmation. We worked on trying to reconcile those differences for seventeen years, but to no avail. I eventually had to face the reality that marriage was constricting and restricting my basic nature and my essential need for life's fulfillment. It was probably doing the same for Lee. I came to realize that my experience of pain, regardless of the physical reasons identified medically, was directly related to the stress of an unfulfilling marriage.

Pain is a message that something is wrong and a message that something has to change. Severe *chronic* pain is usually a message that something very fundamental in one's life has to change.

Divorce was, for many years, totally outside my considerations. We tried, as I have already indicated, for seventeen years to rectify the problems. Eventually I came to realize that in the interest of health, and in spite of considerable trepidation regarding the impact on our three children, that marriage had to come to an end. I can only speak for myself but suspect that all of us are better off because of that decision. I can only imagine how much worse things would have been for Lee, our children, and myself had I continued in the direction of living out that future predicted by the physicians.

It probably differs in degree among all of us, but for me that primary relationship of marriage is an extraordinarily crucial part of my life. To have the intimacy of a close friendship and a partnership in life's journey, to love and to be loved totally, unconditionally, and absolutely, is so important to me that words are completely inadequate to express it. I simply cannot imagine life being fulfilled without that deep intimacy which allows for, indeed demands, the unparalleled opportunity to express love and to be loved. When something which holds the potential for such an experience of heaven is not working right, it can become the worst hell.

The next two years were spent searching for the healing I was determined to find, exploring a wide range of new mind-body techniques, reading an enormous number of books and research papers on the leading edge of medical developments, experimenting with many healing modalities. I knew there were no guarantees of finding a healing, but failure would not be for lack of trying.

Before discussing specifically the mind-body techniques that I found helpful I want to make one preliminary comment. Ever since my first book was published there have been many people who were personally in pain, or who had a loved one who was, calling and writing to get more specific information on my "skills" and "techniques." While appreciating and understanding their desperate longing for answers, I want to make very clear my feelings about such personal specifics.

Each of us is different and I don't believe that my experience necessarily provides the formula for anyone else. There are some underlying generalities that are applicable across the board and I am trying to share those. But this or that technique, or a specific combination of activities, must be tailored to the individual. In a very real sense each person must find their own virgin re-birth into health and wellness. All others of us can do is to share our personal journey, attempt to identify the applicable generalities, and love one another.

I've already mentioned one attitudinal generality—determination to be the victorious captain of your own ship, rather than being a helpless and passive victim. The second, third, and fourth generalities in finding one's own healing are the three dominant themes of Epoch III—holism, empowerment, and transformation. They have been implied in about everything we have been talking about.

Consequently, if you are searching for a healing look beyond the fences of little minds and narrow paradigms. Be skeptical of any "expert" who piously pronounces what is the legitimate territory from which your healing must come and declares others as illegitimate. Don't accept my healing or any one else's, or this or that expert's paradigm, as the final definition of possibilities for your own healing. Fly over the fences like an eagle and search out your own healing ground.

(A lot of health professionals are going to be very nervous about what I have just said—and appropriately so. Indeed, we have learned a lot in medical science about some of the things that work, and some of the things that are simply dangerous. I am not discounting the value of medical knowledge, but don't want to dilute what was just said with a lot of "but, on the other hand" qualifications. Many medical professionals simply do not recognize how much the protection of their mental and financial "turf" allows suffering to continue. The healing ground for many lies somewhere between that protected territory of the establishment, on the one hand, and the New Age Luddites who think that anything that is medical is wrong, on the other hand.)

The medical paradigm does not give adequate credit to methods of tapping the vast healing resources within the person. Nor does it consider strongly enough what a change of consciousness can do for the body. Healing is always more holistic than we think, more empowering than we tend to assume in advance, and usually associated with welcoming a major change in one's life.

All of that notwithstanding, I promised to share the rest of my story. In addition to the "being" of those generalities, there certainly has been some "doing" that has played an important role in my healing.

One technique has been that of utilizing the power of mental imagery. I researched widely and developed my own synthesis of meditation, guided imagery, visualization, hypnosis and biofeedback. *The Spirit of Synergy* discusses this more extensively so I need not deal with it at length here. But make no mistake about it, imagery is a tremendously powerful mind-body technique about which, as a society, we have just begun to learn. Its capacity to train and hone the mind, the potential for bringing about physical changes, and the general healing capabilities are simply tremendous. There is no question in my mind that, as far as techniques go, this was the most powerful in enabling me to go from severe pain, strong medication, and crippling to manageable pain, no medication and a return to a relatively active, fun and productive life.

The second technique has been that of massage therapy. It was a marvelous serendipity that enabled me to discover just the right person to aid me in my healing journey, Keila Weeks. Keila's deep and profoundly loving spirit, her wise and powerful hands and of course, her professional massage therapy knowledge and skill all combined in a synergy with my body-mind-spirit to play a crucial role in the continued healing over the past few years. It is amazing how past experience is embedded in the musculature of our bodies and how the appropriate body-work can release one from the past and enable living into a new day, indeed, into a new body. Again I would have to say, judging from my experience, that the conventional cultural and medical worldview is tragically too narrow. How many people continue in pain because of our protection of narrow thoughts and concepts, because of the false assumption that the mind and body, past and present, are separate?

Finally, perhaps more mundane yet very important, has been the role of exercise and physical fitness. Because of my particular physical challenges I have had to find a personally tailored approach to fitness and exercise. I certainly can't do all that I would like to do and sometimes what I choose to do increases pain in the short term. Nevertheless, the process of keeping the body as active as possible and as strong and flexible as possible is no small matter. Not to be overlooked in importance is my down-right ecstatic enjoyment of athletic activity. It may sound paradoxical, but sometimes the short-term increase of back and hip pain, when it is in the pursuit of soul-level ecstasy, contributes to overall health and well-being. Conversely, the avoidance of pain at all costs may cost one dearly in quality of life.

After a period of practicing imagery in a deeply relaxed state of consciousness, I experienced a sudden and seemingly miraculous reduction of pain, went "cold turkey" off the medication and have never taken it since—something that was supposed to be impossible. There is still a pain challenge—any conventional medical diagnosis of my back would still assume great pain and crippling—but I have learned to manage it most of the time.

Underneath, beyond, above, in and through all the techniques of pain management is the most substantial aid to the increased quality of my life—the "discovery" of my soul-mate, Diana. The ability to fly like an eagle out of the morass of hell and into the ecstasy of heaven—from soreness to soaring—has been because of Diana, "the wind beneath my wings."

Before leaving this discussion of the blessing from hell, there is one additional aspect that should at least be briefly mentioned. When one has been to hell and back there is an intimate connection with others who are experiencing, or have experienced, their version of hell.

Hell is a singular place. In a very real sense hell is experienced in unique ways by each person and, therefore, can include tremendous feelings of loneliness. Consequently, when one is experiencing hell there is a tremendous hunger for someone out there to understand what one is going through. And when one has been to hell and back, one *does* understand, at least to a certain extent. I can empathize with anyone experiencing hell, because of having been there. At the same time, I can tell people experiencing hell that there is good reason for hope.

There is an exit from hell. We don't have to stay there, regardless of what the experts may predict. We can choose to make "it," whatever is causing the experience of hell, an "ex," a has-been. We can change it. We can escape. We can leave by creating an "ex/it." If the cynics say there are no exits, and the skeptics say you won't find one even if there is one, prove them wrong. Become proficient in creating and discovering "ex/its."

The hell of chronic pain, from whatever source, can be awful. But the exit from hell and the ascent into heaven can be full of awe. I experienced the horrible awfulness of hellish pain, but I have also experienced the incredible awe-fullness of the heavenly exit from pain.

The Blessing from Heaven: Love

The most important ingredient in Epoch III spirituality is a new grasp of the ontological nature of love. We cannot, therefore, look seriously at our integrity with our time in history without a very careful consideration of love—how we relate existentially to love as the essential power of the universe, and how we manifest or fail to manifest love in the nitty-gritty moments of our daily living. The integrity of the loving macrocosm with the microcosm of our version of love—that is a central ingredient in our historical integrity.

I am not suggesting that love is just now coming on the scene. It is not new in that sense. Love has been the central force of the universe since creation. Humanity's attempt to understand and describe ontological love has been present in philosophies and theologies as far back as we can remember. Love, for instance, has been the cornerstone and the genius of Epoch II Christianity in spite of how often it has been distorted or forgotten.

What is new about love is the context of the current world in transformation, the dying of the Epoch II value system and the emergence of Epoch III values. This new context is what gives love a new depth and focus. The Epoch III synergy of science and spirituality is bringing us into a new awareness of the essential wholeness of everything, and the central energy of wholeness is ontological love. The Epoch III emphasis upon empowerment brings a new focus on the pragmatic "bottom-line" aspects of love. And the Epoch III emphasis upon change, transition, and transformation brings us face to face with love as faith rather than as a static set of beliefs.

Integrity has to do with wholeness, consequently historical integrity comes to its most important focus in how our individual love stories fit within the cosmic Love Story. As I have tried to understand the flow of my story—the "plot" of my love story, as it were—I have discovered the following chapters.

The first chapter of my love story had to do with my maternal grandfather. I never knew Lem Williams—he died a month before my birth—but I wish I had. Those who knew him say he was quite an independent thinker and a fascinating and unique personality. Lem did a lot of things like most self-sufficient Jack-of-all-trades men did in rural Iowa during the early decades of this century. Mostly, however, he built buildings as a stone and brick mason and harvested ice from the river to deliver to the homes in and around Coon Rapids. He also spent a lot of time reading and always had a dictionary on his lap to quench his thirst for understanding words.

One particular day, as the local newspaper recorded it, the residents of Coon Rapids looked out their windows to see Lem driving up the street in his ice wagon. That was customary. But this time something was different about Lem's wagon. There on the side of his wagon, where usually the word ICE appeared, Lem had painted in large letters the word ALTRUISM. When asked why he had put that particular word on the side of his ice wagon, Lem replied: "I've been studying all the 'isms'—socialism, communism, capitalism, and so on. I've decided the best 'ism' of them all is altruism."

I am delighted to be related to that man and treasure his heritage. Anyone who puts "unselfish concern for the welfare of others" at the top of his list and has the audacity to advertise it in the context of his daily work, has a sense of the spiritual, an emphasis on love, a pragmatic courage, and is making the world a better place.

The second chapter of my love story was written immediately prior to my birth. A year before their pregnancy with me my parents had lost a baby girl just after birth for no known medical reason;

consequently my impending birth took on great concern and intensity. Rather than having the delivery in their home in rural northern Iowa as they had done with earlier births, they went north to a little Mennonite hospital in Mountain Lake, Minnesota.

The night before I was born my mother and father were in prayer and conversation about all their fears and hopes surrounding this event. In a numinous moment they were drawn together in a common commitment—if this child lived they would do all in their power to enable him or her to know and manifest love and to grow into a life capable of serving humanity in special ways.

One of the most remarkable parts of that chapter was that they did not tell me about their commitment through all the years of my total preoccupation with athletics—even to the brink of my becoming a professional athlete—loving me enough not to impose their agenda on how I would invest my life. They did not use that commitment, either as a club to try to control me or as a cry of frustration, during my stormy temper-laden adolescence—a time which would have tried the patience and commitment of saints.

I knew nothing of this pre-birth commitment and prayer until one day in the spring of my senior year of college. That's the next chapter—what happened to cause them to finally tell me.

I was about to graduate from college and was facing a dilemma—should I play professional baseball with the New York Yankees or should I play professional football with the (then) Baltimore Colts. Never had I seriously considered any other professional option—sports it would be, but what sport? I had no idea my life was about to take a completely unpredictable turn.

Cornell College conducted every spring a "Religion-in-Life Week." The speaker that year was Dr. James S. Thomas of the Methodist Board of Education. Lee and I were asked to host Dr. Thomas for a supper with other married couples on campus. We did so and I experienced an evening of discussion with Dr. Thomas. I remember being extremely impressed with his intellectual and spiritual power, but had no inkling of what was to come.

The next evening, mostly out of courtesy to our guest, Lee and I went to the chapel talk by Dr. Thomas. I don't remember what he talked about, and I'm not at all sure that his words had any particular role in what happened next. Suddenly, and here words fail to express the profundity of my experience, my life was totally turned inside-out. In an instant of complete mystical knowing my life turned away from professional athletics and toward love of and service to humanity.

The experience was beyond all the usual senses—I didn't hear voices, I didn't see any visions, no one "touched" me, etc., etc., etc. Perhaps the metaphor that comes closest in description is that of awakening. It was like all my previous life had been in a dream—a marvelous dream, mind you—but now life took on a whole new level of perception. There was no conventional religious symbolism, no "call" from Christ, no institutional loyalty, no dogma or doctrine that stood central to the experience. There was only an absolutely complete knowing that my entire life had been redirected, and a trust and faith that what was meant to be the specific steps in my journey would gradually be revealed to me.

The transformation was as complete as it was sudden. For a twenty-two year old jock who had lived his whole life in love with athletics and preparing to live it professionally, there was a total turning to a new and completely unexpected direction. Although my love for athletics continues as a peripheral activity there has not been a moment of second-guessing that mystical moment and that total transformation of professional direction.

The remarkable insight about my parents and their revelation of their pre-birth commitment occurred a couple of weeks later. I went home to Des Moines to share this dramatic event with them personally for I expected my total turn-about to shock them as it had my friends, fellow athletes, and coaches. After telling them all about the event and my decision to go to graduate school in preparation for the Christian ministry—for that was the primary way, it seemed to me at the time, to manifest my new commitment—I expected surprise if not confusion from them. Neither was the case. They simply looked at each other, smiled, and affirmed me in my decision. Then they told me the story surrounding my birth. What faith! What patience!

The next chapter in my love story was written some three years later. After two years of intensive academic focus in graduate school, with one year remaining, I realized a time-out was needed for some deep personal work. The sudden decision that sent me into the graduate study of theology, with no real prepararation for any overt personal faith journey, left me feeling intellectually stuffed while my soul was starving. I knew church history, biblical literary analysis, the life of Jesus, and what people like St. Paul, St. Augustine, Luther, and Wesley believed. But *I* didn't know what I believed—a poor foundation on which to enter the ministry.

I decided to take a year off before finishing my final year of the Master's degree program at Vanderbilt University Divinity School.

Through a series of providential serendipities I had the opportunity to spend that year off "working" under Dr. George Ball, the campus chaplain at Hamline University in St. Paul, Minnesota. I put working in quotes because they didn't have a budget for an assistant campus chaplain. Dr. Ball, however, agreed to let me help him out in his work duties in exchange for his time in helping me deal with my internal struggle.

I explained to Dr. Ball that I wanted to find out what I really believed, not what other people believed, before taking my last year in seminary. In order to do that I wanted to doubt everything possible and see what was left—then build on that. I was asking him to be a non-threatened and facilitative aid in that process. Heresy was not to be a legitimate barrier to this search for I wanted a free atmosphere for discovering what my soul really believed to be true.

I could not have asked for a better facilitator and friend. George Ball was an incredible help and in no way a hinder to my process. He had no need to impose a belief system nor was he threatened by anything I experimented with in this faith journey.

To sum up a year of intense questioning, experimenting, search, and research, I found that I could doubt everything that was a mental construct, an idea, or an intellectual belief. If the mind could fashion an idea it could find it unfashionable. If I could believe something I could doubt the same thing.

I eventually arrived, however, at the realization that transcending all belief and doubt was the experience of love as the essential core of the universe. Before my body developed, love was in the cellular structure of the universe. My body was simply one manifestation of that loving energy. Before my mind could reason, love was in my soul. Before I was, love brought life, and eventually me, into being. There was something much deeper than my thought processes that *knew* love was the most fundamental force in the universe. Out of my depths came the one thing that I discovered could not be doubted—love.

Because of an ego built on athletic success and a fiercely independent spirit, I was tempted at first to believe my conclusion about love had come all on its own. But in hindsight—it's amazing what age can do to soften an adolescent ego—I am sure it was no coincidence that I grew up in such a loving home, had parents committed to an ethic of love, was powerfully redirected through the loving force of Jim Thomas, and that George Ball was one of the most loving people I had ever witnessed in the nitty-gritty of daily activity.

Since then, everything else has had to take a secondary role to the ontology and ethic of love. No well-constructed belief system, no well-rationalized course of action can take priority over love. I may have a lot of disagreement with some of what St. Paul thought and said, but he was absolutely right when he wrote a letter to the church in Corinth in which he said:

> I may speak in tongues of men or of angels, but if I am without love, I am a sounding gong or a clanging cymbal. I may have the gift of prophecy, and know every hidden truth; I may have faith strong enough to move mountains; but if I have no love, I am nothing. I may dole out all I possess, or even give my body to be burnt, but if I have no love, I am none the better.[2]

St. Paul went on to describe the qualities of love, and then concluded by saying, "There are three things that last forever: faith, hope, and love; but the greatest of them all is love."

Actually what is important is that I *did* come to that insight alone and through a deeply personal and integral search. Just because others have come to the same insight does not dilute, but only strengthens, our own discoveries. We have to make it *our* story, and that is not done simply by "believing in" someone else's journey of discovery. I am convinced that we don't *know* love just by believing in Jesus, or in Paul's letters, or in anyone else who speaks of or personifies love. It has to be our own story of discovery. Unfortunately too many religious institutions place their emphasis upon intellectual belief, rather than in facilitating personal discovery. In the latter we can't be afraid of any territory of doubt through which we travel in order to find our soul's grounding.

The most important chapter in my love story over the past 16 years has been Diana. It goes far beyond being loved thoroughly and unconditionally by the most naturally powerful woman I have ever known; she has also been able to receive, without distortion, the tremendous love I have for her. That is a real gift.

There has also been a marvelous learning dimension, for me at least, in these sixteen years. Diana has taught me, not intentionally nor overtly but just by the nature of her being, what it is really like to be at home in the wilderness of one's soul. There is a depth and profundity to her connection with the animal world that I find utterly fascinating; in her I have experienced what truly empowered femininity is all about—a completion of and a balancing to my sense of the masculine.

The most recent chapter in my love story has involved some very hard lessons on how love's shadow can ruin friendships. Actually, this may be where Sam Keen's reference to fire comes in, for it has been a trial by fire.

Love is a blessing from heaven. But heaven, like anything else of substance, has a shadow. For some, in their Epoch II dualism, heaven was all light and hell all darkness, and generally the latter was projected out onto someone else. But in Epoch III's holism we realize that its all of a whole in a marvelously ordained richness of texture. Love, like the other blessings from heaven, has its shadow.

It has taken some painful experiences in the last few years to break through a naivete I had about love. If one's manifestation of love is naive, one can be blindsided and betrayed. Mine was and I got it—in spades. Out of that transforming fire in the wilderness of love came two lessons for me.

Previously I tended to think that if I was acting out of love and my motives were on the up and up then my own shadow was not involved. It's not quite that simple. I can be acting out of love and still my shadow—the repressed and unconscious dimensions of myself—can and will influence part or all of the relationship. Acting out of love simply does not eliminate the need to try to understand one's own dark side. In fact if our interest is love, it is even more important that we try to understand our shadow.

The second lesson came as a result of thinking that if I was loving toward another person, they would surely be loving in return. I know that probably sounds terribly naive, and if it does you may be ahead of me on this matter—or just more cynical. But because that is basically what I expected, I was unprepared for someone else's hell jumping up to destroy my heaven.

Both these insights lead right back to love—in this case, the aspect of love we call forgiveness. We certainly have no need for a mature and powerful capacity to forgive ourselves if we never confront our own shadow, nor to forgive others if we are never attacked by them. It's easy to love when everything is going along beautifully. The real test of love—and forgiveness is one of the nitty-gritty practicalities of ontological love—is when experiencing the shadow full-force, our own or someone else's.

Blessings In Process: Heroic Journeys

Heroic journeys are blessings in process—in two important ways. In the first place they are *about process*—change, movement, transformation, and evolution. In the second place they are *in process*—never completely finished and the learning never stops. As long as we live, if we are willing to live a heroic journey, we are continually separating from the past, discovering empowerment and returning to serve. Any and all three stages are blessings and a life lived as a heroic journey is a blessing in and of itself.

Before I finish this chapter I want to share two of my blessings in process—one having more general applicability, the process of discovering Epoch III masculinity, and one being more personal, the living and writing of this book.

(A) MASCULINITY—GROWING UP IN EPOCH II, GROWING ON INTO EPOCH III

A thoroughly patriarchal Epoch II gave us immature, adolescent and distorted notions of both masculinity and femininity. We are so much in the transitional time right now that we probably still don't know to what extent our Epoch II stereotypes condition and affect our lives, nor how far we have yet to go in discovering fully mature and healthy notions of sexuality.

This I know for sure—we will not have a healthy humanity until we discover, in our respective wildernesses, mature masculinity, mature femininity, and the relationship between the two. It is not a simple matter with a quick solution. Although the women's movement has been the first to address the Epoch II immaturity, and the men's movement is now underway—the oppressed is always the first to know that a change is necessary, the oppressor only later, if at all—we are still in the transition. Ten or twenty years from now we will see more clearly how even what we believe so fervently now is still only part of the way to full health, wholeness, and holiness.

Make no mistake about it, this is a heroic journey. Anyone who thinks our notions of masculinity and femininity need not change is, in my opinion, very mistaken. Anyone who thinks Epoch III maturation in this area is simple and that we're already there is, in my opinion, very naive. It is one of the most important and difficult transitions involved in this transformational time.

Personally, I can obviously speak only of masculinity—the process of discovery for a man who was raised in Epoch II and who is trying to grow into the maturity of Epoch III. It is particularly difficult because I really enjoyed and felt very much at home in the Epoch II notion of masculinity. For many years it simply never occurred to me there was anything wrong with the image I was living out. I felt fulfilled, I understood what it was to "be a man," I was naturally good at it—why change?

Only after beginning to listen to what the women's movement was saying—to listen deeply and carefully—did I find myself becoming aware of the many overt and subtle discriminations against and disempowerment of women throughout our society, and in our personal relationships. A lot was wrong, and anyone interested in justice and equality had to do something about it.

But at that level it is still an external matter—one can be for justice and equality for women and still not be aware of how deeply the Epoch II patriarchy has distorted our own notions of masculinity and/or femininity. You simply cannot have immaturity in one perception and maturity in the other. Only after considerably more reflection did I realize that external social justice had to be balanced with internal transformation.

I make no pretense to having made it into Epoch III on this matter—but I am working on it. That is why this discussion is "in process." Two brief stories illustrate some of that process.

I was in the middle of thinking about all this when Diana and I had a co-teaching engagement in Hawaii. To squeeze in a mini-vacation we stayed on for a couple of days after our teaching was over. We went off to a more remote place and enjoyed just being with each other, the sun, the water, and the sand. This matter of discovering the difference between Epoch II and Epoch III masculinity and femininity was a frequent subject of our discussion.

Late one night we walked along the beach. The full moon sent shimmering bars of white light riding atop each wave that greeted us at the shoreline. It was as if the moon were trying to send me a message, for regardless of how far we walked the moonlight atop the waves kept coming my way.

I know, of course, how to make rational sense of that phenomenon, but the symbolism took hold of my mind and wouldn't let go. It was as if my mind were caught in the undertow of the tide. I felt the invisible pull, as the waters experience the moon. The moon symbolic of the feminine, and the water symbolic of the unconscious—femininity and waves of consciousness—we were one in the experience of a rising tide.

We stayed at the beach long into the night, lovers oblivious to the passage of time, conversation separated by long periods of silence as our minds and bodies alternated between separate and common journeys. We experienced being husband and wife, male and female, individuals and a twosome, and together participants in an awe-inspiring cosmos.

Questions occupied my whole being. How does Diana incorporate both polarities in such a beautiful combination, predominately manifesting the feminine qualities, yet in her wholeness manifesting a marvelous and appropriate integration of masculine qualities? And in very different ways, and in the interest of my own unique wholeness, how do I appropriately integrate feminine qualities into what I know so well, my version of masculinity?

I thought about how I, acculturated as a male in the Epoch II mainstream assumptions about masculinity, had also come to believe that such notions were truncated, less than whole and healthy. Yet I also felt foreign to some of the alternative versions suggested in this transitional time.

In a transitional time we face a dilemma. To stick stubbornly with the past leaves us unavailable to the creative workings of Spirit, which is always working for our greater health and wholeness. Rigidity and stasis, in my opinion, are anti-Spirit. On the other hand, not all of the past is thrown off as we mature into a more whole future. Nor is every new idea a good idea. But clearly, growth and maturation mean we have to be willing to die to the old and be born into something new.

The matter of masculine-feminine wholeness within the one person is quite an interesting challenge. What were the Bob Keck notions of masculinity that needed to die, and what needed to be born? And how does fear of change distort one's process?—more a factor, I suspect, than we generally think. I have been so at-home with most of the Epoch II version of me, albeit knowing that it was not complete, I wonder what I will mourn if some of it needs to die to give birth to a more whole and healthy Epoch III version.

These thoughts, and the focus on the moon, brought to mind a legend of the Zulu tribe. As legend has it the moon wanted to communicate to the people on earth that death was not to be feared because there is life after death. To communicate this important message to the people on earth the moon selected the hare since he was so fast. But the hare bungled the message and instead of telling the people on earth that death was not to be feared he told us that death was to be feared. The moon was so angry for messing up such an important message that it struck him on the face, splitting his lip. Thus, the hare-lip.

Could it be, I wondered, that the moon was sending a message to me that night atop those waves? Was it pulling a rising tide within me for health and wholeness, something the moon symbolizes, namely, the feminine qualities? And was it telling me death was not to be feared while growing into something new and healthier?

All of that notwithstanding, I could not identify anything about this growing that frightened me. No matter how much I searched, I could not come up with anything about integrating appropriate feminine qualities that gave me concern. Certainly I was secure in my basic masculinity, and expansion or improvement on that did not seem to worry me. That, at least, was what I thought consciously.

We eventually decided to turn in. It had been a glorious day and night, and the sleep was deep and restful. The unconscious, however, does not need to rest and it continued my learning. I had a dream. In the dream Diana and I were traveling through a country where they persecuted women. I was commiserating with her about this, the injustice of it all, when she said to me, "Let's escape into the neighboring country. There they treat women equally." "That's easy for you to say," I replied in the dream, "but there they decapitate men."

If we are willing to listen to our dreams they invariably go deeper than all our intellectual head-tripping of an issue. I knew I was philosophically for equality and justice for women—changes called for as we mature from Epoch II into Epoch III. But I also thought I had no fears about the other aspect of health and wholeness— becoming more integrated personally with feminine qualities. My dream showed that, in fact, I had some fears about that integration; at some level I evidently feared losing my head.

Interestingly, my dream did not indicate a fear of castration but rather a fear of losing my head, my mind, presumably my thinking capabilities. That came as a surprise to me and indicated some of my deep agenda for becoming integral with the emerging Epoch III.

The second story that I will share is perhaps not as profound in its implications, yet brought a little humor into my growth process—a quality sometimes in short demand when we are "serious" about growth and development.

For a number of years I had been consulting with corporations and other organizations, assisting them in enhancing the health and well-being of their employees while diminishing illness, medical costs, absenteeism, etc. One specialty within that large spectrum was the role of stress in disease and how stress management skills can create and maintain a healthy life.

This story came out of one such occasion with a large company in Columbus, Ohio. In the process of discussing stress management, I explained how our current notion of masculinity—one that only allows male executives to be hard-driving, single-minded, tunnel-visioned, hostile if anyone gets in the way—was contributing to early heart attacks. I discussed how a more holistic integration of feminine qualities could result in a healthier masculinity.

After the seminar I was browsing over participants' evaluation forms looking for clues to which subjects had been communicated effectively, which had not, and in general how the session could be improved. I was enjoying quite a nice ego trip, what with all the positive comments, when I was brought up short. One evaluation form was uniquely critical. Instead of answering any of the official questions the participant, presumably one of the male executives, had simply printed in large letters across the entire sheet, "DR. KECK EATS QUICHE." The reference was obviously to the book *Real Men Don't Eat Quiche*. I have to admit to three quick reactions:

"First of all," I thought, "that was a clever evaluation, and I have to give the guy credit for being so creative."

"Secondly," I reasoned, "this must mean I touched a raw nerve with the idea that men should integrate appropriate feminine qualities."

"Thirdly," my head gave way to my gut reaction, "I'd like to get that turkey into a handball court and we'll just see who eats quiche!"

Oh well, so I have a ways to go when someone is questioning my masculinity.

(B) A JOURNEY IN TRANSITION—THE LIVING AND THE WRITING OF SACRED EYES:

This book has been a real soul-level process for me, resulting in an experience of the classic heroic journey. It doesn't feel as though I chose the process, but rather the process chose me. To a great extent my decisions along this journey were not a rational choice to do this rather than that—but simply choosing to be responsive to the Spirit moving in and through this experience.

As in the classic heroic journey there was the separation. Although I had been thinking about, researching for, and writing portions of this book for some twelve years, I was always trying to do it alongside other work. Two years ago the decision was made to dive into the writing full-time until it was finished. This book, my soul was saying, just had to be finished before going on to anything else.

As in all such separations there were deaths, fears, uncertainties, and the faithful openness to whatever the future would hold. At age 55, to stop earning money and gradually use up savings, not certain when the book would be finished, caused considerable financial anxiety. And going into oblivion, as far as the world was concerned, has had its challenges to the ego. What if this book turns out to be totally worthless to the outside world? What if I never make another contribution of any significance? Am I ready to have all my accomplishments exist in the past? If I let my former persona to the world die what would take its place? Who am I becoming? Such issues, in one's mid-fifties, are not simply interesting coffee-table topics for discussion—we're talking existential anguish.

The second stage, as in the classic heroic journey, was empowerment. I had no idea what I was getting into and can't begin to describe adequately all the extraordinary experiences of depth I had during this process. On the one hand, words seem inadequate to do justice to the journey my soul has been through during the living and writing of this book. On the other hand, this book *is* my testimony to the experience of trying to put the exploration of Spirit into words. Much of what you have read and are reading in these pages was new to me as it flowed out onto the page. That has been a fascinating and humbling experience for someone who thought his intellect was in charge of the writing process.

The encounter with power has been such that I feel like a very different person now than I was two years ago. Although the power has come in the form of thoughts and emotions all across the spectrum, I feel an incredible sense of gratitude for the totality of the experience. Each experience has had the paradoxical effect of making me awe-struck with the kind of power we individually can tap into, and at the same time giving an overwhelming and marvelous sense of humility, gratitude, and obligation.

We are incarnations of a powerful Spirit, yet the power is not ours alone. We have access to the power, yet it is beyond any one manifestation or life. And I will say this—it leaves me sad for anyone who has not experienced the power of loving Spirit, who thinks we are separated from the rest of the world, who doesn't find meaning and purpose in life, and who thinks we have to look externally for the power that heals and the power that is holy.

Finally, in the heroic journey, is the return to serve. My journey in, through, and beyond *Sacred Eyes* is still very much in process. I only know that I am committed to serve "in light of" this particular journey. The precise nature of that, of course, remains to be seen. But then, that is why faith is so central to a journey such as this.

II. WHAT ABOUT *YOUR* WILDERNESS, *YOUR* FIRES, AND *YOUR* PRAYERS?
HOW DO YOU FOLLOW THE BLESSINGS OF *YOUR* STORY INTO HISTORICAL INTEGRITY WITH THE COSMIC STORY?

When you go deep into your wilderness what do you find? Do you find that, on the surface, you have been living someone else's story—the story your parents wanted you to live, the story that fits the culture's stereotype for you, or the story your spouse has in mind for you?

What have been your blessings from hell?

What have been your blessings from heaven?

What has been your love story?

In order to "get a life," as the saying goes, you have to live your own story. Your uniqueness, your blessings, your historical integrity can only be manifested if you, as Sam Keen put it, "author/ize" your own story.

In a story told about Mahatma Gandhi, a man had traveled far in order to get a glimpse of the holy man and to take back to his people some jewel of truth uttered by the great Gandhi. As Gandhi was boarding a train the man, feeling that he was going to lose the opportunity, pressed forward through the crowd and yelled, "Please, what can I take back to tell my people? What is your central message?" The crowd noise was such that the man could not hear the reply Gandhi shouted back, in spite of repeated attempts. Finally, just as the train was pulling away, Gandhi hurriedly wrote five words on a paper bag and handed it out the window to the desperate follower. The note read: "My life is my message."

None of us may feel that our life is of the spiritual stature of a Gandhi, but the truth is the same for all of us. In spite of who we may think we are, in spite of all we may think or say we believe, it all comes down to this—our life is our message. In that light, what is your message for the world? What statement does your life make? What message will you communicate when those around you stop listening to what you believe, or think, or say, and simply listen to your life? Will there be an integrity to that message? Will there be an integrity between your life and what you say you believe? Will there be an historical integrity between your life and the time and place of your life?

You need that integrity for a healthy, whole, and holy life. The world needs your integrity, contributed in the interests of a healthy, whole and holy future. So, author/ize your story—now.

> Whatever you do or dream you can, begin it.
> Boldness has genius, magic and power in it.
> Begin it now.
>
> —GOETHE

CONCLUSION

A NEW HEAVEN
AND A NEW EARTH

Then I saw a new heaven and a new earth.
Behold. I am making all things new.
—THE REVELATION OF JOHN

THE TRANSFORMATION IN WHICH WE ARE LIVING IS HUGE—nothing less than the emergence of a new heaven and a new earth and, consequently, a new God and a new humanity. The import of this transformation is indicated by the fact that there has been only one other such soul-level change even closely approximating this one in magnitude and consequence, and that took place between 5,000 and 10,000 years ago. So buckle your seat-belts—we're in for quite a ride as we enter the 21st century and catapult into Epoch III.

There is a particularly tough mental challenge in this interim time, but since Epoch II was precisely about developing our mental capabilities, hopefully we are up to the task. The challenge is this—can we think big enough without losing our capacity for discernment? Can we be bold enough without being naive? In an age when only the exaggerations appear to be coming true, in a time when the most dramatic transformation in thousands of years is taking place, we simply will not perceive the possibilities inherent in this transformation if we stay ensconced within small minds.

Michael Murphy, in his seminal and enormously important book, *The Future of the Body*, was faced with a similar challenge. His advice, when exploring the further reaches of human nature, is to be "open-minded but keep an ear for tall tales."[1] In the metaphor of this book, I would add that it takes sacred eyes to perceive the substance of an unfolding and previously unknown future without being fooled by tall tales, entranced by fads or detoured by aberrations.

A highly developed intellect is crucial to the process of liberating us into an expansive future, but the intellect can also be a prison, locking us into small discoveries of the past. At this time in history, we need minds capable of critical discernment and yet creatively open to that which we had never before imagined.

Perhaps even more difficult is the spiritual challenge facing us. Most of us have had our spiritual life conditioned greatly by institutionalized religion, and *any* institution tends to be conservative—conserving and preserving the past. There is value in that, and there are problems, particularly in a time of major transformation. In a time when Spirit is creating a whole new heaven and earth, our spiritual lives must be open to newness or we'll miss the whole marvelous journey. So, again, balance is called for—a spiritual life that can bring the value of the past into a living, breathing, dancing, creative and evolving spiritualized future.

It is a very challenging time. It is a mind-boggling and spirit-stretching time. But, make no mistake about it, Epoch III will be the dawn of a totally new kind of human existence. Indeed, we are on the threshold of experiencing nothing less than a new heaven and a new earth.

We began our discussion of Epoch III with a visionary statement from the historian Lewis Mumford in which he suggested that the coming spiritual maturity "will unveil new potentialities, no more visible in the human self today than radium was in the physical world a century ago." So the challenge is to overcome myopia, which is defined as "an abnormal eye condition in which light rays from distant objects are focused in front of the retina instead of on it, so that the objects are not seen distinctly; nearsightedness." What a marvelously appropriate definition of our challenge today. With the cultivation of sacred eyes we can overcome the nearsightedness that always threatens to lock our vision into only that which has been, rather than seeing that which is to come.

A New Heaven—(Therefore, A New God)

The old cliche is right—in the beginning we were created in the image of God, and we have been returning the compliment ever since. We have always created God in our own image—in the particular image we had of the world at any given time. Our world-view created our image of God. We are about to make an epoch-sized switch and, no doubt about it, there will be some of us who would rather fight than switch. But we have switched before—from the Mother Goddess to a Father God—and we're going to do it again. Soon.

First of all, we need to be very clear about one thing—*our concepts of God never describe God in any full or complete manner*. They are only our meager attempts to understand God, and fall far short of actually describing the divine Spirit of the universe. We have to be either incredibly arrogant or wildly naive to think that our minds could actually understand, or that our language could sufficiently describe, the spiritual essence of everything that is.

Secondly, our images of God are the result of our deep values, and not the other way around. Soul-level reality precedes mental constructs. Heaven is not "up" or "out"—it is a soul-level kind of place. And since Spirit at this time in history is working out a major transformation of humanity's soul, a new heaven is in the making. In other words, God creates a new heaven, transforms our soul, and we respond by constructing a new image of God.

As we discussed in Chapter Six, the 1960s was the decade in which this soul-level transformation started erupting onto the culture's surface. And it is interesting to see how much experimentation with "God talk" has emerged in the past three decades.

The widespread restlessness with the Epoch II notion of a Father God is testimony to the new heaven taking shape within our soul. In the last thirty years we have seen a growing interest in Goddess worship. Progressive Christian churches have been increasingly addressing a "Mother-Father God." Interest in Native American spirituality has been growing, where they often speak of and to "The Great Spirit." And for those who have been uncomfortable with any religious language, the spiritual impulse is given the name of "Universal Mind," "Mind-at-Large," or "Cosmic Consciousness." Awareness coming from a deep intuitive level is emerging all across the human landscape with experimentation in God-talk. The Epoch II notion of God just won't cut it anymore, for it does not have integrity with the Epoch III soul growing within us.

The suggestion here, however, is that probably none of the above will adequately describe our experience of Spirit in Epoch III. Regarding Goddess worship, I simply don't believe this trans formation is about going back, in spite of how much we need the balancing that fuels that particular movement. This is not about

going back to Epoch I. This is not a devolutionary transformation—
it is, rather, an evolutionary transformation. Nor do I think we will
long be satisfied with the androgynous "Mother-Father" language,
even though Epoch III will clearly transcend the patriarchal images
that have thrust women into second-class spiritual citizenship. And
it is interesting, and understandable, that in concluding an Epoch II
agenda of mental development the people who feel a spiritual
impulse but don't like religious language want to speak of the
Ultimate of the universe as being some kind of Super-Mind.

My suspicion is that all the above are interim efforts—understandable, but probably not what will characterize Epoch III. We
may, in fact, still be too much in the interim to be able to perceive an
adequate Epoch III notion of God. Nevertheless, some of us just
have to give it a try.

Clearly, no one person will name God for us, and I certainly have
no presumption of doing so here. Somehow—eventually—we will
come to a consensus as to what adequately expresses our Epoch III
experience of life's spiritual essence.

One possibility, however, is that which emerges from an historical and evolutionary perspective, for we are two-thirds of the way
through a linear trinity—Mother, Son, and Holy Spirit. Epoch I can
be seen as being the period of the Mother, Epoch II as that of the Son,
and Epoch III as the period of the Holy Spirit. Perhaps a little
elaboration would be helpful.

Epoch I was the period of the Mother, in the sense that we were
born of Mother Earth, had a feminine deep value system, and
worshiped the Goddess. Epoch II was the period of the Son, in the
sense that it was our collective adolescence, we had a masculine
value system, and we worshiped a male notion of Divinity. Consequently, although we worshiped a Father God it has been the period
of the Son in an evolutionary and maturational sense.

Before we were ready for the period of the Holy Spirit, however,
we needed to take a brief sojourn by which to conclude our
adolescence. This brief sojourn has been the modern scientific era—
indeed, it has been a three hundred year sojourn, but that is very
brief in relationship to the full five to ten thousand years of our
Epoch II adolescence. It was a "prodigal son" sort of venture.

As a way of topping off our adolescent ego and mental development, we declared our independence from the Father, decided we
could understand and deal with reality on our own, and left
"home" with an enormous confidence in our own mental abilities—
after all, we dubbed ourselves the doubly wise.

As we discussed in Chapter Five, we intentionally left the worship of the Father, but we did not give up worship—we just worshiped our own mental capacities, as manifested in science and rationalism. We did not need the Father anymore, we thought, for we could understand the universe and ourselves without the immature psychological crutch of religion. We came to believe— indeed, with a fervor of a true believer—that anything "proved" by science was therefore "real." But, in contrast, anything labeled mystical, religious, spiritual, para-psychological, or "occult" was suspect, fanciful and dubbed "unrealistic." It is interesting to note that even Epoch II mainstream psychology—which if it were true to its name would be the study of the soul—wanted so much to be legitimate in the eyes of the scientific gods, that it rejected spirituality altogether as having anything to do with the healthy person.

George Bernard Shaw understood this early on, and he wrote: "There is nothing that people will not believe nowadays if only it be presented to them as Science, and nothing they will not disbelieve if it be presented to them as religion."[2]

Our worship of science, however, did not bring us a meaningful existence. In fact, the more we worshiped at this altar, the more cynical and depressed we became. One famous scientist expresses this meaninglessness by writing: "The more the universe seems comprehensible, the more it also seems pointless."[3] And another says: "The ancient covenant is in pieces: man at last knows that he is alone in the unfeeling immensity of the universe, out of which he has emerged only by chance."[4]

Three hundred years of this ego-trip and "going it on our own" has not brought us to the point of feeling very good about the universe, ourselves, or our place in the universe. We're not really enjoying life very much, and we find it hard to muster any hope for the future. When we are honest with ourselves we admit to a deep despair, a feeling of meaninglessness, purposelessness, and an all-pervasive spiritual malaise.

"Nothing has been more futile," writes history professor Theodore Roszak, "than our effort over the past few centuries to establish values and define sanity with a cultural context that finds no place for the sacred and views life as a marginal anomaly in the universe."[5]

We now are beginning to realize that our "prodigal son" sojourn was not all that it was cracked up to be. Science and rationalism are gods with clay feet. We learned a great deal, gained a great amount of technological progress, yet we feel deep in our heart and soul that something is missing. No longer are we convinced that the reductionistic, materialistic and atheistic perspective adequately describes the world. No longer does a universe devoid of Spirit seem credible. No longer can we believe that high spiritual insights are "nothing but" chemical reactions in the materialistic brain. And no longer are we sold on the notion that the universe, and we ourselves, are dis-spirited machines.

Something is missing, and we are beginning to suspect that we will find it if we return "home." But "home" is not back to the Father God of Epoch II. "Home" is where the Spirit is, at the spiritual core of our life and in the core of all life. "Home" is the shortest of all journey's—back to the "within-ness" of everything and the "ground" of Being-ness. The journey "home" for the "prodigal son" is the shortest of all journeys. It takes but a moment in time, or a flash in perception.

So we come to the transformation into Epoch III, the epoch of time that we could view as the third phase in a linear trinity—the period of the Holy Spirit. To fully understand its appropriateness it helps to consider the other two words that share the same root with the word holy—health and wholeness.

In the evolutionary scheme of things, we developed our bodies (Epoch I) and then our minds (Epoch II). We now come to the time of spiritual maturation (Epoch I II)—thus, the historical period when the Spirit of the Holy comes to the evolutionary forefront. It is also the time for us to discover ontological love as an enormous healing power—thus, the Spirit of Health. And, as we discussed in Chapter Eight, one of the deep primary values of Epoch III is the discovery that this is a holistic universe—thus, the Spirit of Wholeness.

It would be appropriate, therefore, for us to see Epoch III as the period of the Holy Spirit, and to use this as our name for God. The difficulty with this, of course, is the extent to which the term may be inescapably wrapped up in the religious baggage of our adolescence. Clearly, unless we can free ourselves of the limited Epoch II uses of the term, it won't suffice as an Epoch III concept of God.

It may be that the most empowering, most liberating, most accurate and most healing image of God for Epoch III will be that which has surfaced time and again throughout our discussion of Epoch III values, namely, Love . If we come to fully understand the ontological Love that creates and sustains the universe, and that which is the magnetic power pulling us toward health, wholeness, and holiness—there may not be a better notion of "God." Rather than the periodic statements in Epoch II that, among the various other attributes of God, "God is love"—perhaps the Epoch III change is simply to turn it around to an all encompassing "Love is God."

It is Love that has created an evolutionary inwardness to the universe, growing us toward health and wholeness. It is Love that provides the allurement, the gravity, the attractional force that unites everything in a holistic universe. It is Love that heals our past and empowers our future. It is Love that affirms and liberates every person. And it is Love that can reunite the parts of us that get separated and fractured, along with reconciling our estranged brothers and sisters on this planet, and can bring about a re-union and comm-union with Father Sky and Mother Earth. So Love just might be the best Epoch III name for God, *if* we can grow in our understanding of ontological Love.

We either have to liberate our concepts of Holy Spirit and/or Love from the inadequate and immature notions we have had of them in Epoch II, or we will have to come up with something else. Whatever. But make no mistake about it, a new heaven *is* emerging, and we *will* be developing a new image of God.

When that happens we can be certain of this—our image of Heaven and God will be something quite different from the reductionistic notion of a heaven separated from earth, and the divine as different from human. We will no longer tolerate a concept of God that is patriarchal, sexist, racist, nationalistic, or parochial in any way, shape, manner, or form.

It will be a concept of God that is "up close and personal," enabling a thoroughly radical democratization of spirituality. It will be a notion of God that does not need official institutional conduits, nor outside experts or saviors, in order to gain access to the sacred essence of life. It will be a concept that empowers our sense of the Holy, replacing the dis-spirited and "modern" arrogance and spiritual malaise of our Epoch II "prodigal son" phase. It will be a concept that penetrates and permeates every aspect of life, and impacts every institution of culture. It will liberate and affirm *every* kind of person, leaving far behind the immature notions that confer second-class spiritual citizenship on the people outside the inner circle. It will be a sense of Spirit that moves, grows, evolves and is by nature transforming. And it will be a notion of God that is big enough to inspire the new and more mature human being emerging in our time.

A New Earth—(Therefore, A New Human)

A new earth and a new human will be emerging in Epoch III precisely because we have a new heaven. A new heaven inevitably creates a new human.

Spirit, in creating a new heaven, is transforming the soul of humanity. It is calling us forward into adult maturity, a maturity in which we will be balancing our physical, mental, and spiritual capabilities. The new human is being called forth to be a creative participant in the further evolution of life here on planet Earth.

One thing that I have found interesting throughout this fourteen year Deep Value Trend Analysis is how this soul-level transformation is bubbling to the surface in such seemingly disparate minds. From a widely divergent spectrum we hear impressive minds conceiving of, and their voices articulating, the sense of a very new kind of human being emerging across this evolutionary threshold.

From the biologist/essayist Lewis Thomas. . .

> What we call contemporary culture may turn out, years hence, to have been a very early stage of primitive thought on the way to human maturity. What seems to us to be the accident-proneness of state-craft, the lethal folly of nation-states, and the dismaying emptiness of the time ahead may be merely the equivalent of early juvenile delinquency. . . . If we can stay alive, my guess is that we will someday amaze ourselves by what we can become as a species. Looked at as larvae, even as juveniles, for all our folly, we are a splendid, promising form of life and I am on our side.[6]

. . . to the human potential researcher and lecturer, Jean Houston:

> The Rhythm that is coming brings the search for the possible human in ways that it has never been sought before. . . . With the present convergence of the findings of anthropology, cross-cultural studies, psychophysical research, and studies into the nature and function of brain, we are beginning to have in hand a perspective on human possibility as profound as it is provocative. This perspective allows us to turn the corner on our humanity, exploring and experiencing the astonishing complexity and variety of the world of the possible human. It is virtually a new introduction to the human race."[7]

Again, the challenge is to retain our best critical analytical abilities, while at the same time being able to think big enough to understand the possibilities coming true in our time. The new human that is now emerging was unimagined in Epoch II. We will be empowered in ways that will transcend anything we have known in the past. And we will discover a level of health and well-being, as well as the prevention and cure of illness, that has only been described before as "miraculous."

If we can imagine the difference between the human being now and the human being of some ten to twenty thousand years ago, that much difference again—and probably much more—will be growing in the coming decades. Consider how far we have come, from stone tools to the technology of putting a person on the moon. Consider how far we have come in communication technology, micro-surgery, understanding the universe, understanding this planet, etc., etc., etc. Consider how much we have changed since our childhood, before 10,000 years ago, and consider how much more we are likely to change as we get our act together in body, mind, and spirit.

Human life, like all organisms, moves naturally on to the next stage of growth. We developed physically in our childhood, mentally in our adolescence, and now move on to spiritual maturation. Because of our material and mental focus in Epoch II, the tendency is to think of progress only in materialistic or mental terms. But because this transformation is spiritual, just imagine what a different human we will be when we put spiritual maturity together with physical and mental maturity.

This soul-level transformation will change everything about human life. As we discussed earlier, it is a dramatic change in the underground river that creates and nourishes everything on the surface of culture—our more superficial values will change to reflect the deep value changes, our health-care will be approached very differently, as will education, politics, organized religion, and our way of doing business. Indeed, it will be a new earthly reality precisely because within us there is a new heaven taking shape. Earth is re-spiritualized, heaven is terra firmed and in-carnated, and the sacred and the profane are integrated.

When we do become integral with the new heaven within us there will be no more problems of self-esteem and self-worth. We will become whole human beings living empowered lives of love and service. We will begin taking responsibility for our co-creator role on this planet. And we will start contributing a level of creativity not as yet envisioned.

To linger on that point for just a moment, it is a misunderstanding of Epoch III empowerment to think that it leads to egotism. Egotism is an adolescent, distorted, and small notion of empowerment. Egotism comes from an immature ego. In contrast, in Epoch III the empowered and affirmed mature ego knows that we did not create this universal Love-power, and we do not have exclusive use of it. Rather, we are individual, "special case" incarnations of the power that permeates and evolves the universe. It is an incredible blessing that, if followed, is awesome in its capacity to empower us personally, yet connects us with the cosmos at large—an extraordinarily humbling realization.

This is not a time in history in which cowards will feel comfortable, nor will those who find their security in stasis. But neither is it a time for spiritual elitism. Quite the contrary, the ground on which all of us are standing is holy, every cell in every body is filled with the power of Spirit. Courage for this transformational trip comes from the innate spiritual democracy of Epoch III—every person who discovers their historical integrity will be empowered with a spiritual maturity and participate in a synergistic community of other empowered humans.

This is a glorious time in which to be alive. We have the special opportunity to participate in the most powerful transformation ever to come along. Also unique is that it is happening fast enough for us to see some results of our participation. The power and synergy of Love will be remaking heaven and earth, and we are living right in the midst of it. Why you? Why me? Why here? Why now? Why don't we decide to make the most of this opportunity? In the words of Tennyson, "Come my friends, 'Tis not too late to seek a newer world."

AFTERWORD

To your tired eyes I bring a vision of a different world, so new and clean and fresh you will forget the pain and sorrow that you saw before.

Yet this is a vision which you must share with everyone you see, for otherwise you will behold it not.

To give this gift is how to make it yours.

—A COURSE IN MIRACLES

CHAPTER NOTES

CHAPTER ONE
1. Davies, Paul, *Cosmic Blueprint*, Simon & Schuster, 1988, pg 203.
2. Boslough, John, *Stephen Hawking's Universe*, Quill, 1985, pg 121.
3. Ibid., pg 123.
4. Ibid., pg 121.
5. Talbot, Michael, *Beyond the Quantum*, Macmillin, 1986, pg 184.
6. Ibid., pg 122-123.
7. Boslough, op.cit., pg 142.
8. Davies, Paul, *God and The New Physics*, Simon & Schuster, 1983, pg 189.
9. Augros, Robert M., and George N. Stanciu, *The New Story of Science*, Gateway Editions, 1984, pg 69.

CHAPTER TWO
1. Weiner, Jonathan, *Planet Earth*, Bantam Books, 1986, pg 312.
2. Ibid., pg 314.
3. Margulis, Lynn, and Sagan, Dorion, *Micro-Cosmos*, Summit Books, 1986 pgs 72 and 89.
4. Seielstad, George, *At the Heart of the Web*, Harcourt Brace Javanovich, 1989, pg 115.
5. Ibid.
6. Ibid., pg 139.
7. Margulis, op.cit., pg 15.
8. Ibid., pg 95.
9. Watson, Lyall, *Heaven's Breath*, William Morrow & Company, 1984, pg 18.
10. Interview in *Omni*, July 1986.
11. Weiner, op.cit., pg 329 .

CHAPTER THREE
1. Gould, Stephen Jay, *Wonderful Life*, Norton, 1989, pg 24.
2. Sagan, Carl, *The Dragons of Eden*, Random House, 1977.
3. Margulis, Lynn and Dorion Sagan, *Micro-Cosmos*, Summit Books, 1986, pg 48.
4. Ibid., pg 216.
5. *Discovery Magazine*, April, 1990, "Playing Dice With Megadeath," by Jared Diamond, pg 57.
6. *Discovery Magazine*, August, 1990, "Argument Over A Woman," by James Shreeve pg 52.
7. Eisler, Riane, *The Chalice & The Blade*, HarperCollins, 1987, pg 6.
8. Gimbutas, *Language of the Goddess*, pg 316.
9. Eisler, op.cit., pg 7.
10. Ibid.
11. Ibid.
12. French, Marilyn, *Beyond Power*, Summit Books, 1985, pg 27.
13. Mumford, Lewis, *The Myth of the Machine*, Harcourt Brace Javanovich, Inc., 1966, pg 216.

14. Heinberg, Richard, *Memories and Visions of Paradise*, Tarcher, 1989, quoted on pg 216.
15. Eisler, op.cit., pg 21.

EPOCH II INTRODUCTION
1. Eisler, Riane, *The Chalice & The Blade*, HarperCollins, 1987, pg 48.
2. Heinberg, Richard, *Memories and Visions of Paradise*, Tarcher, 1989, pg 39.
3. Ginzberg, Lewis, "The Legends of the Jews," Vol. I - Philadelphia: The Jewish Publication Society of America, pg 71.
4. Fox, Michael W., *The New Eden*, Lotus Press, 1989, pg 16.
5. Berman, Morris, *Coming to Our Senses*, Simon & Schuster, 1989, pg 70.
6. Ibid., pg 71.
7. Thompson, William Irwin, *The Time Falling Bodies Take to Light*, St. Martin's Press, 1981, pg 155.
8. Ibid., pg 156.

CHAPTER FOUR
1. Pagels, E., *The Gnostic Gospels*, pg 60.
2 Berman, Morris, op.cit, pg 46.
3. Sheehan, Thomas, *The First Coming*, Random House, 1986, pg 5.
4. Jong, Erica, *Witches A Plumb Book*, 1981, pg 38 f.
5. Ibid., pg 43.
6. Ibid.
7. Berman, op.cit., pg 192.
8. Ibid, pg 191.
9. Ibid, pg 97.
10. Sam Keen has an excellent discussion of this in his book *Faces of the Enemy*, Harper San Francisco, 1986.
11. *Smithsonian Magazine*, February, 1990, "How a Mysterious Disease Laid Low Europe's Masses" by Charles L. Mee, Jr., pg 76.
12. Ibid.

CHAPTER FIVE
1. Thompson, William Irwin, *Imaginary Landscape*, St. Martin's, 1989, pg 155.
2. Merchant, Carolyn, *The Death of Nature*, HarperCollins, 1980, pg 169.
3. French, Marilyn, op.cit., pg 117.
4. Merchant, Carolyn, op.cit., pg 171.
5. Ibid.
6. Berman, Morris, *The Reenchantment of the World*, Cornell University Press, 1981, pg 31.
7. Merchant, Carolyn, op.cit., pg 193.
8. Capra, Fritjof, *The Turning Point*, Simon and Schuster, 1982, pg 62.
9. Ibid., pg 59.
10. French, Marilyn, op.cit., pg 283.
11. Harrison, Edward, *Masks of the Universe*, Macmillan, 1985, pg 102.
12. Ibid, pg 105.
13. Capra, Fritjof, op.cit., pg 108.
14. Augros, Robert M., and George N. Stanciu, *The New Story of Science*, Gateway Editions, 1984, pg 86.

15. Capra, Fritjof, op.cit. pg 147.
16. Interview in *Medical Self Care*, Fall, 1980, pg 4.
17. Ibid.
18. Preston, Thomas, *The Clay Pedestal*, Scribners, 1986, pg 66.
19. Ibid., pg 72-75.
20. *Science* magazine, June 1986, pg 14.
21. Ibid.
22. Siegel, Bernie, *Love, Medicine & Miracles*, HarperCollins, 1986, pg 25.
23. Kennedy, Donald, "Courses by Newspaper," *Columbus Dispatch*, 4/26/81.
24. Wolfe, Sidney, and Coley, Christopher, *Pills That Don't Work*, Farrar, Straus and Giroux, 1980.
25. Boulder, Colorado, "Daily Camera," July 12, 1990, quoting Dr. Brian Strom.
26. People Medical Society's newsletter, February 1986.
27. Preston, Thomas, op.cit. pg 137.
28. Ibid., pg 138.
29. Boulder, Colorado, "Daily Camera," September 21, 1986.
30. Cousins, Norman, *Head First*, Dutton, 1989, pg 159.
31. Ibid.
32. Ibid., pg 160.
33. Des Moines, Iowa, *Register*, October 20, 21, and 22, 1982.
34. Ibid.
35. Boulder, Colorado, "Daily Camera," June 22, 1990.
36. Ibid., June 19, 1990.
37. Article by Daniel Greenberg, Boulder "Daily Camera," Nov. 27, 1986, pg 3-B.
38. Illich, Ivan, *Medical Nemesis*, Bantam Books, 1976, pg 15.
39. Boulder, Colorado, "Daily Camera," May 8, 1986.
40. *USA Today*, Aug. 24-26, 1990, Report on *Lancet* article.
41. Interview in *Medical Self Care*, Fall, 1980 pg 4.
42. Ibid.
43. Ibid.

CHAPTER SIX

1. Leonard, George, *Walking on the Edge of the World*, Houghton-Mifflin, 1988, pg 9.
2. Ibid., pg 10.
3. Boulder, Colorado, "Daily Camera," June 14, 1990, column by Richard Reeves.
4. Weiner, Jonathon, *Planet Earth*, pg 272.
5. Ibid., pg 294.
6. Brown, Lester, ed., *State of the World—1990*, Worldwatch Institute, pg 173-174.
7. *Worldwatch* magazine, Sep-Oct, 1988, "Unhealthy Alliance" by Lori Heise, pg 19.
8. Research monograph, "Learning Factors In Substance Abuse," quoted in *Noetic Sciences Review*, Summer - 1990, pg 26.
9. *Worldwatch* magazine, op.cit.
10. Ibid.

11. Ibid.
12. Jung, C.G., *Psychology and Religion: West & East*, par. 802.
13. Mooney, Frances Lucindi, *Storming Eastern Temples*, The Theosophical Publishing House, 1976.
14. Thompson, William Irwin, *The Time Falling Bodies Take to Light*, St. Martin's Press, 1981.
15. Harrington, Michael, *The Politics at God's Funeral*, Holt, Rinehart, Winston, 1983, pg 1.
16. Neihardt, John C., *Black Elk Speaks*, University of Nebraska Press, 1968, pg 3-4.
17. Luke, Helen M, *Dark Wood to White Rose*, Parabola Books, 1989, pg xiv.
18. Harrington, op.cit., pg 10-11.
19. Bly, Robert, *Sleepers Joining Hands*, HarperCollins, 1973, pg 48-49.
20. Gould, Stephen Jay, *Wonderful Life*, Norton, 1989, pg 54.
21. Miller, David interviewed in "The Tarrytown Letter," September, 1983.
22. Toffler, Alvin, *Through the '80s*, World Future Society, 1980, and interviewed in "The Tarrytown Letter," Jan., 1984.
23. Yankelovich, Daniel, *Psychology Today*, April, 1981, pg 36.
24. Hawkin, Paul, *The Next Economy*, 1983.
25. de Chardin, Teilhard, *Building The Earth*, pg 23.
26. Whyte, Lancelot, *The Universe of Experience*, Harper/Torchbooks.
27. Platt, John, *The Step to Man*, Wiley, 1966.
28. Reich, Charles, *The Greening of America*, Random House, 1970.
29. Roszak, Theodore, *Person/Planet*, Anchor Press, 19780, pg xix.
30. Leonard, George, *The Transformation*, Delacorte Press, 1972.
31. Harman, Willis, in an IONS letter received 3/1/91.
32. Jung, C.G., *Memories, Dreams, Reflections*, Random House, 1961.

CHAPTER SEVEN

1. Campbell, Joseph, in conversation with Michael Toms, *An Open Life*, Larson Publications, 1988, pg 24.
2. Luke, Helen M, op.cit., pg 4.
3. *The Spirit of Synergy* was published by Abingdon Press in 1978. Now out-of-print, remaining copies are available, through Synergy Associates, Inc., P. O. Box 4589, Boulder, CO 80306. The film *Healing and Wholeness* was produced by and is available through Hartley Productions, Cos Cob, CN.

EPOCH III INTRODUCTION

1. Schumacher, E. F., *A Guide for the Perplexed*, HarperCollins, 1977, pg 1.

CHAPTER EIGHT

1. Bohm, David, *Wholeness and the Implicate Order*, Routledge & Kegan Paul, 1980, pgs 1 and 2.
2. Research regarding the placebo effect can be found documented in: Institute of Noetic Sciences Special Report, May 1987; Norman Cousins, *Anatomy of an Illness*, Norton, 1979, *Head First*, Dutton, 1989; White, Tursky, Schwartz, *Placebo: Theory, Research, and Mechanisms*, Guilford, 1985.
3. Quoted in Dr. Arnold A. Hutschnecker, *Hope*, Putnam, 1981, pgs 232-3.

4. Research regarding the role of mind in cancer can be found documented in 1989 *Brain/Mind Bulletin;* Larry Dossey, *Space, Time & Medicine,* Shambhala, 1982; Arnold Hutschnecker, *Hope,* Putnam, 1981; Carl and Stephany Simonton, *Getting Well Again,* Tarcher, 1978; *Journal of Transpersonal Psychology,* No.1, 1975; *Annals of the New York Academy of Sciences,* Vol. 164 and 125; *Science,* Vol 200; L. LeShan, *You Can Fight For Your Life,* Evans, 1977; James Lynch, *The Broken Heart,* Basic Books, 1977.

4. Quoted in Hutschnecker's *Hope,* pg 232-3.

5. Institute of Noetic Sciences Special Report on MPD.

6. Watson, Lyall, *Lifetide,* Simon and Schuster, 1979, pg 179.

7. Berman, Morris, op.cit., pg 156.

8. Moyers, Bill, *A World of Ideas Doubleday,* 1989, interview with Elaine Pagels, pg 378.

9. Ibid., pg 379.

10. Dossey, Larry, op.cit., pg 222.

11. Mooney, Lucindi Frances, *Storming Eastern Temples,* Quest, 1976, pg 32.

12. *Parabola,* Vol. X, No. 1, pg 25.

13. Mooney, op.cit., pg 13.

14. Berman, Morris, *Coming to our Senses,* Simon & Schuster, 1989, pg 343.

15. Keen, Sam, *Faces of the Enemy,* HarperCollins, 1986, jacket cover.

16. Ibid., pg 25.

17. Jung, C. G., *Aion,* Princeton Bollingen Series, 1959, pg 71.

18. *Parabola,* Vol. III, No. 3, pg 34.

19. Mooney, op.cit., pg 8.

20. Dunne, John S., *The Way of All the Earth,* University of Notre Dame Press, 1972, preface.

21. King, Ursula, *The Spirit of One Earth,* Paragon House, 1989, pg 10.

22. Ferris, Timothy, *Coming of Age in the Milky Way,* Morrow, 1988, pg 368.

23. *Brain/Mind Bulletin,* December 12, 1983.

24. Ibid.

25. De Civitate Dei, XXI, pg 8.

26. "Institute of Noetic Sciences Special Report," May 1987.

27. Wilson, Ian, *Stigmata,* HarperCollins, 1989, pg 7.

28. "Institute of Noetic Sciences Special Report," May 1987.

29. Chopra, Deepak, *Quantum Healing,* Bantam New Age, 1989, pg 17.

30. Kohn, Alfie, *No Contest,* Houghton Mifflin, 1986, pg 21.

31. Morowitz, Harold J., *Mayonnaise and the Origin of Life,* Berkeley Books, 1985, pge 26.

32. *New Age Journal,* Sept/Oct., 1989, pg 110.

33. King, op.cit., pg 176.

34. Ibid., pg 179-180.

35. *East/West Journal,* March 1982, pg 35.

36. Swimme, Brian, *The Universe is a Green Dragon,* Bear & Co., 1984, pg 44-45.

37. Siegel, Bernie, *Love, Medicine & Miracles,* HarperCollins, 1986, pg 180.

38. Kaufmann, *A Miracle To Believe In: They loved a child back to life.*

39. *Brain /Mind Bulletin,* April 20, 1981.

40. Keen, Sam, *The Passionate Life,* HarperCollins, 1983, pg 47.

CHAPTER NINE
1. Dossey, Larry, op.cit., pg 83.
2. Wolf, Fred Alan, *Taking the Quantum Leap*, HarperCollins, 1981, pgs 6 and 151.
3. A *New Age Journal* interview with David Bohm, Sept/Oct. 1989.
4. John 16:7.
5. John 14:12.
6. Dunne, John S., op.cit., pg 48.
7. Eisley, Loren, *The Invisible Pyramid*, Scribners, 1970, pg 81.
8. Masson, Jeffrey, *Final Analysis*, Addison-Wesley, 1990, pg 212.
9. Tillich, Paul, *The Courage To Be*, Yale University Press, 1952, pg 29.
10. Campbell, Joseph, and Toms, Michael, *An Open Life*, pg 26.
11. Roszak, Theodore, *Unfinished Animal*, HarperCollins, 1975, page241.
12. Ibid., pg 7.
13. Quoted in a flyer sent out by *Brain/Mind Bulletin*.
14. Campbell, Joseph, and Moyers, Bill, *The Power of Myth*, Doubleday, 1988, pg 69.
15. Pagels, Elaine, op.cit., pg 128.
16. Cousins, Norman, quoted in cassette tapes on his book *Head First*.
17. Simonton, Carl and Stephanie, *Getting Well Again*, Tarcher, 1978, pgs 53-54.
18. *Science*, Vol. 200, June 23, 1978.
19. Hutschnecker, A., op.cit., pg 234.
20. *Science*, Vol. 200, June 23, 1978.
21. Ibid.
22. *American Health* magazine, July/Aug, 1983, pg 60.
23. *Psychology Today* magazine, Feb, 1987, pg 37.
24. Seligman, Martin, *Learned Optimism*, Knopf, 1990.
25. Rilke, Rainer Maria, *Letters to a Young Poet*, Random House, 1984, pg 34-35.
26. Tillich, op.cit., pg 22.
27. Welwood, John, *Journey of the Heart*, Harper/Collins, 1990, pg 215.
28. King, Ursula, op.cit., pg 183.
29. Seligman, op.cit., pg 16.
30. Singer, June, *Seeing Through The Visible World*, Harper/ S.F., 1990, pg 145.

CHAPTER TEN
1. Jantsch, Erich and Conrad Waddington, *Evolution and Consciousness*, Addison-Wesley, 1976, pg 2.
2. Jantsch, Erich, *The Self-Organizing Universe*, Pergamon Press, 1980, pg 8.
3. *Omni* magazine interview with Ilya Prigogine, May 1983.
4. Toffler, Alvin, *Future Shock*, Random House, 1970, pg 23.
5. Ibid.
6. *The Anotated Alice*, pg 209f.
7. Campbell, Joseph, *Hero with a Thousand Faces*, Princeton University Press, 1949, pg 31-34.
8. Peck, M. Scott, *The Road Less Traveled*, Simon and Schuster, 1978, pg 71.
9. Genesis 32:27 and 32:28.
10. James, William, *Psychology: Briefer Course*, Harper Touchstone, 1961.

11. Campbell, Joseph, *Transformations of Myth Through Time*, HarperCollins, 1990, pg 211.
12. Highwater, Jamake, *The Primal Mind*, NAL, 1981, pg 85.
13. Walsch, Roger, *The Spirit of Shamanism*, Tarcher, 1990, pgs 255-56.
14. *Psychology Today*, December 1983.
15. Prather, Hugh, *I Touch the Earth, the Earth Touches Me*, Doubleday, 1972, book does not have pg numbers.
16. Campbell, Joseph, and Moyers, Bill, *Power of Myth*, Doubleday, 1988, pg 70.

CHAPTER ELEVEN
1. See Morris Berman's, *Coming to Our Senses*, Simon and Schuster, 1989, for an excellent discussion of how our separation from nature was essentially an attempt to make the wild, tame.
2. Lowenstein, Jerold, "Whose Genome Is It, Anyway?", *Discover Magazine*, May, 1992, pgs 28 to 31.
3. All quotes taken from *The Home Planet*, edited by Kevin W. Kelley, Addison-Wesley Publishing Company, 1988.
4. Niehardt, John G., *Black Elk Speaks*, University of Nebraska Press, 1988, pgs. 294-296.
5. Flowers, Betty Sue, Ed., *The Power of Myth*, Joseph Campbell with Bill Moyers, Doubleday, 1988, pg 88.
6 Sheldrake, Rupert, *The Rebirth of Nature*, Bantam 1991, pgs 58-59 .
7 Has appeared many places. This precise version was taken from "Philoxenia," the newsletter of the Robert D. Zimmer Group.
8. *ReVision* magazine, Winter/Spring 1986, pg 79.
9. For a thorough discussion of the NDE research, see Dr. Kenneth Ring's *Heading Toward Omega*, William Morrow and Co., 1984.
10. *Noetic Sciences Review*, Spring 1987, pg 8.

CHAPTER TWELVE
1. Keen, Sam, *To A Dancing God*, HarperCollins, 1970, pg 85.
2. I Corinthians 13:1-3.

CONCLUSION
1. Murphy, Michael, *The Future of the Body*, Tarcher, 1992, pg 9.
2. Shaw, George Bernard, *Plays Extravagant*, Penguin, from the preface of "The Simpleton of the Unexpected Isles."
3. Weinberg, Steven, *The First Three Minutes*, Andre Deutsch, 1977, pg 149.
4. Monod, Jacques, *Chance and Necessity*, translated by A. Wainhouse, Collins, 1972, pg 167.
5. Roszak, Theodore, *The Voice of the Earth*, Simon & Schuster, 1992, pg 17.
6. Thomas, Lewis, *The Fragile Species*, Charles Scribner's Sons, 1992, pg 81.
7. Houston, Jean, *The Possible Human*, Tarcher, Inc., 1982, pgs xvi and xvii.

SUGGESTED READING

With fourteen years of research involved in Deep Value Trend Analysis, and in the writing of this book, there has been a bibliography of literally several hundred books and thousands of articles. To list all of them would be of little use to the average reader of this book. Instead, what I have done is to glean just a few authors from that larger number, for the following "suggested reading" list. In most cases, each of the authors listed have written more than one book—I have listed only one from each author, but the one I would consider to be most relevant to the discussion in Sacred Eyes. There is substantial value, in my opinion, in reading anything written by the following people.

Achterberg, Jeanne *Imagery In Healing*, New Science Library, 1985.

Arditti, Rita, Pat Brennan, and Steve Cavrak, *Science and Liberation*, South End Press, 1980.

Arrien, Angeles, *The Four-Fold Way: Walking the Paths of the Warrior, Teacher, Healer, and Visionary*, Harper San Francisco, 1992.

Augros, Robert M and George Stanciu, *The New Story of Science*, Gateway, 1984.

Barbour, Ian, *Religion in an Age of Science*, Harper San Francisco, 1990.

Bateson, Gregory, *Mind and Nature: A Necessary Unity*, Dutton, 1979.

Berman, Morris, *Coming To Our Senses*, Simon and Schuster, 1989.

Bohm, David, *Wholeness and the Implicate Order*, Routledge & Kegan Paul, 1980.

Borysenko, Joan, *Minding the Body, Mending the Mind*, Addison-Wesley, 1987.

Briggs, John, and F. David Peat, *The Turbulent Mirror: An Illustrated Guide to Chaos Theory and the Science of Wholeness*, HarperCollins, 1989.

Calvin, William H., *The Ascent Of Mind*, Bantam Books, 1990.

Campbell, Joseph, *Transformations of Myth Through Time*, Harper, 1990.

Capra, Fritjof, *The Turning Point*, Simon & Schuster, 1982.

Chaisson, Eric, *The Life Era: Cosmic Selection & Conscious Evolution*, Atlantic Monthly Press, 1987.

Chopra, Deepak, *Quantum Healing*, Bantam, 1989.

Christ, Carol, ed., *Diving Deep and Surfacing: Women Writers on Spiritual Quest*, Beacon Press, 1980.

Colegrave, Sukie, *The Spirit of the Valley: The Masculine and Feminine in Human Consciuosness*, Tarcher, 1979.

Davies, Paul, and John Gribbin, *The Matter Myth: Toward 21st Century Science*, Viking, 1991.

Devall, Bill and George Sessions, *Deep Ecology*, Gibbs Smith, 1985.

Dossey, Larry, Recovering *The Soul: A Scientific and Spiritual Search*, Bantam Books, 1989.

Eisler, Riane, *The Chalice & the Blade*, Harper San Francisco, 1987.

Feinstein, David and Stanley Krippner, *Personal Mythology*, Tarcher, 1988.

Ferris, Timothy, *The Mind's Sky: Human Intelligence in a Cosmic Context*, Bantam, 1992.

Fox, Matthew, *The Coming of the Cosmic Christ*, Harper San Francisco, 1988.

Ferguson, Marilyn, *The Aquarian Conspiracy*, Tarcher, 1980.

French, Marilyn, *Beyond Power: On Women, Men, and Morals*, Summit, 1985.

Fromm, Erich, *The Art of Loving*, Bantam, 1956.

Gimbutas, Marija, *The Language of the Goddess*, HarperCollins, 1989.

Glieck, James, *Chaos Theory: Making a New Science*, Viking, 1987.

Goldenberg, Naomi, *Changing of the Gods*, Beacon Press, 1979.

Griffin, David Ray, ed., *The Reenchantment of Science: Postmodern Proposals*, SUNY Press, 1988.

Griffin, David Ray and Thomas J.J., Altizer *John Cobb's Theology In Process*, Westminister Press, 1977.

Grof, Stanislav and Christina, *Spiritual Emergence*, Tarcher, 1989.

Harman, Willis, *Global Mind Change*, Knowledge Systems, Inc., 1988.

Harner, Michael, *The Way of the Shaman*, Bantam, 1980.

Harris, Errol E., *Cosmos and Anthropos: A Philosophical Interpretation of the Anthropic Cosmological Principle*, Humanities Press Int., 1991.

Harrison, Edward, *Masks of the Universe*, Macmillan, 1985.

Hayward, Jeremy, *Perceiving Ordinary Magic*, New Science Library, 1984.

Heinberg, Richard, *Memories and Visions of Paradise*, Tarcher, 1989.

Henderson, Hazel, *Paradigms in Progress*, Knowledge Systems, Inc., 1992.

Highwater, Jamake, *The Primal Mind*, NAL, 1981.

Houston, Jean, *The Possible Human*, Tarcher, 1982.

Jantsch, Erich, *The Self-Organizing Universe: Scientific and Human Implications of the Emerging Paradigm of Evolution*, Pergamon, 1980.

Jung, C.G., *The Undiscovered Self*, Atlantic Little, Brown, 1957.

Justice, Blair, *Who Gets Sick: Thinking and Health*, Peak Press, 1987.

Keen, Sam, *The Passionate Life*, Harper San Francisco, 1983.

King, Ursula, *The Spirit of One Earth: Reflections on Teilhard de Chardin and Global Spirituality*, Paragon House, 1989.

Kohn, Alfie, *The Brighter Side of Human Nature*, Basic Books, 1990.

Langer, Ellen, *Mindfullness*, Addison Wesley, 1989.

Laszlo, Ervin, *Evolution: The Grand Synthesis*, New Science Library, 1987.

Leonard, George, *The Transformation*, Delacorte, 1972.

Lerner, Gerda, *The Creation of Patriarchy*, Oxford, 1986.

Locke, Steven and Douglas Colligan, *The Healer Within*, NAL, 1986.

Lovelock, James, *Gaia: A New Look at Life on Earth*, Oxford, 1979.

Loye, David, *The Sphinx and The Rainbow*, New Science Library, 1983.

Luke, Helen, *Woman, Earth and Spirit*, Crossroad Pub., 1981.

Mallove, Eugene, *The Quickening Universe: Cosmic Evolution and Human Destiny*, St. Martin's Press, 1987.

Margulis, Lynn and Dorion Sagan, *Micro-Cosmos*, Summit, 1986.

May, Robert, *Physicians of the Soul*, Crossroad, 1982.

Medicine Eagle, *Brooke Buffalo Woman Comes Singing*, Ballantine, 1991.

Merchant, Carolyn, *The Death of Nature: Women, Ecology, and the Scientific Revolution*, HarperCollins, 1980.

Metzner, Ralph, *Opening To Inner Light*, Tarcher, 1986.

Mitchell, Stephen, *The Gospel According To Jesus*, HarperCollins, 1991.

Moss, Richard, *The Black Butterfly: An Invitation to Radical Aliveness,* Celestial Arts, 1986.

Muller, Robert, *New Genesis: Shaping a Global Spsirituality,* Doubleday, 1982.

Mumford, Lewis, *The Transformations of Man,* Torchbook, 1956.

Murphy, Michael, *The Future Of The Body,* Tarcher, 1992.

Naisbitt, John and Patricia, *Aburdene Megatrends 2000,* Morrow, 1990.

Nicholson, Shirley, ed., *The Goddess Re-Awakening, Quest,* 1989.

Olds, Linda, *Fully Human,* Prentice Hall, 1981.

Ornish, Dean, *Dr. Dean Ornish's Program for Reversing Heart Disease,* Random House, 1990.

Pagels, Elaine, *The Gnostic Gospels,* Random House, 1979.

Pearce, Joseph Chilton, *Exploring The Crack in the Cosmic Egg,* Julian, 1974.

Pearsall, Paul, *Making Miracles,* Prentice Hall, 1991.

Peck, Scott, *The Road Less Traveled,* Touchstone, 1978.

Prigogine, Ilya, and Isabelle Stengers, *Order Out of Chaos,* Bantam, 1984.

Rifkin, Jeremy, *Biosphere Politics,* Crown, 1991.

Ring, Kenneth, *Heading Toward Omega: In Search of the Meaning of the Near-Death Experience,* William Morrow and Co., 1984.

Roszak, Theodore, *The Voice Of The Earth,* Simon & Schuster, 1992.

Russell, Peter, *The White Hole In Time,* Harper San Francisco, 1992.

Sagan, Carl, *The Dragons of Eden: Speculations on the Evolution of Human Intelligence,* Random House, 1977.

Sahtouris, Elisabet, *Gaia: The Human Journey From Chaos To Cosmos,* Pocket Books, 1989.

Samples, Bob, *Mind of our Mother: Toward Holonomy and Planetary Consciousness,* Addison-Wesley, 1981.

Seielstad, George, *At the Heart of the Web,* Harcourt Brace Jovanovich, 1989.

Seligman, Martin, *Learned Optimism,* Knopf, 1990.

Sheehan, Thomas, *The First Coming,* Random House, 1986.

Sheldrake, Rupert, *The Rebirth of Nature: The Greening of Science and God,* Century, 1990.

Sherrard, Philip, *The Eclipse of Man and Nature,* Inner Traditions, 1987.

Siegel, Bernie, *Love, Medicine, & Miracles,* HarperCollins, 1986.

Simonton, Carl and Stephanie Simonton, *Getting Well Again,* Tarcher, 1978.

Singer, June, *Seeing Through The Visible World,* Harper San Francisco, 1990.

Stone, Hal and Sidra Winkelman, *Embracing Ourselves,* New World Library, 1989.

Stone, Merlin, *When God Was a Woman,* Harcourt Brace Jovanovich, 1976.

Swimme, Brian and Thomas Berry, *The Universe Story: From the Primordial Flaring Forth to the Ecozoic Era,* Harper San Francisco, 1992.

Talbot, Michael, *Beyond the Quantum,* Macmillan, 1987.

Tarnas, Richard, *The Passion of the Western Mind,* Harmony, 1991.

Tart, Charles, *Waking Up: Overcoming the Obstacles to Human Potential,* New Science Library, 1986.

Teilhard de Chardin, Pierre, *The Phenomenon of Man,* Harper Bros, 1959.

Thompson, Willaim Irwin, *The Time Falling Bodies Take To Light,* St. Martin's Press, 1981.

Toffler, Alvin, *The Third Wave,* Morrow, 1980.

Vaughan, Frances, *The Inward Arc,* New Science Library, 1985.

Walsh, Roger, *The Spirit of Shamanism,* Tarcher, 1990.
Weil, Andrew, *Health and Healing,* Houghton Mifflin, 1983.
Welwood, John, *Journey of the Heart,* HarperCollins, 1990.
Wickes, Frances, *The Inner World of Choice,* Prentice-Hall, 1963.
Wilber, Ken, *Up From Eden: A Transpersonal View of Human Evolution,* Anchor Press, 1981.
Williamson, Marianne, *A Return To Love,* HarperCollins, 1992.
Wolf, Fred Alan, *Taking the Quantum Leap,* HarperCollins, 1989.
Young, Louise, *The Unfinished Universe,* Simon & Schuster, 1986.
Zukav, Gary, *The Seat of the Soul,* Simon & Schuster, 1989.

Recommended Periodicals:

Advances: The Journal of Mind-Body Health; Published by the Fetzer Institute, 9292 West KL Avenue, Kalamazoo, MI 49009

Common Boundary: Bwtween Spirituality and Psychotherapy; Common Boundary, 4304 East-West Highway, Bethesda, MD 20814

Brain-Mind & Common Sense; Interface Press, Box 42211, 4717 N. Figeuroa St., Los Angeles, CA 90042

New Dimensions; New Dimensions Radio, P. O. Box 410510, San Francisco, CA 94141

Noetic Sciences Review; The Institute of Noetic Sciences, 475 Gate Five Road, Suite 300, Sausalito, CA 94965

Parabola: The Magazine of Myth and Tradition; Parabola, 656 Broadway, New York, NY 10012

The Quest; Theosophical Society in America, P. O. Box 270, Wheaton, IL 60189

ReVision: A Journal of Consciousness and Transformation; ReVision, 1319 Eighteenth Street NW, Washington, DC 20036

ADDITIONAL RESOURCES

For a free catalog of guided-imagery tapes, and other resources directly related to *Sacred Eyes*, write:

Synergy Associates, Inc.
P. O. Box 4589
Boulder, CO 80306

ABOUT THE AUTHOR

L. Robert Keck is a writer, lecturer, and consultant, living in Boulder, Colorado.

Dr. Keck brings to his writing an extraordinarily diverse background and a wide range of interests. Academically he received his undergraduate degree from Cornell College in sociology, his master's degree from Vanderbilt University in theology, and a Ph.D. from The Union Institute in the philosophy of health. Professionally Dr. Keck has been a creative innovator in at least three different fields—as a clergyman he was a United Methodist pastor and then an urban minister working on the problems of the city, including poverty housing, public education, and race relations—in higher education he served on the faculties of Hamline University and The Ohio State University Medical School, as well as being the president of Boulder Graduate School—and in health care he was the recipient of numerous research grants, developed and helped launch holistic health centers, and became one of the first and foremost corporate wellness consultants in the United States.

INDEX